God Bless America

12-17-06

Catherine & Fred —

I hope you enjoy this —
Best wishes —

God Bless America

Patriotic Fervor or Historic Reality?

Dean C. Coddington and Richard L. Chapman

iUniverse, Inc.
New York Lincoln Shanghai

God Bless America
Patriotic Fervor or Historic Reality?

Copyright © 2006 by Coddington/Chapman LLC

All rights reserved. No part of this book may be used or reproduced by any means, graphic, electronic, or mechanical, including photocopying, recording, taping or by any information storage retrieval system without the written permission of the publisher except in the case of brief quotations embodied in critical articles and reviews.

iUniverse books may be ordered through booksellers or by contacting:

iUniverse
2021 Pine Lake Road, Suite 100
Lincoln, NE 68512
www.iuniverse.com
1-800-Authors (1-800-288-4677)

ISBN-13: 978-0-595-39345-9 (pbk)
ISBN-13: 978-0-595-85644-2 (cloth)
ISBN-13: 978-0-595-83742-7 (ebk)
ISBN-10: 0-595-39345-4 (pbk)
ISBN-10: 0-595-85644-6 (cloth)
ISBN-10: 0-595-83742-5 (ebk)

Printed in the United States of America

Contents

Preface ix

Acknowledgements xv

Chapter 1: In Pursuit of Freedom—The Seeds that Influenced the Founding of America 1

Chapter 2: Settlement Patterns in Early America—A Diversity of Motivations 21

Chapter 3: The Impact of the Great Awakening—The Emergence of Discontent 43

Chapter 4: Prelude to the Declaration of Independence 64

Chapter 5: The Revolutionary War—The First Months 88

Chapter 6: The Revolutionary War—Years of Survival 109

Chapter 7: The Southern Campaigns: Defeat, Then Victory at Yorktown 127

Chapter 8: The Chaos of the Articles of Confederation and the Need for Change 149

Chapter 9: Managing Change—The Ratification of the New Constitution 168

Chapter 10: The Second Great Awakening—Lasting Influences 184

Chapter 11: Nation Building—Challenges and Triumphs of the First 12 Years 203

Chapter 12: Thomas Jefferson—A Change in Direction? 218
Chapter 13: Mr. Madison's War 243
Chapter 14: Presidencies of James Monroe and John Quincy Adams Position New Country as a World Power 257
Chapter 15: The Role of Christianity in Founding America 269
Chapter 16: God Has Blessed America 282
Chapter Endnotes 295
Selected Bibliography 317
About the Authors 329
Index 333

Dedication

Pastor Charles "Chuck" VerStraten.
Friend and mentor; truly a shepherd of
his flock.

Preface

> *When I read early American history, I find that it was a miracle that this country made it. It was pretty iffy. We were either very, very lucky, or had some help along the way.*
>
> —Participant in authors' survey of meaning of God Bless America.

Most presidents in our lifetimes have closed their speeches with "God bless America." But what does it mean? Christians we queried about this practice had sharply different viewpoints:

- I view this as two things. One, it is a gratuitous greeting (but in this case, a conclusion), much like "have a nice day," or "how are you?" Secondly, it is a political statement to keep a "constituency" appeased. It is carefully composed, crafted and delivered to emote a response. As such, it has more theatrical value than spiritual meaning.

- Remember that the British say, "God save the Queen." It is a way that political leaders rally people by invoking the name of God. They bring God into the equation to gain support.

- It means just what it says: "May God continue to bless America in all things we do, undertake and move forward on."

- It is a statement that God is recognized in this country as the supreme power who orders the course of men and nations.

- It moves me. It makes me believe that the president is truly convinced that there is a God, and it makes me feel that he is truly imploring God to bless America. It is like a prayer, an invocation. It makes me feel more secure with the president's leadership.

We were surprised at the range of opinions on this topic, and these differences motivated us to explore the question of God's blessing of America in more detail. One of the key questions we address in this analysis of early American history is: What is the evidence of God's blessings on the formative years of the United States?

Then there is the issue of whether God blesses certain countries in special ways. We believe the Bible is clear that Israel falls into this category, but have there been others? As a seminary professor said to us, "I don't see America mentioned in the Bible." A related question: Is God using the United States to carry out His plan for the world? On this question we also found a variety of views among Christians:

- I do not believe America is unique in God's sight. In fact, I believe that if Christ doesn't return soon, we will be very much like the Egyptians, the Greeks, the Romans and the Europeans. That is, we were fortunate to be the leader of the world for a season. However, in God's view of history, there is only one kingdom that is blessed—His.
- America is not any more blessed than any other wealthy country. Sometimes we think we are blessed, or unique, because of the giant economic engine that is the United States.
- Yes. The fact is that we have been able to create a viable republic that has lasted over 200 years through a long list of major crises. And the fact is, in spite of what we read and hear about being hated by the rest of the world, millions around the globe continue to aspire to come here and be part of the "American dream."
- He has certainly blessed us more than any other nation with liberty and material comfort. Unique? On the vast wheel of history, that remains to be seen.

We aren't suggesting that the United States is the only country that has experienced God's blessings. We have visited many other countries around the world that appear to be experiencing God's blessings in terms of peace and prosperity. However, a major question addressed in this book is whether or not God intervened in identifiable ways in the United States during its founding years.

Europeans and others around the world consider the United States to be a "very religious" country. This makes many Europeans nervous; they wonder what we are going to do next in God's name. In other words, having a reputation for being a religious country is a liability in the view of many, including a number of citizens living in countries that have historically been friends and allies of the United States.

Our Interest in American History—A Different Perspective

The Wall Street Journal reported that since 9/11, Americans have become infatuated with the Founding Fathers. The president of one publishing house referred to Americans as redefining themselves, both domestically and internationally, and looking at their roots.

We are part of this growing number of Americans who have a renewed interest in, and appreciation for, the founding of our country, and for the Founding Fathers. In our case, like many others, the terrorist attacks on the World Trade Center and Pentagon triggered this passion. We were—and remain—indignant that a handful of terrorists thought they could intimidate this country. Reading about the efforts and sacrifices made by the early immigrants, the writers of the Declaration of Independence and Constitution, and the soldiers and sailors of the Revolutionary War (and their families), fanned the flames of our passion to know more.

However, the nature of our interest in early American history differs from that of many others who have written or continue to write on this subject. At the outset of our research, we were curious about how the religious views of the Founders shaped their ideas regarding how to organize and govern the country. Some of our friends argued that nearly all of the Founders were evangelical Christians; we questioned that claim. Others argued that the Founders were students of European Enlightenment philosophers and that this was the most important factor influencing their thinking; we didn't agree with this assertion either.

Our primary interest—and the focus of this book—is in understanding the impact of religion on the founding of America. As we learned more about early America, we began to see God's hand, or blessings, in three general categories:

- The effect of Christianity on America's heritage.

- The impact of Christianity on the desire for liberty, an important factor setting the stage for the Declaration of Independence and Revolutionary War.
- Divine providence, or intervention, leading up to and during the formative years of America.

Research Approach and Time Frame

In addition to visiting most of the historical sites described in this book, we have relied on popular secular history and biographies. It was reading these books, including several that make no mention of God's blessings, that triggered our interest in seeking a better understanding of the Christian heritage and evidence of divine providence in the founding of America. The body of literature we reviewed included works by authors such as Stephen Ambrose, Bernard Bailyn, Carol Berkin, H. W. Brands, Charles Cerami, Bruce Chadwick, Ron Chernow, Jared Diamond, Joseph Ellis, John Ferling, David Fischer, Thomas Fleming, James Hutson, Walter Isaacson, Paul Johnson, Richard Ketchum, David McCullough, Walter McDougall, Alan Taylor and Gordon Wood. We also tapped the writings of well-known Christian scholars and authors, including Chuck Colson, Stephen Mansfield, George Marsden, Martin Marty, Mark Noll and Bruce Shelley.

Recent authors of biographies of the Founding Fathers and books on early American history often justify their books by claiming that they had access to documents or resources not previously available. With the Internet and a continuation of scholarly research leading to the discovery of new documents, this is undoubtedly true.

In our case, however, we made no effort to access previously unpublished materials; we relied on the writings of the popular historians listed above. We believe that our most important contribution has been to search out and highlight the evidence of God's blessings based on the existing historical record.

We selected the 1500 to 1830 period for several reasons. It includes the decline of the Spanish Empire, the period of early exploration of North America, the first sustainable settlements, the first and second Great Awakenings (religious revivals), the Declaration of Independence and the Revolutionary War, the writing and ratification of the Constitution, the Louisiana Purchase, the Lewis and Clark expedition, the War of 1812, and the first six presidencies. Until the years following the War of 1812 (the James Monroe and John Quincy Adams presidencies) there were serious questions about the long-term viability of the United States and its role in the world.

Alexis de Tocqueville's *Democracy in America*, a thorough and highly respected assessment of the United States following his 1831-32 visit, made this a natural benchmark. Also, several of the Founding Fathers were still alive in the 1820s; John Adams and Thomas Jefferson lived until 1826 and their 158 letters represent an interesting retrospective look at the development of the country. John Quincy Adams, an eyewitness to the first major battle of the Revolutionary War and subsequent events, a prolific writer and orator, and the sixth president, was active until he died in 1848.

Why This Assessment?

What qualifies us to take on such a monumental analysis? Quite frankly, when the idea was first suggested, we could not visualize a more challenging and overwhelming intellectual undertaking. Furthermore, we are not theologians or professional historians. We are Christian laymen who have spent our careers in economic and policy research. Even recognizing these limitations, many of our friends urged us to expand a PowerPoint presentation about God's blessings on the founding of America. For reasons we can't fully explain, we felt compelled to pursue this research and write this book. And, the more time we spent on research, the more important we thought it was to complete and publish the results of our analysis.

This is not a political book; we don't have a political ax to grind. When it came to this research and analysis, we did our best to be analytical and objective, or what the Founders would have referred to as being "disinterested" (a compliment in those days). For example, we searched for evidence of God's blessings on the formation of the country, and where we found that kind of evidence, we reported it in the context of the historical record.

We approached this task humbly, and with the support and encouragement of many relatives and friends. We offer this book to you, the reader, as our best effort at identifying God's blessings on America in the years leading up to 1830. We invite you to review the evidence and draw your own conclusions.

Acknowledgements

As noted in the Preface, this book originated from a series of PowerPoint presentations made before the Legacy Class at Mission Hills Church in Greenwood Village, Colo. The lead teacher of the class, Dr. Harold Westing, an adjunct professor at Denver Seminary, commented, "I think I sense another book." He knew that both of us had written books on a variety of subjects (health care, public policy, Christianity in the workplace), and suggested that we just might have something worthy of publication. Thanks, Harold, for your encouragement and continuing support.

We are especially grateful to our wives, Judy Coddington and Marilyn Chapman, and our families, for their continuing support during the two years it took to prepare this book. They put up with our "intense focus" on research and writing.

We are also grateful to those who served as advisors on this project. The individuals identified below met with us to discuss their perspectives on early American history and read chapters as they were being drafted. We very much appreciate the contributions of each of these individuals:

- Lowell Palmquist, former health system CEO and a long-time friend, read most chapters in their early stages and read the final manuscript before printing.
- Richard A. Coddington, a retired U. S. Public Health Service and Environmental Protection Agency executive, read the manuscript several times and provided valuable feedback.

- Dr. Lynn Coddington, a niece of one of the authors, and an accomplished author, helped us with the introductions to several chapters.

- Dr. Bruce Demarest, professor, Denver Seminary, and his wife Elsie, a retired history teacher in the Douglas County School System in Colorado, both helped with this effort.

- David Nilges, a real estate consultant and friend of both authors, read early drafts of the manuscript and encouraged us to be more bold in offering our interpretation of events.

- Joel Severson, former owner of a large chain of Christian bookstores in Texas, reviewed early drafts of several chapters and assisted us with the development of a marketing plan.

- Bil Rodgers, a professional actor and author of numerous books, encouraged us throughout the writing and publication process. Bil also took the lead in designing the cover.

- Bruce Kidman, a long-time friend of the authors who lives in Santa Fe, reviewed every chapter at least once and offered useful suggestions and encouragement.

Marshall Shelley, a senior executive with *Christianity Today International*, reviewed parts of the manuscript and urged us to move ahead with our project. His father, Dr. Bruce Shelley, a retired professor of Denver Seminary and author of a best-selling book on church history, encouraged us to write this book.

In the conduct of our research, we are especially indebted to two highly-respected authors. Dr. James Hutson of the Library of Congress provided a comprehensive and valuable document, *Religion and the Founding of the American Republic*. Dr. Mark Noll, professor at Notre Dame University, has written several books, including *America's God* and *The Rise of Evangelicalism*, that were invaluable in our research. We thank both Jim and Mark for their contributions.

Others who helped us on this endeavor included John Billington, Dr. Kenneth Coddington, Dr. Jim Frantz, Tom Helms, K. Kalan, Tom Kristopeit, Joe Kulik, Robert Maitan, Marty Pomeroy, Dr. Gerry Sheveland, V. J. Smith, Ellen Stewart, Dr. Gary VanderArk, Rick Webb, and Dr. Craig Williford.

At McManis Consulting, April Costigan helped us prepare many of the exhibits; we are grateful for her assistance. Keith Moore, chairman and CEO of McManis, and a co-author (with Coddington) of almost a dozen health care books, offered numerous invaluable suggestions on the Preface and the final two chapters.

Walt Walkowski, a student at Denver Seminary and a former journalist, provided copyediting services; we appreciated the care Walt put into smoothing out the manuscript. We also thank Rifka Keilson, Katie Egan and the entire staff at iUniverse.

Jeffrey Ward of North Yarmouth, Maine, gave us permission to use his maps of the Long Island and Trenton and Princeton battles. Larry Bowring of Bowring Cartographic permitted us to use his Boston area and Southern campaign maps. We thank both Jeff and Larry for their help.

George Lundeen, sculpture of the bronze of Thomas Jefferson, which appears on the cover, graciously permitted us to use a photograph of his work for our cover. The bronze is located at White Fence Farm, a restaurant in the Denver area. We thank both George and the owners of White Fence Farm.

CHAPTER 1

▼

In Pursuit of Freedom— The Seeds that Influenced the Founding of America

To impose religious uniformity, seventeenth-century Europeans tortured, maimed, and murdered individuals, fought wars, and displaced populations.

—James Hutson, *Religion and the Founding of the American Republic*, 3.

Following his return from a trip along both coasts of South America, a friend asked one of the authors: "Why are the forms of government, economies, religious preferences and cultures of South and Central American countries so different from the United States? A visiting lecturer on board ship raised this issue, and I didn't have a good answer."

Related to our friend's question, this chapter considers these and other matters:

- Immediately after Columbus's voyages, Spain and Portugal quickly gained control of Mexico, the West Indies (Caribbean Islands), and Central and South America. Why did the Spanish and Portuguese move so fast while other European countries (especially England and France) delayed for decades?

- What impact did the Protestant Reformation, the establishment of the Church of England, the translation of the Bible into English, and the teachings of John Calvin have on the initial settlement and development of British North America?

- What effect did the great European wars of the 17th and 18th centuries have on the number and types of European immigrants to North America?

- What role did science, technology, and capitalism play in the initial settlement of North America?

- Where did the slave trade have its greatest impacts?

For John Jay, an important but often overlooked Founding Father, it was apparent the events in Europe prior to the settling of the North American colonies were not a product of chance. Writing late in his life, he said that a proper history of the United States, "...would develop the great plan of providence for causing this extensive part of our world to be discovered, and these 'uttermost parts of the earth' to be gradually filled with civilized and Christian people and nations...In my opinion, the historian, in the course of the work, is never to lose sight of that great plan."[1] Our purpose in this chapter is to attempt to understand this plan.

Impact of Luther, Henry VIII, the Bible and Calvinism

The beginning of the Protestant Reformation, King Henry VIII's break from the Roman Catholic Church, early efforts to translate the Bible into understandable English and John Calvin's philosophy and teaching were all important in setting the stage for the settlement and culture of North America.

Martin Luther. As a young man, Luther was nearly struck by lightning. In a mixture of fear and relief, he vowed to become a monk after calling out to St. Anne for help. Following through on the vow, he became a zealous monk but found his efforts lacking. He feared and, at times, hated God; he worried incessantly

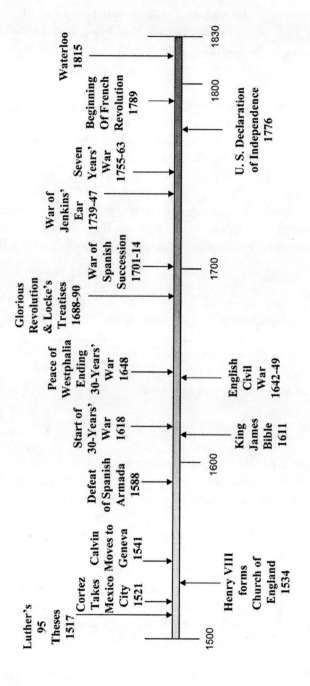

about his salvation; he wondered how he might have a loving, joy-filled relationship with his Creator. Finally, in 1515, following untold hours of fasting, prayer and Bible study, he concluded that man was justified by faith in Christ only, not by church ritual or dogma.

Two years later, incensed by the sale of indulgences (parishioners paid the church for forgiveness of their sins) to raise money to complete St. Peter's Basilica in Rome, Luther began to preach against many of the teachings and practices of the Roman Catholic Church. Luther's opposition to the church culminated in his nailing 95 theses (or propositions) to the door of All Saints' Church at Wittenburg on October 31, 1517. This marked the beginning of the Reformation, an event that reverberated through Europe and North America. Luther was subsequently declared a heretic by the Catholic Church and given 60 days to recant. He refused to back down and escaped; a friendly prince hid him in Wartburg Castle.

Martin Marty, a theologian and historian, summarized the revolution led by Luther: "Catholic reformers agreed with this (Luther's) attack in part, but wanted to make changes within the church, not being thrown out or going into exile from it. Those who were Protestant lost patience, status, or, in some cases, limb and life. Europe was never again to be united in faith. The exploring and settlement of North America was also henceforth to reflect the battles over faith that divided Europe."[2]

Before he died in 1546, Luther translated the New Testament into German, and revised the Latin liturgy into German. By then, leadership of the movement he had started passed on to others. However, Luther's influence, directly and indirectly, set the stage for the first settlements in North America.

As discussed in the next chapter, many of the early immigrants to North America were Protestants and products of the Reformation. The immigrants included the Huguenots (French Protestants) who were either killed or driven out of France in the 16th century; many of the Dutch and Germans who settled in the Middle Colonies; and the Puritans, who disagreed with many aspects of the Church of England. During the first 100 years of North American colonization, a high proportion of the immigrants were products of the Reformation.

Henry VIII and the Church of England. Largely as a result of impatience with the Roman Catholic Church for its unwillingness to annul his marriage with Katherine of Aragon (her sin was that she failed to produce a son and heir), King Henry VIII broke from the Catholic Church and established the Church of England, which was Roman Catholic in all but name and allegiance to the pope. Henry VIII married Anne Boleyn in January 1533 and a year later, he took on the title of supreme head of the Church of England. However, "To the end of his life, Henry VIII remained a devout Catholic who deplored Lutheran and other heresies, but he had to maintain a balance between the radical evangelicals at his court, who were pressing for ever wider reforms and secretly flirting with Protestantism, and the conservatives, who would have given anything to turn the clock back."[3]

It was under Queen Elizabeth I (1558-1603), daughter of Henry VIII and Anne Boleyn, that the Church of England assumed its character—neither Roman nor Reformed. Elizabeth's Thirty-Nine Articles, which were essentially Protestant but contained several Catholic elements, represented a compromise, or as some called it, "the middle way" between Catholicism and Protestantism.[4] Reacting negatively to the Thirty-Nine Articles, a small band of Puritan separatists (we know them as the Pilgrims) left England to spend 12 years in the Netherlands prior to sailing for North America. These "religious revolutionaries," who were perhaps the philosophical forefathers of today's religious conservatives, were influential beyond their numbers as the second wave of settlers (after Jamestown) in the New World.

Translation of the Bible into English. Prior to the reign of Henry VIII, there was a strident and growing Protestant movement in England. Dissidents included John Wycliffe, a professor at Oxford and a Bible translator, William Tyndale, Miles Coverdale and others who, in several cases, gave their lives so that the Bible could be translated into English and made available to the general population.[5]

The ebb and flow of church and royal support for a Bible in the "vulgar" language of the people has been the subject of several books. By 1600, the Geneva Bible (also referred to as the "Queen Elizabeth Bible") was commonly used in England; 86 editions had been printed between 1568 when it was first published up to the time it was superseded by the King James Bible.

In 1603, shortly after he assumed the English crown, King James I called a conference between Church of England officials and leaders of the growing Puritan movement. On the second day of what is referred to as the Hampton Court Conference, one of the Puritans challenged the king to sponsor a new Bible; the king embraced the proposal with a fervor that caught the Church of England hierarchy off guard. "Before the end of July the following year, the king had approved fifty-four translators arranged into six companies, two to meet at Westminster under its dean, and two each at the universities of Oxford and Cambridge under the direction of their royal Hebrew professors."[6] The new Bible became commercially available in 1611 and although it was not an immediate success in terms of sales, "The King James Version held undisputed sway in the English speaking world for more than two centuries..."[7]

What were the implications of the publication of the King James Bible for the colonization and culture of early America? The new Bible was released within four years of the Jamestown settlement, and it was widely available in both North America and England; many colonists learned to read from this version of the Bible. "Up to and through the Civil War, publishing and distribution of the Bible dwarfed all other literary enterprises in the new nation."[8]

John Calvin. Calvin (1509-1564) was born just outside Paris and entered the University of Paris at age 14. Following receipt of a master's degree he planned a career as an attorney and scholar. However, shortly after graduation, Calvin experienced a conversion experience and identified himself with the Protestant cause. Because of his religious beliefs and writings, he was forced to flee France and ended up in Geneva where he headed a religious community for most of his remaining years.

Calvin's central focus was the sovereignty of God. The movement he founded was especially strong in Scotland and Northern Ireland, where Presbyterians were dominant. Other denominations that had a strong Calvinistic bent were the Dutch and German Reformed churches, and many Congregationalists (Puritans). In France, Calvinism was important in spawning the Huguenots, a Protestant group that was gaining influence before thousands were massacred by French Catholics on St. Bartholomew's Day, 1572.

According to one historian, "...the consequence of faith to Calvin—far more than to Luther—is strenuous effort to introduce the kingdom of God on earth."[9]

This, of course, was the primary focus of the Pilgrim separatists and the Puritans who came to New England in relatively large numbers in the 1630s. Along the same lines, Calvin taught that not even popes or kings had claims to absolute power. "Calvin never preached the 'right of revolution,' but he did encourage the growth of representative assemblies and stressed their right to resist the tyranny of monarchs."[10]

Calvin taught that Christianity impacts the character of believers. One historian wrote that while God's saving grace is not based on good works, "the true Christian finds in the law (the Bible) the divine pattern for moral character." He went on, "This rigorous pursuit of moral righteousness was one of the primary features of Calvinism. It made character a fundamental test of genuine religious life and explains Calvinism's dynamic, social activism. God calls the elect for his purpose!"[11]

The Calvinistic flavor of early Christianity led people to believe in divine providence. Martin Marty noted that in Switzerland, "the more staid and systematic lawyer John Calvin began to envision a further reformed church based on both grace and a strong sense of divine providence or control in history. The Calvinist version was to have more voice in America..."[12]

In summary, the Reformation initiated by Martin Luther, Henry VIII's break with the Roman Catholic Church, ready access to the King James Bible, and John Calvin's teachings about divine providence and the sovereignty of God all had important implications for the political landscape in Europe and the subsequent settlement of North America. Nearly all of the immigrants to North America were Protestants, either from the Church of England or Puritans who tried to purify the Anglican Church. Calvinism was the dominant brand of Christianity in New England and the Middle Colonies (New York, New Jersey, Pennsylvania and Delaware).

Spanish Settlement of Mexico and South America Influenced Colonization of North America

While the growth in Protestantism was setting the stage for immigration from northern Europe, Spain was already seeding strong Catholic influences in the New World. For example, less than 30 years after it was discovered, 10,000 Spanish-speaking Europeans were living on the Island of Hispaniola (present-day

Haiti and the Dominican Republic), growing their own food, and establishing trading patterns with Europeans.[13]

Well before the first permanent European settlement in North America, 250,000 Spanish immigrants had arrived in the New World, mainly settling in Mexico and South America. As one example of how Spanish domination preceded the colonization of North America, Hernando Cortes' attack and occupation of heavily populated Mexico City took place in 1521, 100 years before the Pilgrims landed at Plymouth Rock.

Until 1570 almost all of the Spanish immigrants to the Americas were young men; however, the number of immigrant women increased in subsequent years. "By 1574 the Spanish had chartered 121 towns in the Americas, and another 210 followed by 1628."[14] Again, much of this preceded the Puritans first wave of immigration to the Boston area.

By 1585 bullion mined in South America and Mexico amounted to one quarter of the Spanish Crown's total revenue.[15] Between 1500 and 1650, for example, 16,000 tons of silver was transported from the New World to Spain. (To put this in perspective, the silver imported from the Americas tripled Europe's supply of this precious metal.) Much of this wealth was used to pay soldiers, finance local administration and support Spain's allies. "Huge sums also went for special undertakings—the direct costs of the Armada sent against England amounted to more than 10 million ducats, about twice the empire's total annual budget…"[16]

This huge flow of wealth originating in the New World caught the attention of France, which began to sponsor piracy. The English, under Sir Francis Drake, joined in the piracy forcing the Spanish to ship gold and silver bullion in large and expensive convoys. The losses to pirates and the added cost of convoys reduced the profitability of the mining operations in the Americas, which in turn contributed to the erosion of Spain's influence in both Europe and the New World.

Recognizing that obtaining wealth by piracy was a hit and miss proposition (as well as morally wrong), France and England began to consider the possibility of permanent colonies in the Caribbean and North America. The Spanish were concerned about this potential intrusion into a part of the world they had monopolized; however, by the end of the 16th century, there was little they could do to stop it.

The defeat of the Spanish Armada in 1588 was a pivotal event influencing the future of North America. It established English sea power after more than a century of Spanish domination. The Armada, which included 130 ships and 27,000 men, was headed for the Dutch Republic to pick up additional troops for an invasion of England. However, a battle with 197 British ships off the coast of England, plus a severe storm, left the Spanish fleet decimated. One-third of the Spanish ships did not make it back to their homeports with a loss of 11,000 men.[17] One historian concluded, "The invincibility of Spain had become a myth, and England's rise was an event of epochal significance, especially for North America, a large part of which was to become part of its empire."[18]

The further deterioration of the Spanish Empire. Following the near destruction of its Armada, the influence of Spain and its empire continued to erode. Portugal broke away in 1640 after 60 years of subordination to the Spanish Crown. At this same time, there were major rebellions in the Basque Provinces. "By mid-century, Spain, formally still a great dynastic state, was no longer the dominant European power she had been a 100 years earlier."[19]

The decline of the Spanish Empire also correlated with the forced conversion of an estimated 300,000 Jews (they were referred to as New Christians), the Inquisition in which a substantial number of the New Christians were tortured and executed, and the deportation of 170,000 Jews. "Being a true Jew was declared 'the greatest, most perilous and most contagious of crimes'…The loss of Jewish talent harmed Spain for centuries, but the Catholic sovereigns at the time overlooked the loss in order to glory in doing the will of God by creating a Spain spiritually united for mission."[20]

Economically, financially and morally, the Spanish Empire was in terrible shape. The empire declared bankruptcy in 1596, a few years after the disaster of the Spanish Armada, and then again in 1607, 1627, 1647 and 1653.[21] Despite the decline of the Spanish Empire, England and France found it prudent to steer clear of the Spanish in the West Indies and Florida, and consequently looked for opportunities to explore and colonize the northern coast of North America. Spanish military outposts in Florida were not strong enough to stop the English from landing settlers in the Chesapeake and New England, the Dutch from settling on the Hudson River and lower Manhattan Island, and the French from developing villages along the St. Lawrence River and in Acadia (present-day Nova Scotia).

Motivations for colonizing North America. Prior to the defeat of the Spanish Armada, Queen Elizabeth read Richard Hakluyt's *Discourse of Western Planting*. This plan laid out the reasons for England to encourage colonization of America: "Timber, fish, furs, and perhaps precious metals would enrich England and reduce its dependence on imports. Colonies would provide burgeoning markets, especially for England's now depressed woolen trade. Emigration would open a safety valve draining off vagrants, criminals, the unemployed, and religious dissidents such as the Puritans. Above all, colonies over the water would make the North Atlantic an English lake while providing bases from which to strike at the Spanish Main."[22]

The French put less emphasis on colonizing, and instead focused on fishing, fur trading and commercial ventures. Along with English and Basque fisherman, the French had long experience in fishing for cod off the coasts of Newfoundland, Greenland, Labrador, Nova Scotia and as far south as Maine. But France did not have the navy or financial resources to engage in large-scale colonization, nor did French citizens show interest in immigrating to North America.

The Dutch Republic, finally free from Spanish domination after 1650, has long been recognized as having the most diverse and tolerant culture in Europe. Furthermore, the Dutch had a strong navy, and several reasons for establishing settlements in the area between the Chesapeake and New England. Their motivations were largely commercial (e.g., fur trading with the Indians, recognition of the value of the New York harbor, and as a place for people who wanted to relocate to the New World).

The Impact of European Military Conflicts

The Thirty-Years' War and other conflicts on the European continent had a major influence on early America. Thousands of people (nearly all of them Protestants) immigrated to the new country seeking economic opportunity, land, peace and freedom of religion. Many individuals and families from northern Europe settled in the Middle Colonies. These settlers, who came from the Dutch Republic, Scotland, Germany, Sweden, Denmark, Norway and Ireland, represent an important part of the Christian heritage of America, and their successors played key roles in the Revolutionary War.

Thirty-Years' War (1618-1648). Although nearly all of the fighting in this war took place on the European Continent, primarily in the area now occupied by Germany, the impacts on the colonization of North America were important. One historian summarized it this way: "Less a single war than an era of wars, the Thirty Years' War marked the passing of Spanish hegemony in western Europe and its replacement by France." He went on, "...Catholic France, the 'eldest daughter of the Church,' under the leadership of a cardinal, joined Dutch Calvinists and Swedish Lutherans in asserting the rights of German princes against the Catholic Habsburgs."[23] The miseries of the Thirty-Years' War were prolonged until the Peace of Westphalia ended the fighting.

This war took a tremendous toll on the population of Germany, which declined 35 to 40 percent over the 30 years. The economies of the principalities and countries impacted by the war were in a shambles. In the decades that followed this conflict, tens of thousands of Germans and Scandinavians immigrated to North America.

English Civil War (1642-1649). In June 1642 the Parliament, controlled by Puritans, gave King Charles I a 19-part ultimatum. When the king rejected these demands, Parliament began to recruit and organize military volunteers. The Parliamentarian side, called "Roundheads" because they had their hair cut short displaying the shape of their heads, included many in the middle classes. King Charles' followers included mostly Catholics and members of the Church of England.

The king's armies won most of the early battles. However, midway through the war, the Scots joined Oliver Cromwell's Roundhead army, and the forces of Parliament began to win more victories. In the summer of 1645 Cromwell's forces surrounded Oxford (headquarters of the king's army), and later in the year, the king's army surrendered. King Charles I gave himself up in May 1646 and was beheaded in 1649.[24]

The success of the Puritans in the English Civil War dried up the supply of English men and women wanting to immigrate to New England. With the hope that they could maintain control of their lives and patterns of worship, Puritans had no reason to leave England. Since New England was economically dependent on the steady influx of newcomers, the sharp decline in immigration depressed its economy.[25]

However, the Puritan administration in England soon proved to be despotic and unpopular. The rules established by the Puritan-controlled Parliament were more stringent than those under King Charles I. Many Englishmen wished for the return of a king, and in 1659, just 13 years after the Puritans won the civil war, 10,000 Scottish soldiers marched into England and, without meeting armed resistance, installed the executed king's son, Charles II, as King of England.[26] The reign of the English Puritans was over.

The Glorious Revolution (1688-1689). The Glorious Revolution was a non-violent change in leadership, which came 40 years after the English civil war. King James II (son of King Charles II), a Catholic who was opposed by the Church of England, was replaced by his son-in-law, William of Orange and wife Mary (daughter of King James II). With 500 ships and a force of 11,000 troops, William of Orange (who was head of state of the Dutch Republic) crossed the English Channel and landed in southwest England; his army met no resistance in its march to London. The new king and queen, who were Protestants, agreed to follow the laws of the land (the Magna Carta) and work closely with Parliament. In retrospect, this series of events set the stage for Great Britain's growth in worldwide power and prestige.[27]

War of Spanish Succession (1701-1714). By claiming the vacant Spanish throne for his grandson, King Louis XIV of France threatened to take control of Spain and merge the two nations, thus destroying the balance of power in Europe. England strongly resisted such a move. In the resulting conflict, the British won a surprising series of victories in Europe, marking England's emergence as the top military power in the world.[28]

This war spilled over into North America with mixed results. For example, British troops and Carolina volunteers attacked the Spanish garrison in St. Augustine, but were repulsed. The French rallied Indians and burned several frontier towns in New England. In 1710, the combination of the Royal Navy and New England volunteers captured Port Royal in Acadia. In 1711 the English attempted to capture Quebec from the sea, but were turned back by stormy weather.

The Treaty of Utrecht ended the War of Spanish Succession. This treaty established the boundaries of Spain, Portugal, France, Belgium and the United Provinces (corresponding roughly to the present-day Netherlands and Belgium). Spain retained most of its colonial possessions in South America and Mexico, but the Spanish Empire would never again rise above being a second-rate world power.[29] Another important feature of the Treaty of Utrecht was that France and Spain agreed that the two empires would forever remain separate.

One of the consequences of this war was that "the English committed the future of their empire to maritime commerce rather than to European territory— a dramatic shift that elevated their American colonies to new importance."[30] The British navy was larger than the combined French and Spanish navies, and had more combat experience. On the other hand, since the French had continuing concerns over maintaining their European borders, they devoted most of their financial resources to building their army.

War of Jenkins' Ear (1739-1748). English ship's master Robert Jenkins appeared in Parliament with evidence that Spanish buccaneers had stolen his cargo, and for good measure, cut off his ear. "Jenkins kept it pickled in a jar and now displayed it to great effect."[31] When the Spanish refused British demands that the Spanish desist from seizure of foreign vessels, Britain declared war on Spain.

Within a year, this conflict merged into what was known as the War of the Austrian Succession. A coalition of French and Prussian (German) armies fought to take provinces away from the Habsburg empress of Austria. England's King George II, a native of Hanover, feared for the security of his ancestral province, and entered the war on the side of Austria. This meant that England and Austria opposed Spain, France and Prussia.

This war had several implications for the new British settlements in North America. First, because of Georgia's close proximity to the Spanish forts in Florida, Governor James Oglethorpe organized 2,000 Georgia and South Carolina militia to attack St. Augustine. However, even with the help of the British navy, the militia failed in its mission; Oglethorpe was later court martialed in London.[32] This marked the second failed British and American attempt to dislodge the Spanish from Florida.

In 1744 3,000 New England volunteers, under Governor William Shirley of Massachusetts, successfully attacked Louisbourg, a French fortress and naval station on Cape Breton Island, Nova Scotia. However, much to the consternation of New Englanders, the British returned Louisbourg to the French as part of the 1748 treaty ending the war. This decision contributed to the colonists' growing dissatisfaction with British rule.[33]

Seven-Years' War. By the middle of the 18th century, Spanish influence continued to decline, and England and France emerged as the two world superpowers. It didn't take long after the treaty ending the War of Jenkins' Ear before England and France were at it again. In addition to North America, where it was referred to as the French & Indian War, fighting in the Seven-Years' War took place in Europe, India, the Philippines and the Caribbean.

When peace was concluded in 1763, England had won control of most of North America and had emerged as the most powerful country in the world: "The Peace of Paris is a good marker of a new world order. It had replaced that dominated by Spain and Portugal, the only great colonial powers of the sixteenth century; both had long passed their zenith by 1763. It registered the ascendancy of Great Britain in the rivalry with France overseas which had preoccupied her for nearly three-quarters of a century. The duel was not over, and Frenchmen could still be hopeful that they would recover lost ground. Great Britain, none the less, was to be the next great imperial power."[34]

This war had two especially important implications for the colonies. First, the British believed that the colonists should pay a substantial share of the costs incurred in defeating the French, and the failure to reconcile this and several other contentious issues contributed to the Revolutionary War. Secondly, the sea power of Great Britain continued to grow more dominant, a factor that prolonged the war for independence.

The Development of Capitalism, Science and Technology

Wherever northern Europeans went in the world in the 1500s and 1600s, they found that their ships and technology were more advanced than that of the civilizations they contacted. This situation also applied to agriculture, clothing, transportation, and the ability to make war. For example, the English were the first to develop round-bottom boats that enabled them to more efficiently sail in the oceans, carry larger cargoes and arm themselves with more and better cannon. They were the first to develop the technologies for making clothing out of wool. Their practices of crop rotation, deeper plowing, and the use of horses were superior to most other countries. The firearms of the Europeans were far advanced compared with the weapons of native populations.

What did this have to do with the settlement of America? It meant that Native Americans in both continents were no match for the English, French, Spanish, Dutch and other European immigrants. The scientific and technological prowess of the Europeans, combined with the diseases brought by the visitors (including the African slaves), completely overwhelmed the natives.

What does all this have to do with God? Professor Rodney Stark argued persuasively that Christianity was the religion that fostered the development of science, technology and capitalism in Europe, especially in England. He wrote that the conflict between the scientific revolution in the years preceding the 16th century and Christianity (primarily Roman Catholics) has been misrepresented: "Some wonderful things were achieved during this era (referring to the 'Dark Ages'), but they were not produced by an eruption of secular thinking. Rather, these achievements were the culmination of many centuries of systematic progress by medieval Scholastics (scholars), sustained by the uniquely Christian twelfth-century invention, the university. Not only were science and religion compatible, they were inseparable—the rise of science was achieved by deeply religious Christian scholars."[35]

Thus, capitalism, science and technology were key factors facilitating the massive movement of Europeans to North and South America. Furthermore, according to Stark's analysis, the historic Christian culture of Europe was the major contributor to the scientific and technological lead enjoyed by the Europeans.

The Enlightenment in Europe was Backdrop for Both the French and American Revolutions

The "Enlightenment" is generally considered to have run for a little more than 100 years, from the 1680s to the 1790s. What was the Enlightenment? What impact did it have in Europe and North America? How did the Enlightenment differ in France, Great Britain, and in North America? One of the themes we develop in this book is the relationship between Enlightenment thinking and Christianity in the settlement, growth and governmental structures of North America.

Many Enlightenment thinkers and philosophers, "...believed that unassisted human reason, not faith or tradition, was the principal guide to human conduct. Everything, including political and religious authority, must be subject to a critique of reason if it were to commend itself to the respect of humanity. Particularly suspect was religious faith and superstition."[36]

France was best known for its secular Enlightenment philosophy. Important French philosophers included Voltaire, Rousseau, and Montesquieu. One of their major accomplishments was the production of the *Encyclopedie,* which at the time was a significant source of written knowledge. The French philosophers were generally anti-church and opposed to Christianity.

In her book on the Enlightenment, Gertrude Himmelfarb argued that the French Enlightenment was only part of the total picture. She observed that the connection between the anti-church and anti-crown philosophers and the French Revolution has led to an overemphasis on the French Enlightenment. There were at least three Enlightenments: one in France, another in Scotland/Great Britain (e.g., Isaac Newton, David Hume, Adam Smith, Edward Gibbon) and a third in America (Jefferson, Franklin and Hamilton). "Thus, the British Enlightenment represents 'the sociology of virtue,' the French 'the sociology of reason,' the American 'the politics of liberty.'"[37]

At the time of the Glorious Revolution in England, John Locke, an influential philosopher who was part of the Scottish Enlightenment, developed a rationale for government and its relationship to the people. He published his *Two Treatises on Government* in 1689 and 1690, in which he argued that people were born free and that God had not put any one person above another. He also made this important and revolutionary point: governments are not supreme authorities; they can be replaced by society if they violate established principles.[38]

Factors Influencing Immigration to the New World

During the 17th century, the peak period of emigration from England to North America, English leaders thought that their country was over populated. Thus, England's rulers encouraged emigration to the colonies, where laborers could raise commodities for the mother country and where political dissidents could be exiled. However, late in the 17th century and into the early part of the 18th century, opinion shifted: "the home government became more tolerant of religious diversity; English manufacturing expanded, increasing the demand for cheap labor; and the realm frequently needed additional thousands for an enlarged military."[39]

As a result of these changes, the flow of English men and women to America almost dried up by the 18th century, with the majority of the new immigrants coming from Germany, Scotland, Ireland and the Scandinavian countries. Prior to 1700, for example, 350,000 immigrants to the North American colonies came from England. By comparison, from 1700 to 1775 that number dropped to 80,000, half of whom were felons.[40]

By the 1750s Germans were arriving in North America at the rate of more than 5,000 per year. "The colonial emigration was a modest subset of a much larger movement of Germans out of the Rhineland. Between 1680 and 1780 about 500,000 southwestern Germans emigrated, but only a fifth went to British America."[41] Much of this massive emigration was attributable to the aftereffects of the Thirty-Years' War. The rulers of a fragmented Germany continued to levy high taxes and conscript young men for military service.

As noted earlier, the French did not encourage immigration to the New World. In fact, most Frenchmen who came to Canada expected to return to France; it was typically viewed as a temporary assignment.

Not all immigrants crossed the Atlantic willingly. Over a 350-year period (1500 to 1850), European ships made an estimated 40,000 trips from the West African coast, with three-quarters of them succeeding in bringing human cargo to American ports. The total number of people taken from Africa was 11.0 million; 9.5 million survived the trip. Most of the African slaves were transported to the West Indies, Brazil and elsewhere in South America. Only 3.8 percent of this forced migration of Africans landed in British North America.[42]

The high attrition rate for slaves deposited in the West Indies was one reason so many were required. For example, "During the 18th century at least one-third of the slaves died within three years of their arrival on the island of Barbados." In addition to tropical diseases, the slaves suffered from a low birthrate, a diet deficient in protein, and harsh fieldwork. By comparison, in the British North American colonies, where slaves were better fed, the 250,000 slaves imported had increased to 576,000 by 1780. In sharp contrast, although 1.2 million slaves had been imported in the previous two centuries, by 1780 the British West Indies had a slave population of only 350,000.[43]

The Seeds that Grew into Early America

Several forces swept Europe in the century preceding the settling of the New World, and they played a critical role in shaping America's future. Clearly, the interplay between Christian sects in Europe was a significant factor causing the settlement of the New World. Additionally, Christians shaped the culture of North America. Was there also an overall guiding hand at work? Consider the following:

- After a fast start in colonizing Mexico, the Caribbean and South America, Spain's role as leader of a major world empire declined. If the Spanish Empire had not experienced serious setbacks, there is at least a 50 percent probability that most of North America would have been settled by the Spanish rather than by immigrants from England and other northern European countries.

- It is interesting to ponder the impact on Spain of its efforts to forcibly convert and exile its relatively large Jewish population in the 15th century. The Muslim sultan of Turkey, the recipient of large numbers of Jewish refugees, said, "Do you call this king (referring to the king of Spain) a statesman, who impoverishes his land and enriches mine?"[44] As noted earlier, the loss of Jewish talent arguably harmed the country and contributed to the decline of the Spanish Empire.

- Even with the decline of the Spanish Empire, England, France and the Dutch continued to respect Spanish colonial power and military might. These countries focused their initial settlements on the Chesapeake Bay, New York, New England and Canada, well north of Spain's small garrisons in eastern Florida.

- Spain and Portugal were major slave traders; together they accounted for more than 95 percent of all slaves transported to the Americas. If these countries had not experienced decline, it is possible that issues relating to slavery in North America would have been even more severe than they were (e.g., more slaves would have been imported). The implications of such a scenario are difficult to comprehend.

- The War of Spanish Succession ended plans for a merger of France and Spain. If these two countries had become a single nation, it is unlikely that English influence in North America would have been as dominant as it was. The eventual development of North America as a predominantly English-speaking, Protestant country might not have occurred.

- By 1700, when English immigration to New England and the Chesapeake region dropped off, poor economic and social conditions in Germany, Sweden, Ireland, Scotland and the Dutch Republic led to large numbers of colonists from these countries. The result was a more heterogeneous mix of people in the colonies than would have been the case with continued dependence on England. This, in turn, affected the desire of many Americans for independence from England.

- Martin Luther, King Henry VIII and John Calvin led movements that were of the utmost importance in establishing Protestantism in Europe and eventually in North America. Most of the English Puritans who came to New England were Calvinists—a belief system that closely integrated their Christian beliefs with freedom and the proper role of government.

- As England and France settled into their respective roles as world powers, England opted for a strong navy, and France invested heavily in its land forces. (Think about Napoleon Bonaparte's conquests following the French Revolution.) The strengths of these two countries, and their almost continuous conflicts, came into play in settling North America; during the Revolutionary War, England had the ability to transport relatively large numbers of soldiers and supplies across the Atlantic.

- The outcome of the French & Indian War was pivotal in shaping the British North American colonies. With the help of colonists, England gained control of nearly all of America north of Mexico and Florida. If England had not prevailed, the ramifications for the eventual development of North America would have been staggering. Even with a British victory, issues over financing the war-related debt sharply divided the American colonies and England.

- The science and technology that aided northern Europeans in their settlement of America was stimulated by Christian theology and scholarship, which had its origins in the Catholic Church during the Dark Ages.

Then there was the impact of the King James Bible. "By the early years of the United States...Scripture had become the national book par excellence...The revitalization and expansion of Protestantism in the early republic rested upon a widely shared confidence in the trustworthiness of the Bible. Broad familiarity with its contents characterized both ordinary people and elites."[45]

Consistent with John Jay's statement that led off this chapter ("a proper history of the United States...would develop the great plan of providence for causing this extensive part of our world to be discovered, and...gradually filled with civilized and Christian people and nations"), there appears to be a pattern of divine providence in terms of the timing of events in Europe, their impact on the initial exploration and settlement of North America, and in the development of the country during its first 200 years.

In his popular pamphlet, *Common Sense,* Thomas Paine argued that the discovery of America opened up space for religious dissidents who could not find a safe place in Europe. "The Reformation was preceded by the discovery of America, as if the Almighty graciously meant to open a sanctuary to the persecuted in future years, when home should afford neither friendship nor safety."[46] Paine also said, "This new world hath been the asylum for the persecuted lovers of civil and religious liberty from *every part* of Europe."[47]

The events described in this chapter contained the seeds of government, economics, culture and religion for the New World. What remained was for these seeds to be planted. The next chapter describes "the planting." Be forewarned; the planting was far more complex and turbulent than you may have understood it to be!

CHAPTER 2
▼

Settlement Patterns in Early America—A Diversity of Motivations

I always considered the settlement of America with Reverence and Wonder, as the Opening of a grand scene and design of Providence, for the illumination of the Ignorant and the Emancipation of the slavish part of Mankind.
—John Adams in James Hutson, *The Founders on Religion*, 15.

A typical comment from friends when we talk about the founding of America: "Our forefathers, the Pilgrims, came over on the Mayflower and settled in Plymouth in order to escape religious persecution. They set the tone for the expansion of Christianity in America. That is our heritage."

The truth is far more complex. For example, here are summaries of three early European efforts to settle North America:

- In 1587, under the leadership of Sir Walter Raleigh, a group of 117 settlers, including 17 women and nine boys, represented the first serious effort to plant a sustainable English colony in North America. (Two years earlier, there had been an attempt to build a fort near the same location; however, this group of 107 men sailed back to England.) The Roanoke colony disappeared while awaiting supplies from England. When the ship finally arrived (it had been delayed by threats to England from the Spanish Armada), all traces of the colony had vanished. The only clue to their disappearance were the letters "CRO" carved in a tree. This was believed to be an abbreviation for Croatoan, an island near present day Cape Hatteras on North Carolina's Outer Banks.

- The sign on the edge of Thomaston, Maine announces, "Thomaston, 1605." A cross and several plaques near the harbor recognize George Weymouth's visit in June 1605, two years before the first permanent North American settlement at Jamestown. After spending several days in the area, Weymouth kidnapped five Indians and returned to England. One of these men, Squanto, later played a key role in helping the Pilgrims survive in Plymouth.

- In August 1607, the same year the first group of English immigrants arrived at Jamestown, 100 settlers landed at a site on the Kennebec River, about 10 miles south of Bath, Maine. During the time they were there, the men built a 30-ton, 50-foot ship, *Virginia of Sagadahoc*, the first large ship built by Englishmen in the New World. However, the colonists became disillusioned with cold weather and lack of food, and by the death of their leader, George Popham. Half the group departed in late 1607 and the remainder sailed the *Virginia of Sagadahoc* to England the following year.

As these examples illustrate, the initial exploration and settlement of North America represents a messy and confusing picture. In addition to Roanoke Island and Popham Beach, there were abortive attempts to plant colonies in Quebec, Nova Scotia, Maine and Florida. It is generally believed that none of these were successful, although no one can be absolutely sure. For example, there is archeological evidence of a European settlement on Maine's Pemaquid Peninsula in the early 1600s; the small community was abandoned in 1676.

The same mixed bag is true of the motivations of the people who immigrated to North America. While the conventional wisdom is that most early settlers came to America seeking freedom from state-sponsored religions, our research indicates that many made the hazardous journey seeking adventure, release from bondage, and in search of land and jobs. The Pilgrims, Puritans and Quakers are examples of those largely motivated by a desire to pursue their own religious preferences. However, most of the other early settlements (e.g., Jamestown, New Hampshire, New York, Delaware, New Jersey and the Carolinas) were promoted by groups of investors looking for high financial returns, or by individuals seeking economic opportunities. The Georgia settlement was different still—a utopian dream of "Enlightened" English aristocrats who wanted to prove that downtrodden and intractable people could be rehabilitated into productive citizens.

Alexis de Tocqueville tells us that the origins of the people who came to the New World explain much about how America developed. "Providence has given us a torch which our forefathers did not possess, and has allowed us to discern fundamental causes in the history of the world which the obscurity of the past concealed from them. If we carefully examine the social and political state of America, after having studied its history, we shall remain perfectly convinced that not an opinion, not a custom, not a law, I may even say not an event, is upon record which the origin of that people will not explain." While acknowledging that the early settlers had different goals in coming to America, and that they came in waves over a 100-year period, Tocqueville concluded that "These men had, however, certain features in common, and they were all placed in an analogous situation. The tie of language is perhaps the strongest and the most durable that can unite mankind. All the emigrants spoke the same tongue; they were all offsets from the same people...they were more conversant with the notions of right and the principles of true freedom than the greater part of their European contemporaries."[1]

Exploratory Visits

There are many examples of explorers—Henry Hudson, Jacques Cartier and George Weymouth—visiting the coast of North America prior to efforts aimed at establishing permanent settlements. The summary that follows represents the tip of the iceberg and is intended to provide a flavor of early exploration of the coast of North America.

The Vikings. It is likely that Vikings from what is now Norway and the Scandinavian countries visited the Canadian Maritime Provinces, Maine and the coast of New England around 1000 AD.[2] The Norse called the southern part of their exploration Vinland, where they found wheat or rice, large trees and rich grazing lands.[3] The remains of Vinland are on the northern tip of Newfoundland.

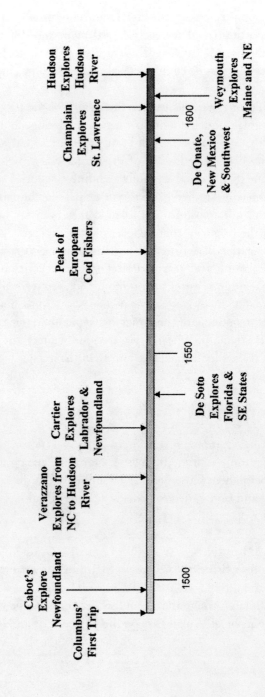

John and Sebastian Cabot. Just five years after Columbus, and again in 1508, John Cabot explored from Newfoundland to Cape Cod searching for a northwest passage to China. He and his crew were "the first Europeans since the Vikings to spot the North American mainland."[4] However, because of fear of Spanish naval power, there was no follow-up to the Cabots' explorations in terms of attempts at colonization. Sebastian Cabot, who was haunted by the disappearance of his father and the crews of four ships, "was particularly conscientious in seeking the support of Divine Providence."[5]

The cod fishers. By 1500 AD, or even earlier, ships from several European countries were fishing for cod off the shores of Newfoundland, Nova Scotia and Maine. "By 1508, 10 percent of the fish sold in the Portuguese ports of Douro and Minho was Newfoundland salt cod. By 1510 salt cod was a staple in Normandy's busy Rouen market."[6] In 1583, Sir Humphrey Gilbert counted 36 English, French, Spanish and Portuguese ships fishing off Newfoundland.[7]

Giovanni da Verazzano. In 1524 the King of France commissioned Verazzano, an Italian, to explore the North America mainland north of major Spanish activity. Verazzano sailed from Carolina's Cape Fear north to the Hudson River. After several months, Verazzano returned to France.

Jacques Cartier. Cartier commanded two ships that sailed for the New World in 1534, exploring present-day Labrador and Newfoundland. Returning from France the next year, he sailed past present-day Quebec City and Montreal on the St. Lawrence River. Cartier, who attempted to plant a colony in Quebec City, reported seeing Indians with complexions as white as Europeans![8]

Hernando de Soto. De Soto, a Spaniard, left Cuba in 1539 to explore Florida and much of what is now the southeastern United States. He was searching for a great city, which would be laden with gold and silver; he was also looking for an east-west river or waterway, opening up the long-wished-for passage to Asia. "Cutting a wide swath through Georgia, Alabama, Mississippi, Arkansas and Louisiana, de Soto found neither his capital city nor his watery way west. His followers made their way to the Gulf of Mexico, then by barges to Mexico, returning after more than four years of pointless plunder empty-handed and utterly disillusioned."[9]

Samuel de Champlain. In 1603 the French crown gave Champlain authority to explore the St. Lawrence Valley "...with an eye to imperial gain and French colonization...For the next several years, Champlain laid the foundations for France's future empire in North America's interior."[10]

Henry Hudson. In 1609 Hudson, an Englishman employed by the Dutch, explored the Hudson River and initiated fur trading with the Mohawks. The initial Dutch settlement near Albany came later, around 1614.

Unsustainable Efforts at Colonization

Following these and other voyages of exploration, and prior to the establishment of Jamestown, there were several attempts to land people on the coast of North America with the intent of establishing permanent colonies. Roanoke and Popham Beach were mentioned earlier. For a variety of reasons, most of these efforts failed.

1541, St. Lawrence River. More than 65 years before Jamestown, the French attempted to plant a colony along the St. Lawrence River. The group, led by Jacques Cartier, was defeated by cold, scurvy and Indians. "With nothing but corpses to show for the expensive effort, the French abandoned further attempts at permanently colonizing the St. Lawrence Valley until the next century."[11]

1562, Savannah River and northern Florida. French Huguenot (Protestant) settlements were established in present-day Georgia and northern Florida. The first effort on the Savannah River, led by Jean Ribault, was almost immediately destroyed by disease, starvation and Indian attacks. A second Huguenot settlement, on the St. John River in 1564, was known as Ft. Caroline. A year later, the Ft. Caroline Huguenots were massacred by Spanish forces.

1587, San Agustin, Florida. The Spanish consolidated their Florida colonies at San Agustin (near present-day St. Augustine). A fort had been built in 1565 giving the Spanish claim to the first settlement in North America. During the 1590s and early 1600s, Franciscan friars established missions along the Atlantic coast north of San Agustin and west along the Florida Gulf Coast. At the peak in 1675, 40 friars ministered to 20,000 native converts who worshiped at 36 churches.[12] Although the Spanish never established a permanent colony in Florida, they held the area until 1820.

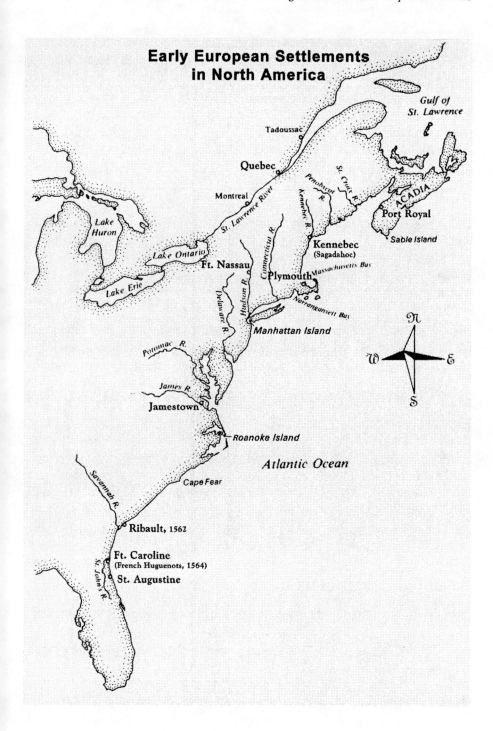

1604, Port Royal, Nova Scotia. Comte de Monts, a Huguenot, led 120 settlers (all men) to Sainte Croix Island off the coast of Acadia, which the British later named Nova Scotia. About half the group died the first winter, and Monts moved the survivors to a site across the Bay of Fundy to what is now Port Royal. In 1607, the handful of men who had survived, including Champlain, gave up and sailed back to France.[13] In 1610, Jean de Poutrincourt returned to Port Royal with supplies and 25 new settlers who found the habitations of the Monts group intact. The primary objectives of this new colony were fur trading and conversion of the Indians to Catholicism.[14]

Three years later, an attack by a ship from Jamestown dealt a serious blow to Port Royal. Although the Virginians destroyed their buildings, the inhabitants of Port Royal were in the fields working and were spared. After the attack, a handful of French remained in Port Royal acting as middlemen for the fur trade; no new settlers arrived until 1623.

In 1632, the French succeeded in establishing a settlement near the mouth of the LaHave River, on the Atlantic side of Nova Scotia. Isaac de Razilly arrived in "Acadie" with 300 men, three Capuchin Fathers and a small number of women and children. However, four years later most of the LaHave residents moved to Port Royal. By 1650, there were 50 French-speaking families living in the Port Royal area.[15]

1608, Quebec City. Champlain returned from France and used the experience gained at Port Royal, plus his knowledge of the St. Lawrence Valley, to establish a fur-trading base near present day Quebec City. Champlain began the winter of 1608-1609 with 28 men; eight survived. Even after being re-supplied, the number of residents of Quebec were small: 16 men in 1616 and 60 persons in 1620. It wasn't until 1617 that the first French family arrived.[16,17]

Sustainable Settlements

In this summary of the settlements that eventually became the 13 British North American colonies, our emphasis is on the origins of the immigrants, motivating factors leading them to immigrate to the new world, and the diversity of their religious beliefs and practices.

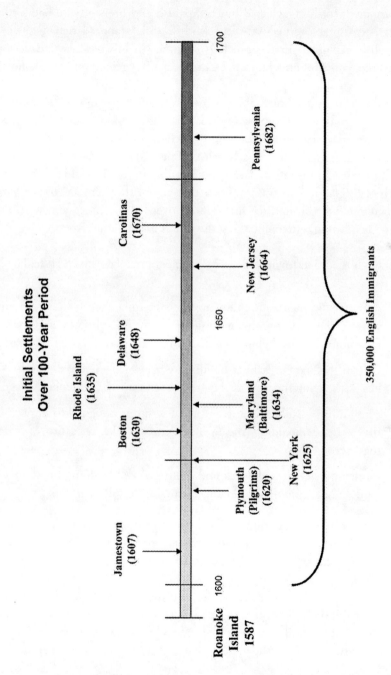

Jamestown (1607). Neglected by the Spanish and French, who had settled in Florida and Canada respectively, the Mid-Atlantic seaboard remained open to the English. As noted in the previous chapter, Spain's weakened naval power reduced the danger of attacks on the Chesapeake Bay region and points north.[18]

In early 1607 three small ships—*Godspeed, Discovery* and *Sarah Constant*—sailed from London to the New World. "This first colony, later called the Virginia Company, included 59 swaggering, self-appointed gentlemen, a few artisans, and one minister of the Church of England. On May 14, the day they arrived, they held a communion service according to the rites and doctrines of the Church of England."[19] It was a miracle that any of the members of the Virginia Company made it through the first winter (over half did not), and were able to sustain an enduring settlement along the shores of the James River.

Although the Jamestown settlement was a commercial venture, it had a Christian flavor:

- As noted, immediately following their landing they held a communion service. They were obviously grateful to be on land and have the five-month voyage behind them, and they thanked God for safe passage.
- One of the first permanent buildings was a small Anglican church. A replica of the church is part of the present Jamestown Settlement village.
- The minister, Robert Hunt, preached sermons designed to impress all of the settlers, including the "gentlemen," of the necessity of working together.
- Hunt ministered to the sick and dying, as well as doing his share of the hard work required to build and maintain the colony.

The economic turning point for Jamestown came in 1612 with the discovery that tobacco grew well in the soil and climate along the James River. By 1618, the colony was exporting 50,000 pounds of tobacco per year.

In 1619, 12 years after the first settlement, the Virginia Company sent its first 90 women to the colony. In that same year 20 Negro slaves were purchased from a Dutch man-of-war; other than household and personal slaves who came with a few of the settlers, this was the first shipment of slaves to North America.[20]

By 1622 the Virginia Company had transported 10,000 people to the Chesapeake Bay region, but only 1,132 were still alive and living in America. Jamestown was adjacent to a large swamp, which was good for defense against possible Spanish or Indian attacks, but bad for health. There were problems with mosquitoes (carriers of malaria), contaminated shallow wells, and stagnant river waters that did not carry away garbage and excrement, thus promoting typhoid fever."[21, 22]

Monhegan Island and the Kennebec River, present-day Maine (1618). Monhegan, off the coast of Maine, was a European fishing port two years before the Pilgrims arrived. The original settlers were part of a mutinous crew of Englishmen who built a village on the island. Maine historian Charles Coffin said, "And when the Pilgrims at Plymouth scraped the bottom of their corn bin in 1622 and starvation stared them in the face, Monhegan fed them...loading them down with fish."[23] In what Coffin cites as an example of Maine and American hospitality, the residents of Monhegan did not take payment for the food they provided.

Coffin also claims that as early as 1615 the coast around the Kennebec was "studded with fishing settlements" and traders. "Before 1623, there were flourishing settlements along the Kennebec, at Sagadahoc (now Bath), and at Merrymeeting..." By 1634, masts for Royal Navy ships were being cut along the Kennebec. "In 1635, there were, not counting fishermen and trappers and traders, almost 150 families set up in steady housekeeping by the Kennebec."[24]

Plymouth (1620). In 1607 William Bradford led a group of Puritans from England to the Dutch Republic. His congregation had been denounced, and had decided to separate from the Church of England. This group of Puritan separatists objected to Queen Elizabeth's 39 Articles, which they believed included too many remnants of Catholicism.

After several years of negotiations, 50 of these separatist Puritans decided to leave for North America. They were joined on the *Mayflower* by a group of 50 Englishmen, who were seeking a new life in America. Before landing, the Puritan separatists and the men entered into a covenant relationship—the *Mayflower Compact.*

The Mayflower Compact, 1620

In the name of God, amen. We whose names are under-written, the loyal subjects of our dread Sovereign Lord King James by the Grace of God of Great Britain, France, Ireland, King, Defender of the Faith, etc. Having undertaken, for the glory of God and advancement of the Christian Faith and honor of King and country, a voyage to plant the first colony in the northern parts of Virginia, do by these presents solemnly and mutually in the presence of God and one of another, covenant and combine ourselves together into a civil body politic, for our better ordering and preservation and furtherance of the ends aforesaid, and by virtue hereof to enact, constitute and frame such just and equal laws, ordinances, acts, constitutions and offices from time to time, as shall be thought most meet and convenient for the general good of the colony. Unto which we promise all due submission and obedience. In witness whereof we have hereunder subscribed our names at Cape Cod, the 11th of November, in the year of the reign of our Sovereign King James of England…Anno Domini 1620.[25]

In many respects, the *Mayflower Compact* was the first written constitution in North America. This document represents evidence of the Christian heritage of what was to become the United States.

In the spring, the colonists learned that disease (perhaps measles) had wiped out nearly all of the local Indians. "The last Pawtuxet survivor was an Indian named Squanto who had been snatched off to England, where he learned language well enough to serve as a middle man with the few Indians in the area. They agreed on a treaty with Chief Massasoit that lasted half a century."[26] As noted earlier, Squanto was one of five Indians kidnapped by George Weymouth's crew 15 years earlier. Bradford referred to Squanto as "a spetiall instrument sent by God."[27]

Although only half the colonists survived the first winter, good crops and more immigrants stabilized and strengthened the colony. Ten years later, at the time John Winthrop and his group (the Massachusetts Bay Company) arrived, a few hundred English settlers were living in the Plymouth colony. In 1691, the

British Crown issued a new charter for Massachusetts extending its authority over Plymouth; the Pilgrims were absorbed into Puritan society.

New Hampshire (1623). Under the auspices of three merchants of Plymouth, England, David Thomson led a group of men in establishing a European settlement near present-day Portsmouth. In that same year, the Laconia Company (jointly owned by Ferdinando Gorges and John Mason) sent a small group of men under Edward and William Hilton to the area. In 1629 Gorges and Mason divided their holdings, with Mason ending up with the territory south of the Piscataqua River (present-day New Hampshire). Thus, Thomson's small colony fell under the control of Mason and the Hiltons.[28] A year later, Mason sent Captain Walter Neal to "perpetuate the settlement" along the Piscataqua. Impressed by the thick growth of wild berries along the west bank of the river, Neal moved the settlement close to what is called "Strawberry Banke," now a restored 10-acre historic site adjacent to downtown Portsmouth.

By 1640 the growing population of Puritans flowing out of Massachusetts spawned new settlements to the northeast. "...some Puritans settled along the coasts of New Hampshire and Maine, where they mingled uneasily with fishing folk, nominal Anglicans who came from the English West Country."[29] For a variety of reasons, the leaders of the towns of Dover, Exeter and Portsmouth agreed to place themselves under the control of Massachusetts. This arrangement lasted until 1741 when New Hampshire was chartered as a separate colony.

New York (1625). In 1614 the Dutch established Fort Nassau on the Hudson River near present day Albany and another small settlement at the mouth of the river on Manhattan Island. These men were fur traders, not settlers. It wasn't until 1625 when Peter Minuit, sponsored by the West India Company of the Netherlands, arrived with the first immigrants intent on establishing a permanent settlement on Manhattan Island. (The purchase of Manhattan Island from the Indians took place a year later.) By 1629, New Amsterdam on the south end of the island had a population of 300.[30]

In 1647, four years after serious Indian fighting, New Amsterdam began to grow. Its new governor, Peter Stuyvesant, and the West India Company began promoting the advantages of living in New Amsterdam, including openness to a diversity of religious sects. New residents from many European countries and from New England led to a population of more than 4,000 by 1650.[31] By 1664, when the English took over and changed the name to New York, there were more than 10,000 inhabitants, including French Huguenots, Catholics (from Belgium), Puritans, and Sephardic Jews. The Dutch took back New York in 1673, but held it only briefly. "Fifteen months after retaking the colony, with the signing of yet another peace treaty, the Dutch gave it back."[32]

Massachusetts Bay Company (1630). A decade after the Pilgrims landed at Plymouth (and two years after a group of 30 men, women and children under Roger Conant had arrived in Salem, north of Boston), John Winthrop led nearly 1,000 Puritans to what is now the Boston area. Over the next 10 years, more than 14,000 Puritans emigrated from England to Massachusetts, dramatically increasing the population of New England. By 1650, New England had 22,000 residents, about the same number as the Chesapeake region (Virginia and Maryland combined).[33]

In his famous "Citee on the Hill" sermon delivered aboard ship, Winthrop said that Puritans immigrating to New England were entering into a covenant relationship with God. If they succeeded in living lives that pleased God, "the Lord will be our God and delight to dwell among us as his own people, and will command a blessing upon us in all our ways, so that we shall see much more of his wisdom, power, goodness and truth than formerly we have been acquainted with (in England)."[34]

One historian noted that "Puritan values helped the colonists prosper in a demanding land. In the process they developed a culture that was both the most entrepreneurial and the most vociferously pious in Anglo-America. Contrary to the declension model (decline from a higher, pristine state) promoted by some historians, the increasing commercialism of New England life at the end of the seventeenth century derived from Puritan values rather than manifested their decay."[35] The Puritans of New England strongly believed that the success or failure of their society was dependent on whether or not they obeyed the designs of divine providence. "They believed, for example, that God smiled upon the quest of liberty."[36]

The first printing press in America was set up in Cambridge shortly after the arrival of the settlers. The initial printing run included 1,700 copies of *The Bay Psalm Book*. "By 1744 the book was in its twenty-sixth edition, reaffirming with each new printing that Puritan congregations would no longer be wholly dependent on England for religious books or even interpretations of sacred text. With this one publication the colonists had made a dramatic statement in developing their own culture of prayer and spirituality in the New World."[37]

Maryland (1634). During his 1629 visit, Lord Calvert, the First Baron Baltimore, fell in love with the Chesapeake region. In 1632 the Crown set aside 12 million acres at the northern head of the Chesapeake Bay as a second colony, to be named Maryland after the queen of the new monarch, Charles I.[38] Under Lord Calvert's younger brother, Leonard Baltimore, the first contingent of colonists arrived on two ships and dropped anchor at a site on the Potomac River called St. Mary's City. All told, the first wave of immigrants included 17 Catholic men and their wives (the first significant number of Catholics to arrive in British North America), 200 Anglicans and a few indentured servants.[39]

Rhode Island (1635). Roger Williams came to the Boston area (initially to Plymouth and then to Salem) in 1631. In a sermon, he referred to the Massachusetts Bay Company as a fraud since it derived from what he considered to be the criminal English Crown. "He also protested the (local) laws on compulsory church attendance, tithes, and the swearing of oaths."[40] In 1635, on the basis of rumors of his impending arrest, Williams and several followers left Salem and settled near Narragansett Bay (present day Providence). He was soon joined by other dissidents, including Anne Hutchinson and William Coddington, who became the first governor of Rhode Island.

Rhode Island's constitution, developed by Williams in 1640, separated church and state, eschewed religious tests, and established assemblies elected by heads of families. Rhode Island received a charter from Parliament in 1644.

Connecticut (1635). Only five years after establishing Boston, a group of Puritans, including Thomas Hooker, John Winthrop, Jr. and 100 others settled the town of Hart's Ford (Hartford). "In 1662, the English government issued a royal charter to the colony of Connecticut that incorporated New Haven, Hartford, Windsor, New London, and Middletown."[41]

Delaware (1648). In 1638, while heavily engaged in Germany's Thirty-Years' War, Sweden granted its West India Company a charter to found New Sweden at Fort Christina, near present-day Wilmington, Del. Ten years later about 400 colonists, mainly Swedes and Finns (referred to as "Forest Finns" because of their expertise in clearing forests), had settled in the area, were clearing land and beginning to farm.[42,43] In 1655 the Dutch Republic took Delaware from Sweden, and integrated it into Manhattan and other Dutch holdings in what were referred to as the Middle Colonies.[44] The English took control of Delaware in 1664.

New Jersey (1664). The Duke of York awarded New Jersey to two English noblemen, who in turn sold their interests to two sets of investors, one from Scotland and the other led by English Quakers. New Jersey was then divided into two colonies, with the Scots taking East Jersey near New York and the Quakers occupying West Jersey along the Delaware River. East Jersey, which attracted Dutch farmers, Puritans from New England and Scottish immigrants, was more multi-ethnic than West Jersey, populated primarily by Quakers. The two Jerseys reunited in 1702. The consolidation of a diverse people led to unusual tolerance of religious beliefs.[45]

Carolina (1670). Carolina, which included land that is now North Carolina, South Carolina and Georgia, was initially settled by people of English ancestry who had lived in Barbados. Many were from families who had owned sugar plantations, but found that the small island of Barbados could no longer support them in the lifestyle they wished. A group of English aristocrats, called the Lords Proprietors, eight powerful political favorites of the king, owned Carolina. These men remained in England and left early colonization to the people of Barbados.[46]

In 1650, before the settlement at Charles Town, there were a number of small villages around Albemarle Sound (north of the ill-fated Roanoke Colony) that were part of the Chesapeake settlements. These colonists resented their inclusion in Carolina. To mollify the Albemarle Sound people, North Carolina was established in 1691 as a distinct government with its own assembly.[47]

This division left Charles Town as the capital of South Carolina. The Goose Creek Men, the dominant early settlers from Barbados, stifled religious diversity, and in 1702, only 30 years after the initial settlers had arrived with a promise of religious freedom, the assembly barred non-Anglicans from holding public office. The Church of England was established as the colony's official tax-supported church.[48]

Although the Carolinas initially provided cattle and lumber to the British West Indies, and tar for ships, there was an opportunity to produce rice, a labor-intensive crop. By 1740 the Carolinas had become the British Empire's great rice colony, just as the Chesapeake region specialized in tobacco and the West Indies in sugar.[49]

Pennsylvania (1682). As a young Englishman, William Penn came under the influence of a Society of Friends (Quaker) itinerant preacher. Despite family resistance and four stints in prison, Penn stuck with his new religion. Because of his family's connections with the Crown (his father was a naval war hero), he was given a charter to establish a colony in what is now Pennsylvania.

Penn arrived in 1682 on one of 18 large ships bearing the vanguard of the 11,000 immigrants who came the first decade.[50] By 1750 there were more Quakers living in the colonies than in Britain. In America they possessed a community of their own, one in which they held the powers of government. At the time of his arrival in Pennsylvania, Penn said: "It is impossible that any people or government should ever prosper, where men render not unto God, that which is God's, as well as to Caesar, that which is Caesar's."[51] Penn and the Quakers were soon followed by another large influx of European emigrants who brought with them a variety of religious backgrounds. "As early as 1683 Francis Daniel Pastorius purchased fifteen thousand acres on which to build Germantown for his company of Rhenish Quakers and Mennonites. An influx of Welshmen left their place names all over Pennsylvania's first counties. Scots-Irish, Swedes, and Dutch added to an ethnic mix as cosmopolitan as New York's."[52]

Georgia (1733). James Oglethorpe conducted colonists across the Atlantic to found Savannah. This colony, which was the brainchild of a group of London philanthropists and social reformers, represented a mix of wealthy merchants, landed gentry, and Anglican ministers. "They hoped to alleviate English urban poverty by shipping 'miserable wretches' and 'drones' to a new southern colony, where hard work on their own farms would cure indolence. By this moral alchemy, people who drained English charity would become productive subjects working both to improve themselves and to defend the empire on a colonial frontier."[53] The new colonists represented a variety of Protestant sects, plus a few Jews; there were no Catholics. By 1751 the strict rules of the philanthropists proved unworkable and Georgia developed into a plantation society similar to that of South Carolina.[54] One historian summed up the situation this way: "Georgia was intended to be a model colony of the Age of Enlightenment...The colony itself prospered; but the experiment in reason, justice and science failed."[55]

Founding of the 13 Colonies—Anything but Homogeneous

- Virginia—commercial venture.
- Massachusetts—Pilgrims and Puritans.
- Rhode Island—religious dissidents.
- Connecticut—Puritans
- Maryland—Roman Catholics and Protestants.
- New York—Dutch; commercial motivations.
- New Jersey—Quakers and others; commercial motivations.
- Delaware—Swedes, Finns and others.
- Carolinas—planters and slaves from Barbados.
- Pennsylvania—Quakers, Scots, Irish, Germans.
- Georgia—utopian community (England).

North American Settlements Beyond Colonial America

Although not part of the original 13 colonies, there were two other noteworthy settlements—Santa Fe and New Orleans—in the first 100 plus years of what is now the United States.

Santa Fe (1610). In 1598 Don Juan de Onate led 500 Mexicans into what is now northern New Mexico and established the capital at San Juan Pueblo. In 1610, Don Pedro de Peralta, the governor, moved the capital 25 miles south to Santa Fe. During the next 70 years, Spanish soldiers and officials, as well as Franciscan missionaries, tried to subjugate and convert the 100,000 Indians in the area.

In 1680 Pueblo Indians revolted against the 2,500 Spanish colonists, killing 400 of them. The remainder escaped to Mexico. Pueblo Indians occupied Santa Fe until 1692-93 when don Diego de Vargas reestablished Spanish control. In 1846, during the early phases of the Mexican American War, General Stephen Kearny took Santa Fe and raised the American flag over the Plaza. In 1848, as part of the Treaty of Guadalupe Hidalgo, Mexico ceded Santa Fe and New Mexico to the United States.

New Orleans (1718). The finances and manpower drain required to fight the War of the Spanish Succession left France unable to invest significant resources in Louisiana. "In 1708, Louisiana consisted of merely 122 soldiers and sailors, 80 slaves, and 77 habitants, scattered along the Gulf Coast. Instead of developing plantations, the early colonists lived by a mix of fishing, subsistence gardening, livestock herding, wildlife hunting, and petty trading with the natives."[56]

Following the Treaty of Utrecht, however, the Company of the Indies, authorized by the French crown, established a colony 125 miles up the Mississippi River near present-day New Orleans. To attract settlers, the company granted long and narrow pieces of land along the Mississippi River. "Between 1717 and 1730, at considerable expense, the Company of the Indies transported 5,400 European colonists and 6,000 African slaves to Louisiana…Most of the Europeans were French, but a substantial minority (about 1,300) were German Catholics, who proved the most industrious and prosperous of the early colonists."[57] The French also used Louisiana as a penal colony.

The lack of food and difficult living conditions, plus severe outbreaks of disease, dramatically reduced New Orleans' population. Some immigrants left for Florida where many died. By 1731 only one-third of the original European colonists were still alive. However, from 1740 on, with better farming and acquired immunity to disease, the situation improved.[58]

The Acadians (or Cajuns) who came to Louisiana were a remnant of the more than 6,000 French settlers the British deported from Nova Scotia in 1755, during the early days of the French & Indian War. Some were expelled to France, where they lived for three decades. In 1785, on the eve of the French Revolution, 1,700 returned to North America settling in Louisiana.[59] "Today these French Cajuns (a slurred version of "Acadian") still reside in or near the marshes and Louisiana bayous…"[60]

Religious Diversity in Early America

Although many of the colonies (e.g., Virginia, New Hampshire, New York, New Jersey, Delaware and the Carolinas) were initially founded as commercial ventures, the Christian religion of almost all the new immigrants was important to them. We know, of course, that it was all-important for the Pilgrims of Plymouth, the Puritans of Massachusetts and Connecticut, and the Quakers of New Jersey and Pennsylvania.

Geographic variations in religion. Because Massachusetts was adequately supplied with Cambridge and Oxford-trained clergy, this colony was especially significant in establishing an early Christian heritage in North America. "All were committed to the idea of a godly society as one in which literacy was general and opportunities existed for the transmission of learning."[61]

Most of the pre-1700 settlers in other colonies were Protestants of a Calvinistic persuasion. These Calvinists, which included most of the Dutch who initially settled the Hudson River and Manhattan Island, believed that while church and society were separate spheres of human activity, they were both under the control of God.[62]

Historian James Hutson noted that there were fewer people in Virginia (and points south) than in the northern colonies and that their religion was not a passion. "But there were plenty of devout men and women south of the Potomac, and so many in the other colonies, that there can be no doubt—none whatsoever—that religion was the salt that flavored life in seventeenth-century British North America."[63]

Economic incentives important. Kenneth Latourette, who specialized in church history, agreed with those who focus on the economic incentives to migrate to America. "The overwhelming proportion of settlers came to the colonies for economic or social rather than religious motives. They were mostly from the underprivileged and by migrating to the New World sought to better their financial or their social standing."[64]

Another historian concurred: "Myth insists that the seventeenth-century English colonists fled from religious persecution into a land of religious freedom. In addition to omitting economic considerations, the myth grossly simplifies the diverse religious motives for emigration. Not all colonists had felt persecuted at home, and few wanted to live in a society that tolerated a plurality of religions. Perfectly content with the official Anglican faith of the homeland, many colonists sought to replicate it in the colonies. And although some English dissenters, principally the Quakers, did seek in America a general religious freedom, many more emigrants wanted their own denomination to dominate, to the prejudice of all others. Indeed, at the end of the seventeenth century, most colonies offered *less* religious toleration than did the mother country."[65]

Regardless of why they came to North America—for land and economic opportunity, to escape European wars and taxes, for adventure, to escape bondage, or for religious freedom—most of the new immigrants were Protestant Christians of one denomination or another. In some colonies, such as New York, New Jersey, Rhode Island, and Pennsylvania, the new residents quickly learned to live together while pursuing better lives. The ability of people of different denominations to find ways to live in harmony is part of America's Christian heritage.

The Status of the Colonies in 1730—A Recap

Looking back at the colonies a century after John Winthrop and his band of Puritans established Boston, here is the picture that emerges:

- By 1730, the European population of the colonies was about 500,000.

- Other than a limited number of ex-convicts, immigration from England had dried up; most new immigrants, who were arriving at the rate of about 7,000 per year, came from Germany, Scotland, Ireland, Netherlands, and the Scandinavian countries. Although English was the language of choice, many tongues—and accents—were common in America.

- More than 90 percent of the residents of the colonies lived on farms or widely scattered villages. Except in larger cities (Boston, New York, Philadelphia and Charles Town were the big four), professional, ordained ministers were in short supply.

- London was the focus of most colonies. Because of poor roads and lack of communications, commerce was primarily back and forth with England. Colonists typically did not have personal relationships with people in other colonies up and down the eastern seaboard.

- About one-quarter of the original immigrants and their descendents were Congregationalists (Puritans), but this denomination had been diluted with the Half-Way Covenant, which allowed people who were not full members to partake in communion and have their children baptized. Furthermore, since non-members could not hold public office, the Half-Way Covenant represented a way to get around the old, more stringent rules.

- There was an almost uniform opinion that America was God's chosen land. Harvard historian Bernard Bailyn said that the colonists carried the idea "…that the colonization of British America had been an event designed by the hand of God to satisfy his ultimate aims…this influential strain of thought, found everywhere in the eighteenth-century colonies, stimulated confidence in the idea that America had a special place, as yet not fully revealed, in the architecture of God's intent."[66]

- Although Harvard, William & Mary, and Yale had been established, there were no officially sanctioned, degree-granting colleges or universities in America. Harvard was established primarily to train clergy.

The bottom line: After more than 100 years, the colonies were populated by people who originated in England, Scotland, Ireland, Germany, several other European countries, Barbados and Africa (the slaves). Other than their predominant Protestant Christianity, the English language, and a desire to make a living for their families, they had little in common. However, between 1730 and 1770 this changed dramatically, largely because of an intense colony-wide religious revival referred to (after the fact) as the Great Awakening.

CHAPTER 3

The Impact of the Great Awakening—The Emergence of Discontent

The Great Awakening was not a misnomer...It was great because it was an event—or rather a series of events—that had a wider scope and impact than any previous episode in American history.
        —James Hutson, *Religion and the Founding of the American Republic,* 25.

In June 1775 a company of men from New Hampshire joined the Continental Army, fighting with distinction at Bunker Hill. That fall, the survivors of this historic battle were among the 1,100 troops who followed Benedict Arnold up the Kennebec River to attack Quebec City in what proved to be an ill-fated expedition. Along the way, they spent three days camped at Newburyport, Mass., where they worshiped at Old South Church before leaving for Canada. Oddly, at least to contemporary minds, the troops talked the rector into opening the casket of George Whitefield, an evangelist who died in 1770, so that they might cut out swatches of his clothing to carry with them as good luck charms.

Alas, the scraps of George Whitefield's coat proved no more reliable protection than the average medieval saints' relics or discarded tissues from today's rock stars, but they tell us a great deal about Whitefield's status in his own time. This man of God, an Oxford-trained itinerant preacher on both sides of the Atlantic, delivered sermons from the steps of American courthouses and in fields to thousands of avid listeners. He was the Billy Graham of mid-18th century England and America, a cultural icon with few peers, the most famous man in the colonies in his time.

Yet more than 200 years after Whitefield's death, if you visit Newburyport, chances are that most people you meet will not have the slightest idea who George Whitefield was. You will find an old port town promoting its many historic buildings dating back to its days as a shipbuilding center, when a number of its most prominent residents were shipbuilders or captains. Most of the town's tourist brochures and booklets do not mention Whitefield. In fact, in a recent visit to the Newburyport visitor's center, only one of the two women working there knew that Whitefield's remains were buried at Old South Church. Obligingly, she called the church to find out if anyone was there; no one answered the phone. When asked about the lack of interest in Whitefield, she reiterated that "Newburyport has many old houses and has an illustrative history going back to Revolutionary times." In other words, very few people care about an old, dead evangelist.

Whitefield's fall into obscurity parallels that of the Great Awakening, the religious revival movement of the mid-18th century in which he was the most visible personality. To read colonial history as it has been recently reported by several prominent historians, one would be hard pressed to find so much as a mention of the Great Awakening, much less Whitefield, Jonathan Edwards, or any of its other prominent leaders.

Although John Adams is known to have said, "The Revolution was in the minds and hearts of the people; a change in their religious sentiments, of their duties and obligations...This radical change in the principles, opinions, sentiments, and affections of the people was the real American Revolution,"[1] many well-known historians omit discussion of the Great Awakening. For example, David Fischer, a professor at Brandeis University, does not mention the Great Awakening in his 850-page book, *Liberty and Freedom*. His only reference to religion is a paragraph about John Adams' efforts to assure freedom of religion in Massachusetts in 1820.[2] Given the large-scale Christian conversions in America described in this chapter, and their impacts on a desire for liberty and freedom—the central theme of Fischer's book—this strikes us as a serious omission.

Some academic historians go even further and either claim that the Great Awakening has been over-rated or deny that it happened. For example, in his book, *Inventing the Great Awakening*, Frank Lambert questions whether significant, intercolonial religious revivals actually took place in the middle of the 18th century, or whether the whole thing was the result of publicity (hype) by the revivalists. Jon Butler, a Yale history professor, writes that the growth in pluralism of churches is the real story of the mid 18th century and that the revivals were over-stated. "Private letters from ministers to each other, read at public occasions on both sides of the Atlantic, created a 'concert of prayer' that made the revivals of the 1740s and 1750s seem even more momentous than they were."[3] A New England historian attributes much of the "temporary" revival in Maine to an earthquake which drove people to search for spiritual answers.[4]

From our perspective, the more we have studied the early history of America, the more we have become convinced that the series of spiritual revivals that swept the colonies in the mid 1700s were tremendously important. We agree with historian Paul Johnson; "Whatever we call it, however, there was a spiritual event in the first half of the 18th Century in America, and it proved to be of vast significance, both in religion and in politics. It was indeed one of the key events in American history."[5] Johnson continued that the Great Awakening "made not only parish boundaries seem unimportant but all boundaries. Hitherto, each colony had seen its outward links as running chiefly to London. Each tended to be a little self-contained world of its own. That was to remain the pattern in the Spanish colonies for another century, independence making no difference in that respect. The Great Awakening altered this separateness. It taught different colonies, tidewaters and piedmonts, coast and up-country, to grasp and appreciate what they had in common, which was a very great deal."[6] Furthermore, George Whitefield was the first American celebrity, "equally well known from Georgia to New Hampshire."[7]

As discussed in the previous chapter, 100 years after the Puritans landed in Boston, Christianity in North America did not differ much from the patterns of the old country. Most churches were structured along the lines of the European model with ministers having unquestioned moral authority, and with churches typically upholding class distinctions among members and the community as a whole. "All of this (the revivals) fit perfectly into the large antiauthoritarian pattern in colonial America, giving the First Great Awakening a political as well as social impact."[8]

This chapter provides an overview of how this series of revivals unfolded, and the resulting spiritual, social and political ramifications for the colonies. Topics discussed include:

- How the revivals, beginning in New Jersey around 1725 and in Massachusetts in 1735, set the stage for more dramatic awakenings up and down the eastern seaboard.

- How three key players in the Great Awakening—John and Charles Wesley, and their protégé George Whitefield—developed their religious "enthusiasm" and ended up as leaders of the spiritual revivals in both Great Britain and North America.

- George Whitefield's impact on America, especially during his second trip to the colonies in 1739-1741.

- The effect of the spiritual revivals on the structure of churches and denominations before the war for independence.

- The impact of the Great Awakening on the social structure of the colonies, and the relevance of these structural changes to a growing desire for independence.

Religious Revival Breaks Out in America in the Mid-1720s

The first colonial revival generally considered to be part of the Great Awakening began in an unlikely place: a Dutch Reformed Church in New Jersey. About the same time, Gilbert Tennent, a Presbyterian minister, led a revival in New Jersey. A few years later, another much-publicized revival broke out in a Congregational (Puritan) Church in Northampton, Mass. The spiritual explosion in America had begun.

Raritan Valley revival. In 1721 Theodore Frelinghuysen, the pastor of Dutch Reformed churches in the Raritan Valley of New Jersey, began proclaiming the need for an inner transformation rather than the mere outward performance of religious ceremonies.[9] A recent immigrant from Holland, Frelinghuysen was

Dean C. Coddington and Richard L. Chapman   47

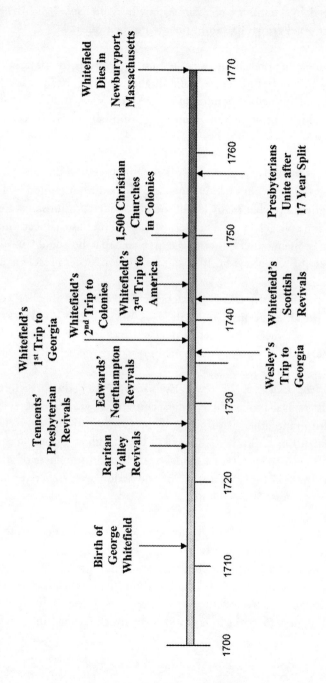

influenced by German protestants known as pietists, "who believed that most Christians had grown flaccid in practicing their faith."[10]

Although his preaching provoked criticism from the pastors of other Dutch Reformed churches in the area, Frelinghuysen soon had a wide following. "Yet lay men and women responded to his fresh message, and his 'emotionally-powerful preaching brought an increasing number of new converts' into the churches."[11]

The Tennents. In 1727 Gilbert Tennent became minister of the Presbyterian Church in New Brunswick, New Jersey. He had been trained by his father, William Tennent, in what many established Presbyterian ministers scornfully referred to as a "log college" (a rural academy focusing on basic education and godliness). Gilbert Tennent quickly became convinced that he should model his ministry after that of Frelinghuysen. It wasn't long before other preachers followed.[12]

Additional Presbyterian ministers were prepared in the "log college," and the revival spread, especially among the Scottish and Irish immigrants. Graduates of the first "log college" founded similar colleges for the training of ministers, and this generated a stream of young men preaching the urgency of conversion.[13]

Jonathan Edwards. In the early 1730s, under the preaching of Jonathan Edwards, revival broke out in Massachusetts. A graduate of Yale, Edwards followed his grandfather as minister of the Congregational Church in Northampton, west of Boston in the Connecticut River Valley. "Speaking slowly, distinctly, and with great solemnity, he made vivid the loathsomeness of sin. In the winter and spring of 1734-1735 a wave of conviction swept over the community and hundreds professed conversion."[14]

Edwards organized small groups, divided by age and gender, to meet in private homes for Bible study and fellowship. "By March 1735 other towns in Hampshire County were experiencing the same communal turn to heartfelt, all-consuming faith. News circulated rapidly about the dozens, and then hundreds, who were 'brought to a lively sense of the excellency of Jesus Christ and his sufficiency and willingness to save sinners, and to be much weaned in their affections from the world.'"[15]

Edwards' account of the Northampton revival, known as the *Faithful Narrative*, was published in England in 1737. It was an immediate best seller and an instant classic. Edwards' publication was more than a record of God's work; it was an authoritative description of how "…our ascended Savior now and then takes a special occasion to manifest the divinity of this Gospel by a plentiful effusion of his Spirit where it is preached: then sinners are turned into saints in numbers, and there is a new face of things spread over a town or a country."[16] Although the language is quaint, Edwards pretty well describes "the effusion of the Spirit" in America during the Great Awakening.

"The pattern was becoming widespread. Clearly something was going on. More and more individuals were being deeply affected by the gospel. Large numbers of people became serious about their need for God. Next came revival."[17]

Meanwhile, Back in England

John and Charles Wesley were the sons of a Church of England pastor, and attended Oxford, where they tried to be good Christians. They were founders of what was referred to, derisively, as the "Holy Club," "Bible moths," Enthusiasts," or "Methodists." In modern day parlance, the Wesleys and many of their friends were seekers after personal salvation and a deeper walk with Christ. The Wesleys never intended to separate from the Church of England. Their goal, until they were pressured to change late in their lives, was to be a force for spiritual growth and good within the established Anglican Church.

The Wesleys travel to Georgia. In late 1735 John Wesley accepted an invitation to sail to Georgia to minister to English settlers and Native Americans. He insisted that his younger brother, Charles (the famous hymn writer), accompany him. When the Wesleys and two colleagues boarded ship for America, they found they would be traveling with a group of Moravians, protestant refugees driven out of Bohemia and Moravia (in modern-day Czech Republic) by pressure from Catholic Austria. This sect was offered sanctuary by Nicholas Ludwig von Zinzendorf at his substantial estate in southwest Saxony (in present-day Germany). The Moravians were pietists, meaning they were born-again Christians with a focus on a continuing personal relationship with Christ (the same definition as often used for evangelicals).

Aboard the ship bound for Savannah, the Wesleys and their fellow passengers ran into a series of violent storms. John Wesley, who was afraid he was going to die, was deeply impressed by the Moravians' lack of fear. The Moravians calmly sang hymns of praise as the sea broke over the deck splitting the mainsail in pieces. The combination of the storm and close contact with the Moravians and their evangelical Christianity had profound long-term impacts on England, America and the rest of the world.

Both on board ship, in Georgia and later in England, John Wesley's contacts with the Moravians changed his life. When John Wesley left Georgia in December 1737 (his brother Charles had returned to England earlier), "his ongoing High-Church seriousness was still a rich spiritual soil, and into that soil had now been planted a quickening Moravian seed."[18] Was it divine providence that a great storm threatened to destroy the ship carrying the Wesleys to Georgia? It was during this storm that John Wesley realized that the faith of the Moravians was special, and he decided to learn more once they landed.

George Whitefield arrives on the scene. Whitefield was born of innkeeper parents in Gloucester, England, in December 1714. During his youth, he was a mediocre student who showed a talent for acting; he appeared to be headed for a career on stage. However, at age 18, he entered Oxford University where he financed his education by doing laundry, cleaning rooms, and serving food to the wealthier students.[19]

During his first few months at Oxford, Whitefield read William Law's, *A Serious Call to a Devout Life*, and said, "God worked powerfully upon my soul, as He has since upon many others, by that and his other excellent treatise upon *Christian Perfection*."[20]

Although he didn't know the Wesleys personally, Whitefield had heard of them. He finagled an invitation to meet Charles Wesley, who provided additional books that described the experiences and works of a number of pietist leaders. As a result, Whitefield was drawn more deeply into the Wesley's network. "From time to time Mr. Wesley permitted me to come unto him, and instructed me as I was able to bear it. By degrees he introduced me to the rest of his Christian brethren. They built me up daily in the knowledge and fear of God, and taught me to endure hardness like a good soldier of Jesus Christ. I now began, like them, to live by rule, and to pick up the very fragments of my time, that not a moment of it might be lost. Whether I ate or drank, or whatsoever I did, I endeavoured to do it all to the glory of God...I joined with them in keeping the stations by fasting Wednesdays and Fridays and left no means unused, which I thought would lead me nearer to Jesus Christ."[21]

In late 1736, following graduation from Oxford and ordination as a Church of England pastor, Whitefield received a letter from John Wesley urging him to come to Savannah; he decided to go. In the 12 months it took to make travel arrangements, Whitefield's status completely changed; he began to preach. "Whitefield, the novice young preacher of justification by faith, was transformed into a national sensation...Beginning in August and continuing through December he was mostly in London, where unprecedented throngs flocked to hear his sermons."[22]

Whitefield's Impact on the Great Awakening

Whitefield arrived in Georgia in early 1738, but was back in England by the end of the year. He got along well in America where he preached an average of twice a day and four times on Sunday. While in Georgia he established several schools and took the initial steps to build an orphanage (the colony had many orphans), a project he continued to promote throughout his ministry in America.

By the time Whitefield had returned to London, the Wesleys had been fellowshiping with the Moravians for several months, and it had changed their lives. "Whitefield's return to London in December (1738) stoked the flames of renewal to an even higher pitch." At a meeting on January 1 and 2, 1739, attended by Whitefield and several others, John Wesley reported, "About three in the morning, as we were continuing instant in prayer, the power of God came mightily upon us, insomuch that many cried out for exceeding joy, and many fell to the ground."[23] It was a prelude to the future.

It is miraculous that three young men whose lives dramatically changed the world were together for one of the most dynamic prayer meetings on record. John and Charles Wesley began a ministry within the established Church of England that had profound impacts on the hearts and minds of people in Great Britain for the next 50 years; after the Revolutionary War, Methodism became the fastest growing denomination in the United States. The Wesleys were joined by George Whitefield, who was to become the most dynamic preacher of God's word who had ever ministered in Great Britain and the colonies. That these three individuals should begin their association at Oxford, and then individually carry out ministries that affected millions of people on both sides of the Atlantic strikes us as incredible. It is difficult to believe that this was an accident; it has all the appearances of divine providence.

Whitefield's second trip to America. In August 1739, less than a year after returning from Georgia, Whitefield once again left for North America. In his months in England, Whitefield had been banned from preaching in Anglican churches in Bath and Bristol, and took the radical step of preaching outdoors (he called it "field preaching"). The results were sensational. His experiences in England, both the preaching and the promotional methods, set the stage for his outdoor preaching in the colonies.

After arriving in Philadelphia in late October 1739, he preached there and in New York for several weeks before traveling south to Delaware, Virginia, North Carolina, South Carolina, and on to Georgia, where he arrived in January 1740. Here is a summary of what happened in Philadelphia during his first visit: "By late afternoon, November 8, 1739, hordes of Philadelphians had converged on the city center. Seldom if ever had so many men and women crowded into the town of twelve thousand. Throughout that cold Thursday word circulated that George Whitefield, a young Anglican preacher, would preach that evening. Too big to assemble in one of the city's nine or ten churches, the throng stood quietly before the evangelist as he mounted the courthouse steps."[24]

After spending the winter months in Georgia, Whitefield returned north. "Through April and May he preached to audiences numbering upwards of 15,000 in Philadelphia and New York, and to smaller but still substantial gatherings in outlying communities. Crowds would be even larger in New England that fall, but even in the spring more people were gathering in one place to hear Whitefield than had ever been assembled at one place to that time in the European history of North America."[25]

In 1740 he traveled north through Rhode Island and on to Boston, then to western Massachusetts, and down the Connecticut River Valley to Hartford and New Haven. In Boston, 23,000 assembled on the Boston Common to hear him preach; this was more than the population of the city! He returned to England late in the year. In the summer of 1741, fresh from his huge success in America,

Whitefield traveled to Scotland for 13 weeks of preaching. The results were good but did not match "the hurricane of grace that Whitefield had brought to New England."[26]

Whitefield's style, appearance and emotional impact. "In public, Whitefield was a born actor. He preached without notes, had a splendid voice that Benjamin Franklin calculated could be readily heard by 25,000, and was a master of painting vivid pictures that would draw an audience emotionally into the theme of the text...Seldom did he preach a sermon in which he did not weep and reduce multitudes to tears."[27] The contrast between Whitefield's insignificant appearance—he was short, slight and cross-eyed—and commanding performance encouraged the impression that God inspired his preaching.[28]

The proportion of Americans who came to hear George Whitefield during his trips to the colonies is unknown, but from all reports, nearly everyone in the Middle Colonies (Pennsylvania, New Jersey, New York and Delaware) and New England heard him at least once during his 1739-1741 tour. Historian James Hutson referred to Whitefield as America's first cultural hero and compared his influence to that of George Washington during and after the Revolutionary War.[29]

Here is one account of Whitefield's arrival in a small town in Pennsylvania: "As the time approached the country roads would, as one farmer described it later that week, reverberate 'like a low rumbling thunder' and be engulfed by clouds of dust as throngs pressed toward the place, as though fleeing for their lives."[30]

When Jonathan Edwards finally met Whitefield, and heard him preach, it changed his life. "As Edwards watched Whitefield preach to a crowd of several thousand at Suffield on Tuesday morning, October 21, he was witnessing the dawn of a new age—the age of the people. Awakenings were familiar in the Connecticut Valley, and Edwards played a key role in one that touched as many people there as did Whitefield. Yet there were some notable differences. Whitefield's tour was a truly international phenomenon. It was also the first intercolonial cultural event, the beginning of a common American cultural identity. Moreover, like most everything else that succeeded in America, it was founded not so much on what was imposed from above as by the popular response generated from below."[31]

Franklin an admirer of Whitefield. Benjamin Franklin was favorably impressed by the religious fervor that accompanied Whitefield's preaching. Franklin enjoyed the discomfort of the leaders of the established churches, especially the Presbyterian Church in Philadelphia; he had tangled with the senior minister on several occasions. Furthermore, he saw religious renewal as a way to improve the morality and virtue of the citizenry. He also developed a nice business printing and distributing Whitefield's sermons.

Franklin wrote this about Whitefield's nightly outdoor revival meetings in Philadelphia: "On Thursday, the Rev. Mr. Whitefield began to preach from the Court House gallery in this city, about six at night, to nearly 6,000 people before him in the street, who stood in awful silence to hear him. The crowds grew larger through the week."[32]

Franklin was impressed with the effect that Whitefield had on the people. "Never did the people show so great a willingness to attend sermons. Religion is become the subject of most conversation. No books are in request but those of piety."[33] Consistent with Franklin's comments, another historian points out that, "Until almost the dawning of the American Revolution, theologians exercised a singular authority in American print culture. Until late in the eighteenth century, they were, in each decade, the most-published authors in America."[34]

In addition to his evangelistic efforts, and fundraising for his orphanage, Whitefield had a major impact on the print media. Many of his sermons were printed, distributed and widely read. He encouraged the publication of many books that he thought would be beneficial to new Christians, and wrote his own journal. "Publishers clamored for his business...He was simply big business."[35]

Whitefield's additional trips to America. In 1744 Whitefield was accompanied by his new wife Elizabeth on his third trip to the colonies; they stayed until 1748. Whitefield found that the fires of revival were still burning. "Revivals had increased both in number and power since his last visit. In fact, the revival was changing the colonies, bringing them together and giving them a common vision."[36]

Whitefield made four additional trips to America, and while his impact did not match that of his second visit in 1739-1741, the zenith of the Great Awakening, his popularity and success continued. Over the 30 years of his ministry, he visited each of the colonies at least twice. It is estimated that he preached more than 18,000 sermons in America.[37] Although controversial with ministers of some established churches who opposed "emotionalism," in his day he was the most famous, and popular, man in the British North American colonies.[38]

In Portsmouth, N. H., at the age of 56, Whitefield preached his last sermon, where it was reported that his delivery was powerful. Later that day he rode a few miles to Newburyport, Mass. to stay at the home of a local parson. After a fitful night, he got up at dawn, looked out the window at the rising sun, and died of what was believed to be an asthma attack. His remains were buried in a crypt under the altar of the Old South Church, a congregation he helped found a few years earlier. Thousands of mourners traveled great distances to attend his funeral.

Impacts on Social Structure and Culture in the Colonies

Paul Johnson wrote that the Great Awakening crossed sectarian (denominational) boundaries, "made light of them indeed, and turned what had been a series of European-style churches into American ones. It began the process which created an ecumenical and American type of religious devotion which affected all groups, and gave a distinctive American flavor to a wide range of denominations."[39]

Another historian noted that George Whitefield challenged traditional sources of authority by attacking "…the prevailing upper-class notion that the uneducated masses had no minds of their own." Whitefield spread the message that "…God did not operate through the elite corps of learned clergy and their aristocratic allies."[40] Is it any wonder that the leaders of traditional churches in both England and the colonies felt threatened by Whitefield and attempted to minimize the importance of the religious revivals?

Mark Noll explained it this way: "Whitefield's preaching broke traditional rules; it called for direct, immediate response; it encouraged the laity to perform Christian services that were the historical preserve of the clergy…Whitefield's speech drove home the lesson that it was not formal education or a prestigious role in the community that ultimately mattered but the choice of an individual for or against God. Whitefield was the colonies' most visible symbol of changing conceptions of hierarchy; he represented a new confidence in the religious powers of the people and a sharp, if implicit, rebuke to the authority of tradition."[41]

In commenting on the conventional wisdom of the time that a hierarchical structure in society was necessary for good government, Harvard historian Bernard Bailyn noted that circumstances in America challenged such assumptions. "The wilderness environment from the beginning had threatened the maintenance of elaborate social distinctions; many of them in the passage of time had in fact been worn away. Puritanism, in addition, and the epidemic evangelicalism of the mid-eighteenth century (the Great Awakening), had created challenges to the traditional notions of social stratifications by generating the conviction that the ultimate quality of men was to be found elsewhere than in their external condition, and that a cosmic achievement lay within each man's grasp."[42]

By aiding the breakdown of class barriers and authority, the Great Awakening contributed to a desire to separate from England. "Revolutions have always begun with an insurgent minority, and the American Revolution was no exception. Whether for white colonists of the middle and lower social orders or for the enslaved, the Great Awakening provided a 'radical model' for revolutionary activists…"[43]

Growth in Churches and Denominations

In the years preceding the Great Awakening, many of the colonists were on the rolls of churches that were part of established denominations (e.g., Congregational, Presbyterian, Dutch Reformed). Church membership and attendance was mediocre, in some places well below European standards. The Quakers and Puritans had lost ground in comparison to their founding years. However, from 1740 on, the situation changed dramatically. New churches and denominations began to take shape, and they had a significant impact on the growth of Christianity in America and on the revolutionary spirit of the people.

Number of churches in 1750. Immediately following the peak of the Great Awakening, when the population of British North America stood at around one million, there were just under 1,500 churches in the colonies:[44]

Denomination	No. of Churches (Region)
Congregational	450 (mostly in New England)
Anglican	300 (mainly in Virginia and the South)
Quakers	250 (Pennsylvania)
Presbyterians	160 (mostly in Middle Colonies)
Baptists	100 (New England and South)
Lutherans	95 (Middle Colonies)
Dutch Reformed	78 (Middle Colonies)
German Reformed	51 (Middle Colonies)
Total	1,484

In addition, there were a few Catholic churches, primarily in Maryland, and Jewish synagogues in Newport, New York City and Charles Town.[45]

Historian Alan Taylor estimated that at an average of 90 families per church, at least two-thirds of the colonists were "churched" in a broad sense. This estimate is confirmed by Mark Noll; his research indicated that 40 to 50 percent of all adults regularly attended church in the years following the Great Awakening.[46] James Hutson's study of religion and the founding of the American Republic contained a higher estimate—75 to 80 percent of the population attended church with some regularity.[47]

Another historian, Walter Latourette, summarized the impact of the revivals on the growth of Christianity in the colonies: "The Great Awakening was evidence of vigour inherent in the Protestantism of the Thirteen Colonies. Here was a vitality which through succeeding decades was to reach a growing proportion of the partially de-Christianized population, was fairly steadily to augment the percentage of church members, and was to continue the mass conversion of which the Great Awakening was the beginning. Out of the Great Awakening came a large increase in churches, of young men entering the ministry, of earnestness among the rank and file of professing Christians, and of missions."[48]

It wasn't just the numbers; the Great Awakening had a special impact on men and youth. "The conversions seemed especially impressive and divine because they included so many men and young people, the colonists ordinarily underrepresented in full church membership."[49] Furthermore, many of these men and their sons later joined the Continental Army and put themselves in harm's way for their new country.

Baptists. Isaac Backus of Connecticut was representative of the individuals whose zeal energized Baptists in America. Converted during the Great Awakening, and a Congregationalist until 1756, Backus was convinced of the Baptist way by two events—a tax on all citizens to build a town church, and disagreement about infant baptism. When Backus was ordained as a Baptist preacher in 1756, there were 36 Baptist churches in New England; when he died in 1804, there were 312.[50]

The growth of Baptist churches in the south was spurred by the Philadelphia Baptist Association. Two brothers-in-law, Shubal Stearns and Daniel Marshall, both of whom had been deeply affected by the preaching of George Whitefield, responded to appeals from the Piedmont area of North Carolina. Beginning in 1754 Marshall worked with Stearns for several years, and then pushed south into Georgia. By 1790, half of all Baptists in the United States lived in the five southern states.

From fewer than 100 churches in the 13 colonies in 1740, the number of Baptist churches increased to almost 500 by 1776.[51] As a group, Baptists were especially strong supporters of the Revolutionary War.

Presbyterians. Although the evangelistic preaching of Whitefield, the Tennents and others, caused a schism among Presbyterians, the denomination reunited in 1758. During the 17 years of separation, the number of Old Side (traditional) ministers dropped from 28 to 23, while the number of New Side (evangelical) clergy climbed from 22 to 73. The number of Presbyterian churches in the colonies increased from 160 in 1750 to nearly 600 by 1776.[52] Most Presbyterian churches were strong supporters of independence from England.

Congregationalists. From its fervent days under the leadership of John Winthrop and the other Puritan founders, the Congregational churches in New England gradually declined in religious zeal. Thirty years later, in 1662, the church instituted the Half-Way Covenant, which led to continuing decline in the vigor of Congregational churches: "The secularization of the churches had become almost complete by 1679. Immorality and irreligion had become alarmingly prevalent. Public calamities—shipwrecks, droughts, conflagrations, pestilence, war with the Indians, etc., came thick and fast and were attributed by the more godly to the decay in religion and morals."[53]

Although several conferences were called to deal with declining interest in full church membership, not much changed. In fact, for Congregational churches, there was further decline: "Skepticism and indifferentism were being somewhat widely diffused. Conversions were rare, and deep religious experiences were not only unlooked for, but were regarded by many as savoring of fanaticism. Preaching here, as in England, had lost much of its fervor."[54]

Even though there were serious disagreements about "enthusiasm," or what might be called excessive emotionalism, the number of Congregational churches began to grow during the Great Awakening. By 1776, for example, the number had reached 668, compared with 423 in 1740, about the time Whitefield arrived in New England. Furthermore, Puritans—and the disciplined thinking and publications of Puritan theologians and leaders like Jonathan Edwards—were disproportionately important in the development of religious thought in America.[55]

Methodists. Methodism initially grew more rapidly in Great Britain than in the American colonies. Even though Whitefield was part of the Methodist movement within the Church of England, he did not promote Methodism during his preaching tours in North America. As a result, in the years prior to the Declaration of Independence, Methodism in the colonies was almost invisible.

Methodism received its biggest boost when 26-year old Francis Asbury arrived in America in 1771. When he first set foot in the colonies as an itinerant preacher, there were 300 people enrolled in American Methodist societies. At his death 40 years later, there were 300,000. As discussed in a later chapter, the most rapid growth of Methodism followed the peace treaty ending the Revolutionary War and occurred during the period of settlement of the interior of the country, mainly Kentucky, Ohio, Tennessee, western Pennsylvania and New York.

Impact of the Great Awakening on Institutions of Higher Education

Prior to 1740 Harvard (1636), Yale (1701) and the College of William & Mary (1693) were the colonies' first and only colleges. All three were founded to train ministers and to support the established churches in Massachusetts, Connecticut and Virginia.

Religious enthusiasm accompanying the Great Awakening, and the general prosperity of the country, led to a rash of new colleges: "By the time of the Revolution nearly every major Christian sect had an institution of its own: New-Side Presbyterians founded Princeton; revivalist Baptists founded Brown; Dutch Reformed revivalists founded Rutgers; a Congregational minister transformed an Indian missionary school into Dartmouth; and Anglicans and Presbyterians worked together in the founding of King's College (later Columbia) and the College of Philadelphia (later the University of Pennsylvania)"..."Between 1746 and 1769, twice as many colleges were founded in the colonies as in the previous hundred years; between 1769 and 1789 twice as many again as in the preceding twenty years."[56]

Even though the colleges were sectarian (denominational), the competition had a liberalizing effect. "While the founding sect in each case could hope to dominate, it dared not monopolize its own institution...While the college president usually came from the dominant sect, it was commonly necessary to conciliate hostile sects by including their representatives among the trustees. King's College, which as an Anglican institution, possessed on its first governing board ministers of four other denominations; Brown's board, although dominated by Baptists, included a substantial number of Congregationalists, Anglicans, and Quakers."[57]

The Great Awakening and the desire of a growing number of Americans for more educational opportunities stimulated the growth in colleges and universities. Of course, following the Revolutionary War, the need for an educated citizenry became critical to the success of the republican form of government called for in the Constitution.

The Great Awakening—A Recap

Historian James Hutson concluded that the Great Awakening was important for several reasons: It "...was great because it was part of a movement that embraced the entire English-speaking world. And...it was great because it created a style of religion—evangelicalism—whose 'distinguishing marks,' in the words of Jonathan Edwards, dominated the American spiritual landscape until the Civil War and continues to be a powerful factor in American religious life."[58]

Referring to the revivals, Alan Taylor, a professor at the University of California–Davis, said: "During the mid-eighteenth Century, British colonial America experienced a dramatic and sweeping set of religious revivals collectively known as the Great Awakening...By no means did all colonists become evangelicals, but the latter were sufficiently numerous and interconnected to influence the entire culture and society."[59]

The research of historians Walter McDougall and Paul Johnson supports the importance of the Great Awakening. McDougall noted that Boston's Charles Chauncy, a Congregational minister who was a leader in the opposition to Edwards and Whitefield, and to enthusiasm, called the revival "'a small Thing'...He was wrong. The social, ecclesiastical, and political effects of the revivals led by Whitefield and his imitators proved indelible."[60] Johnson reported that as many as three out of four colonists participated in the revivals.[61]

Another historian wrote that to compare the mid-18th century revivals with more recent revivals, such as those led by Billy Graham, is to miss the importance of the Great Awakening. "What was once of critical importance to the majority of the people is now of marginal interest. We inevitably will underestimate the effect of the Awakening on eighteenth-century society if we compare it to revivals today. The Awakening was more like the civil rights demonstrations, the campus disturbances, and the urban riots of the 1960s combined. All together these may approach, though certainly not surpass, the Awakening in their impact on national life."[62]

As noted earlier, the preaching of Whitefield and others led to a restructuring of society, primarily a breakdown of hierarchy and class distinctions. Many colonial leaders, especially traditional churchmen like Boston's Charles Chauncy, thought this was destructive and divisive; they vigorously opposed it. However, in retrospect this shift in culture and society helped set the stage for the war for independence, and America's emergence as an independent nation.

Unification of colonists. James Moore, author of *One Nation Under God*, said, "With the growing legion of ministers and evangelists preaching up and down the eastern seaboard, God and prayer were becoming exciting and integral elements in the lives of ordinary people. This virtual explosion of religious revivalism, not to mention the solace that the colonists found in turning to prayer, would help bring the colonies closer together at the dawn of the American Revolution." Moore went on: "Prayer was used by the Founding Fathers as a coalescing tool to bring together widely disparate colonies, communities, and churches."[63]

David Harrell and his co-authors summarized the impact of the Great Awakening this way: "The first great popular movement spanning all the thirteen colonies, the Awakening helped create a sense of community that could begin to be called 'American.'"[64] Historian Robert Middlekauff said that it was the combination of the Great Awakening and the French & Indian War that were the major forces uniting the colonists to declare their independence.[65]

Christianity and liberty. Writer and speaker Stephen Mansfield posited that George Whitefield was the *Forgotten Founding Father* (the title of his book). "Whitefield's support of the American cause took many forms...he increasingly merged political and spiritual themes in his sermons. He spoke often of liberty and obligations of church and state to preserve it."[66]

Walter McDougall summarized Whitefield's preaching: "Last but not least, the message that individuals enjoyed free will under God and bore responsibility for their own destiny encouraged and justified the colonists' habitual defiance of external control...He (Whitefield) offered the colonies a cause: liberty under God and before man."[67]

Historians Larry Schweikart and Michael Allen explained the importance of the revivals of the mid 18th century: "The Great Awakening had galvanized American Christianity, pushing it even further into evangelism, and it served as a springboard to the Revolution itself, fueling the political fire with religious fervor and imbuing in the Founders a sense of rightness of cause."[68]

Historian Middlekauff concurred, "Although Americans entered the revolt against Britain in several ways, their religion proved important in all of them, important even to the lukewarm and indifferent. It did because, more than anything else in America, religion shaped culture." He continued that the Great Awakening "recalled a generation to the standards of reformed Protestantism, which had prevailed at the time of the founding of America…At the same time it produced a concentration on morality and right behavior, a social ethic supple enough to insist on the rights of the community while it supported the claims of individualism."[69]

Another historian summed the impact of the Great Awakening this way: "Measured by the numbers involved or its intellectual and social significance, the Great Awakening was a major movement in the eighteenth century. It released forces that were to have lasting effect on American theology and church life and, indirectly, on politics as well."[70]

So, did the Great Awakening really happen? Did it have important ramifications for the country? The answer to both these questions is an unequivocal "Yes." The timing and scope of the Great Awakening represents compelling evidence that these spiritual revivals were significant and contributed to the drive for American independence. Without this series of spiritual renewals—and the coming together of geographically separated and diverse people across colonial borders—it is unlikely that the 13 colonies would have been able to agree on a Declaration of Independence and persevere in the eight-year Revolutionary War.

Chapter 4

Prelude to the Declaration of Independence

The plain fact is that, had American clergymen of all denominations not assured their pious countrymen, from the beginning of the conflict with Britain, that the resistance movement was right in God's sight and had His blessing, it could not have been sustained and independence could not have been achieved.

—James Hutson, *Religion and the Founding of the American Republic*, 40.

Historian Walter McDougall raised this question: "Was the American rebellion caused by conflicts over wealth or ideology, a backward-looking Whig mentality (in England) or a future-oriented American dream, a secular discourse of human rights and equality or an evangelical discourse of corruption and virtue?" His answer? "...all of the above, because the whole experience of the colonists dating back to 1607...made self government, religious freedom, economic opportunity, and territorial growth inseparable."[1]

Related to McDougall's question, a young Boston lawyer asked 91-year old Levi Preston, a veteran of Lexington and Concord, why America rebelled. Preston replied: "Young man, what we meant in going for those Redcoats was this:

we always had governed ourselves, and we always meant to. They didn't mean we should."[2]

This chapter describes four different but related series of events which preceded the Declaration of Independence:

- The coalescing of the leadership of the colonies in support of independence, at least partially in reaction to events in Boston, resulting in three sessions of the Continental Congress.
- Rebellion by residents of the Boston area leading to armed conflict (the battles of Lexington and Concord, and Bunker Hill), and the eventual British evacuation of Boston.
- Benjamin Franklin's transformation from an admirer of Great Britain and King George III to an ardent advocate of independence.
- The ill-fated efforts—one military and the other diplomatic—to bring Canada into the conflict on the side of the 13 British North American colonies.

All of these activities proceeded in parallel in the years leading up to 1776 and culminated in the Declaration of Independence.

The Colonies Come Together

In 1772 a group of younger members of the Virginia House of Burgesses, including Thomas Jefferson, Patrick Henry, Richard Henry Lee, Francis Lightfoot Lee and Dabney Carr, began meeting privately in the evenings at the Raleigh Tavern in Williamsburg. As a result of these meetings and several House of Burgesses resolutions, it was agreed to open communications with the other colonies. The Virginia committee of correspondence provided both a communications vehicle and a structure for the colonies to coordinate their efforts.

Governor Dunmore of Virginia either did not understand the importance of the resolutions and setting up the committees of correspondence, or he chose to ignore these actions. In reporting to London, he said, "some resolves which show a little ill humour in the house of Burgesses, but…so insignificant that I took no matter of notice of them."[3]

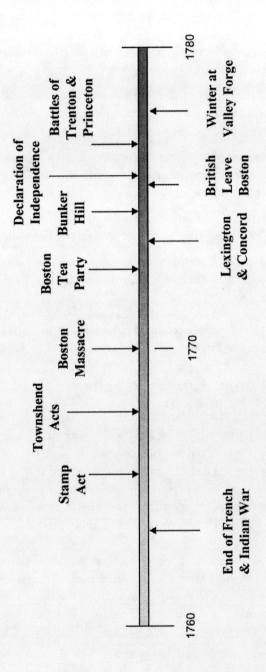

When word of the Boston Tea Party (described later in this chapter) reached Williamsburg in early 1774, Jefferson and others who were part of the Raleigh Tavern group agreed that Virginia should take a swift and unequivocal stand in support of Massachusetts. "As a means of arousing Virginians from lethargy, this group hit upon the idea of calling for a day of general fasting and prayer."[4] Jefferson played a key role in drafting the resolution calling for these acts of devotion, which passed the House of Burgesses unanimously. This time Governor Dunmore took the action more seriously; he summoned the burgesses to the counsel room and dissolved them. Immediately after being put out of business, the burgesses reassembled at Raleigh Tavern and agreed, in writing, to stop using tea and to boycott other commodities sold by the East India Company. "Even more important, the signers agreed that 'an attack, made on one of our sister colonies, to compel submission to arbitrary taxes, is an attack made on all British America.'"[5]

After returning home to Monticello, Jefferson began work on what would become a 23-page pamphlet, *A Summary View of the Rights of British America*. In 1774, when this document was written and distributed, it was considered extreme. However, the circulation of his paper elevated Jefferson to the front ranks of champions of American rights. Many of the points Jefferson made in *A Summary View* were used when he later took the lead in drafting the Declaration of Independence.

Actions in Virginia and other states, provoked by British actions in Boston, led to a series of meetings in Philadelphia. These sessions held during the 1774-1776 period were called the Continental Congress.

1774 session. On September 5, 1774, 50 delegates gathered at the City Tavern in Philadelphia and decided to hold their meetings in the Carpenter's Hall. The purpose of the convention was to show King George III that the colonies were united. After discussing several issues, such as whether each delegation would have a single vote or whether votes would be based on population (they agreed on one vote per colony), they addressed the question of beginning each session in prayer. John Jay of New York and John Rutledge of South Carolina expressed concern that "we were so divided in religious sentiments, some Episcopalians, some Quakers, some Anabaptists, some Presbyterians, and some Congregationalists," that it would be uncomfortable for some to "join in the same act of worship." Samuel Adams, not known as particularly devout, rose and said he "was no bigot, and could hear a prayer from a gentleman of piety and virtue."[6] Two days later, Reverend Jacob Duche opened a session of the Continental Congress by reading from Psalm 35; he added 10 minutes of spontaneous prayer asking God to support the American cause. One member said that Duche's prayer was "worth riding 100 miles to hear."[7]

Here is part of Reverend Duche's prayer that touched the assembly: "Be Thou present O God of Wisdom and direct the counsel of this Honorable Assembly; enable them to settle all things on the best and surest foundations; that the scene of blood may be speedily closed; that order, Harmony, and peace may be effectually restored, and Truth and Justice, Religion and Piety, prevail and flourish among the people."[8]

George Washington attended the 1774 session and was one of the few men present known to most of the delegates. Several members of the Congress had heard of Samuel and John Adams, and Patrick Henry of Virginia, but had never met them. Furthermore, many delegates had never traveled outside their home colonies.

When the first Congress completed its work in late October 1774, there was a celebration dinner at City Tavern. "Although not everyone in Congress had agreed on every issue, delegates from twelve diverse colonies (Georgia was not present) had achieved a remarkable degree of unity."[9] Given that this was the first meeting of a geographically diverse group of colonists, this strikes us as evidence of divine providence.

1775 session. In April 1775, prior to resumption of the second Continental Congress, John Hancock, the president of the Congress, called for a day of total abstinence from work and recreation: "In circumstances as dark as these, it becomes us, as Men and Christians, to reflect that whilst every prudent measure should be taken to ward off the impending judgments...at the same time all confidence must be withheld from the means we use; and reposed only on that God (who) rules in the armies of Heaven, and without His whole blessing, the best human counsels are but foolishness...Resolved...Thursday the 11th of May...to humble themselves before God under the heavy judgments felt and feared, to confess the sins that have deserved them, to implore the Forgiveness of all our transgressions, and a spirit of repentance and reformation...and a Blessing on the...Union of the American Colonies..."[10]

The second session began in May, and moved to the assembly room of the Pennsylvania State House, now known as Independence Hall. Benjamin Franklin, who had just returned from his lengthy stay in England, and Thomas Jefferson were among the 15 new delegates out of a total of 65.

Jefferson arrived in Philadelphia in late June, two days before Washington departed for Boston to take command of the Continental Army. Although Jefferson knew the members of the Virginia delegation, he was not personally acquainted with any of the other delegates. Since Jefferson's writing skills were well known, one of his first assignments was to draft the declaration ordering General Washington to take command of the patriot forces in Boston.

In July Jefferson was asked to be part of a small committee to respond to Lord North's proposals. Jefferson took the lead in drafting the resolutions in which Congress firmly rejected North's ideas. Both of the documents, *The Declaration of the Causes and Necessity of Taking up Arms* and the response to Lord North's plan, were widely published in newspapers across the colonies.

In its Articles of War, adopted on June 30, 1775, the "…Congress devoted three of the four articles in the first section to the religious nurture of the troops. In Article 2 it was 'earnestly recommended to all officers and soldiers to attend divine services.'"[11]

1776 session. David McCullough wrote, "On February 27, word arrived that Parliament, in December, had prohibited all trade with the colonies and denounced as traitors all Americans who did not make an unconditional submission. The punishment for treason, as every member of Congress knew, was death by hanging."[12]

A few days later, on March 16, the Continental Congress declared a national fast. Part of the wording on the proclamation said: "In times of impending calamity and distress; when the liberties of America are imminently endangered by the secret machinations and open assaults of an insidious and vindictive administration, it becomes the indispensable duty of these hitherto free and happy colonies, with true penitence of heart, and the most reverent devotion, publickly to acknowledge the over ruling providence of God; to confess and deplore our offences against him; and to supplicate his interposition for averting the threatened danger, and prospering our strenuous efforts in the cause of freedom, virtue, and posterity."[13]

During the 1774 and 1775 sessions of Congress, Samuel Adams had been an aggressive advocate of independence. However, he realized that he should hold back on the rhetoric and let events unfold, and that these events were more important than anything he might say. Writing to Samuel Cooper in April 1776, Adams said: "We cannot make events. Our business is wisely to improve them. There has been much to do to confirm doubting friends & fortify the timid. It requires time to bring honest men to think & determine alike even in important matters. Mankind are governed more by their feelings than by reason. Events which excite those feelings will produce wonderful effects...One battle would do more towards a Declaration of Independency than a long chain of conclusive arguments in a provincial convention or the Continental Congress."[14]

Adams' trust in events and feelings proved correct; the colonists were soon outraged to learn that King George III had hired German mercenaries (Hessians) to put down the rebellion. The King's action pushed the doubters over the top in terms of deciding it was time to separate from England. A representative from Connecticut "roared that it was the height of infamy for the king to have hired such brutes."[15]

Samuel Adams' keen observation about how events drive change casts doubt on the opinions of those who argue that Enlightenment thinking (reason) was the most important factor in achieving American independence. While we—the authors—value rational thinking based on sound analysis, we agree with Adams that the emotions of the people were critically important, and in early America, these emotions were largely shaped by Christian beliefs that were an outgrowth of the Great Awakening.

John Adams, Samuel's cousin, was a leader in all three sessions of the Continental Congress. "Adams joined in floor debate day after day, arguing a point, pleading, persuading, and nearly always with effect. No one spoke more often or with greater force. 'Every important step was opposed, and carried by bare majorities, which obliged me to be almost constantly engaged in debate,' he would recall."[16]

While the Continental Congress was meeting in Philadelphia, Thomas Paine, a recent immigrant to America, wrote a pamphlet that galvanized opinion against King George III and in favor of independence. The 50-page pamphlet, *Common Sense* (the title was suggested by Dr. Benjamin Rush), was released in January 1776 and was an immediate sensation. More than 150,000 copies were in circulation by spring, and most copies were read by more than one person. Historian Robert Middlekauff referred to *Common Sense* as a "sermon disguised as a political tract."[17] "In Washington's estimation, the 'unanswerable' tract worked a magnificent change in the minds of men and women."[18]

Harking back to the Enlightenment and Great Awakening, historian Walter McDougall said: "Paine's remarkable pamphlet cemented the alliance between the Awakened and the Enlightened, summoned them to a just war, and promised a kind of heaven on earth if they won. That is why some historians miss the point when they denigrate the role of religion in the American rebellion. Perhaps religious language was just 'window dressing' for colonists primarily engaged in a political or economic struggle. Perhaps some clergy did climb on the bandwagon of what was otherwise a 'profoundly secular event.' But to stress the absence of Biblical language in the documents of the American founding while dismissing the torrents of religious rhetoric in the speeches, sermons, and tracts exhorting rebellion and war can only lead to a false conclusion."[19]

Following the release of *Common Sense*, John Adams wrote his own pamphlet, *Thoughts on Government*. Adams began, "It has been the will of Heaven…that we should be thrown into existence at a period when the greatest philosophers and lawgivers of antiquity would have wished to live…a period when a coincidence of circumstances without example has afforded to thirteen colonies at once an opportunity of beginning government anew from the foundation and building as they choose. How few of the human race have ever had an opportunity of choosing a system of government for themselves and their children? How few have ever had anything more of choice in government than in climate?"[20]

Following British rejection of proposals to find solutions to the problems facing the colonies, Richard Henry Lee of Virginia rose to present one of the most important motions considered in any of the three congressional sessions: "Resolved (Lee began):…That these United Colonies are, and of a right ought to be, free and independent states, that they are absolved from all allegiance to the British Crown, and that all political connection between them and the state of

Great Britain is, and ought to be, totally dissolved."[21] John Adams seconded the motion. Following hours of intense debate—candles were brought in as the discussion went into the evening—Congress adjourned for the weekend. On the following Monday, several members succeeded in having a final vote delayed for 20 days, until July 1, to allow delegates from the Middle Colonies to send for new instructions. Nevertheless, it was also agreed that no time should be lost in preparing a declaration of independence. A committee of five—John Adams, Jefferson, Franklin, Roger Sherman and Robert Livingston—was appointed to begin drafting such a document.[22]

Since Jefferson was known as both a strong patriot and excellent writer, the group asked him to prepare a first draft. After spending a week on the document, "...Jefferson submitted it separately to Adams and to Franklin for their suggestions and corrections before presenting it to the full committee. Both men made alterations in their own handwriting on Jefferson's draft, producing a unique and historic document that still survives today. Jefferson then made a fair copy for the committee, which made a few changes and reported it to Congress on June 28."[23]

The entire Congress debated the draft for three days, making a number of changes. Here is the final addition made by the Congress as a whole: "...with a firm reliance on the protection of Divine Providence."[24] Although the draft was finalized on July 4, the final engrossed parchment was not officially signed until August 2.

Historian John Ferling summarized the seriousness of the situation this way: "On July 2, 1776, the United States leapt into the dark. During the next quarter century the new nation struggled toward daylight. It came close—closer than many in our time realize—to failing to establish itself as an independent nation. Furthermore, once independence was achieved, an almost equally desperate struggle followed to preserve the wartime union of states under an acceptable, popular national government."[25]

John Adams' letter to his wife Abigail reflected his ideas of how to celebrate the Declaration of Independence: "The second day of July 1776 will be the most memorable epoch in the history of America...it will be celebrated by succeeding generations as the great anniversary festival. It ought to be commemorated as the Day of Deliverance, by solemn acts of devotion to God Almighty."[26]

Abigail Adams wrote to John that the Declaration of Independence was read from the balcony of the State House in Boston. She reported that the assembled throng paid great attention to every word, and then when it was done, "the cry from the balcony was God Save our American States, and then 3 cheers which rended the air, the bells rang, the privateers fired...the cannon were discharged...and every face appeared joyful."[27]

Personal repercussions from signing the Declaration of Independence. There were good reasons for the signers to be concerned about British reprisals. "In a wrathful spirit of revenge, the enemy singled them out for harsh vengeance."[28] Here are a few examples:

- The two sons of Richard Stockton were put on British prison ships where they were severely beaten and suffered malnutrition. Following a prisoner exchange that freed his sons, Stockton was a broken man and never recovered. Furthermore, his horses and family silver were stolen, furniture burned and library destroyed.

- The homes of signers were marked for destruction; one-third suffered this fate. Five were captured and imprisoned and two others barely escaped captivity.

- Phillip Livingston's business in New York was confiscated. Two other New York signers, William Floyd and Francis Lewis, suffered from the British scorched earth policy. Their woodlands, farms and homes were destroyed. Lewis's wife was taken prisoner and thrown in prison and forced to sleep on the floor; Washington eventually arranged for her exchange for two wives of British officials.

- John Hart's crops and gristmill were destroyed. He was chased for several days, and when he finally returned home, he found his wife dead and their 13 children scattered; his health was broken.

Action in the Boston Area Triggers Desire for Independence

Following the French & Indian War, which was expensive for Great Britain, the Crown and Parliament began searching for new revenue sources to pay off the large debts the country had incurred. Since British leaders believed that the war benefited the American colonies, they thought that colonial North America should bear a significant part of the cost. In an effort to collect these funds, the Stamp Act (a requirement to purchase a notary stamp for all sorts of printed material ranging from pamphlets to diplomas to newspapers) was to be implemented in late 1765.

Both the Stamp Act and the Townshend Acts (new duties on paper, lead, glass and paint which came later) ran into strong resistance from Samuel Adams and the Sons of Liberty. There were branches of the Sons of Liberty in several American colonies, and Adams was a leader in setting up committees on correspondence so the branches could coordinate their efforts.

Boston Massacre. In October 1768 three regiments of British troops, requested by the governor to enforce British law and protect civil officials, arrived in Boston. Eighteen months later, a British sentry in front of the Custom House in Boston (where taxes were collected) was taunted by a small band of men and boys. "The time was shortly after nine. Somewhere a church bell began to toll, the alarm for fire, and almost at once crowds came pouring into the streets, many men, up from the waterfront, brandishing sticks and clubs. As a throng of several hundred converged at the Custom House, the lone guard was reinforced by eight British solders with loaded muskets and fixed bayonets, their captain with drawn sword. Shouting, cursing, the crowd pelted the despised redcoats with snowballs, chunks of ice, oyster shells, and stones. In the melee the soldiers suddenly opened fire, killing five men."[29]

As a leading Boston attorney at the time, John Adams was retained to defend the British soldiers. This was an extremely unpopular assignment; however, Adams thought it was the right thing to do. Of the eight British soldiers, six were acquitted; two were found guilty of manslaughter and branded on their thumbs. In other words, Adams got the soldiers off lightly. Following several months of peace, British troops were withdrawn from Boston.

Boston Tea Party. On December 16, 1773, an incident took place that was the straw that broke the camels back in English/colonial relationships. Lord North had given the East India Company permission to haul three shiploads of tea to Boston for sale at below market prices. Boston merchants, who often obtained tea by smuggling, were outraged at the prospect of these shipments of tea undercutting their market. A crowd of 7,000 met at the Old South Church and about 1,000 men went down to the harbor where Indian costumes and war paint were available for the 50 men who climbed aboard the three ships and threw the tea overboard. The Boston Tea Party lasted two hours.

The British were incensed and within three months they closed the Port of Boston to all traffic. Furthermore, the British government made the Tea Party "...a pretext to punish New England so severely the other colonies would knuckle under to avoid the same fate."[30] One additional step was to shut down Massachusetts' provincial and town governments, and place the colony under martial law by naming General Thomas Gage its new governor.

The Intolerable Acts. England went even further in punishing Massachusetts. "In June 1774, Parliament's Quebec Act established another authoritarian government in Canada, extended its boundaries to include all western lands north of the Ohio River, and permitted the Catholic Church to practice and expand freely throughout." The colonists dubbed these as the Intolerable Acts because they "violated every spirit of English colonization and ground underfoot everything the colonies stood for and dreamed of achieving in harness with Britain."[31]

Edmund Burke, a member of the House of Commons and a supporter of the colonies, gave a three-hour speech arguing that Britain should govern America by their consent. Burke ended with a motion to rescind the Intolerable Acts and leave taxation to the colonies' own assemblies; his motion failed by a wide margin.

British troops return to Boston. Following the Boston Tea Party and the imposition of the Intolerable Acts, the British Crown declared Boston to be in a state of insurrection, and ordered troops back to the city. General Gage arrived in May 1774 with four regiments (each regiment had close to 500 men). By that fall there were 3,000 British soldiers in Boston.[32]

During the winter of 1774-1775 there were a limited number of British incursions into communities surrounding Boston; however, no shots were fired. On April 14 General Gage received instructions from London urging him to undertake a "decisive action" that would break what the British considered to be a rebellion.[33]

Lexington and Concord. Late in the evening of April 18, 1775, 11 months after the British troops had arrived, 700 redcoats boarded boats and crossed Boston's

Back Bay with the intent of taking an ammunition dump in Concord, and hopefully capturing Samuel Adams, who was reported to be spending the night there. The British plans were not a well-kept secret; Paul Revere and William Dawes rode inland to spread the alarm. In the early morning of April 19, the British were met at Lexington by a group of Minutemen (volunteers who drilled three times a week and were available on short notice); someone fired and 18 Americans fell. The British marched on to Concord, only to find most of the munitions had been moved and Adams had disappeared.

After a few hours in Concord, the British turned back to Boston, mission unaccomplished. By afternoon, as many as 3,000 Minutemen had arrived from several towns and skirmished, Indian-style, along the route from Concord to Boston. "The battlefield was in reality a gauntlet, about 16 miles long and never more than three or four hundred yards wide."[34] When the British reached Boston, 270 soldiers had been killed, wounded or were missing. Minutemen losses were 49 killed, and 150 wounded.[35]

Bunker Hill. British troops in Boston were vulnerable to artillery placed on either Bunker Hill to the north or Dorchester Heights on the south. Thus, the British recognized the need to keep the American militia from occupying these higher positions. In June 1775, two months after the Lexington and Concord clash, the Americans learned that the British intended to occupy one or both of these hills. A decision was made by the Americans to fortify Breed's Hill, which fronted Bunker Hill. With last minute reinforcements from two New Hampshire regiments, 1,500 Americans dug in on Breed's Hill.

General Gage, who had been insulted by the effrontery of the Minutemen along the road back from Concord, and motivated by three new generals who would eventually play pivotal roles in the war—William Howe, Johnny Burgoyne and Henry Clinton—plus reinforcements bringing his total force to 5,000, decided to teach the rebels a lesson. After shelling (and burning) Charleston at the foot of Breed's Hill, the British crossed the Charles River and started up the slope. The Americans waited until the British were within 50 yards, and then opened fire. "The British reeled back, then charged twice more until almost half their force of twenty-two hundred was dead (or wounded)."[36] The British captured the hill late in the afternoon after militiamen ran out of ammunition and most slipped away; 400 Americans were killed, including Dr. Joseph Warren, one of New England's best-known patriots.

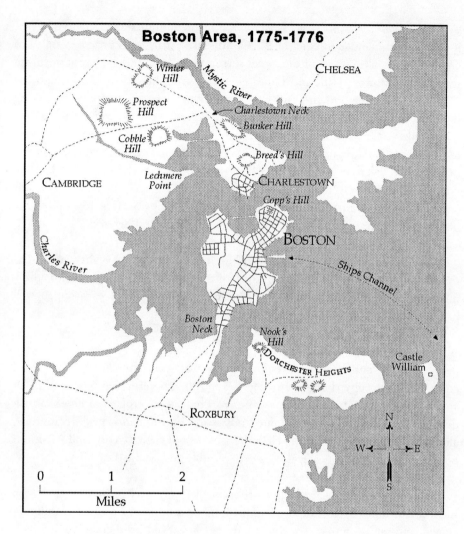

At first, Americans viewed Bunker Hill as a defeat; however, as time went by they began to see it as a victory. Nathaniel Greene of Rhode Island, who was to become one of Washington's most valuable generals, said, "I wish I could sell them another hill at the same price."[37] The losses associated with Bunker Hill stunned the British army as well as the public at home; it threw them on the defensive for more than a year. Bunker Hill also had long-term ramifications for the conduct of the Revolutionary War; in the future, the British tended to avoid frontal assaults on established American positions.

George Washington arrives in Boston. Congress commissioned George Washington as commander-in-chief of the Continental Army with orders to travel to Cambridge to take charge of the forces surrounding Boston. He arrived in July, a month after Bunker Hill, and found chaos. "As Washington rode through the New England encampment, the stench indicated that the troops were risking their health by not digging privies. He quickly discovered that commonly no one gave or obeyed any orders." However, there were immediate changes for the better. Generals Washington and Lee were on the lines every day. One of his early orders issued less than a month after he arrived was straightforward: "And in like manner (the general) requires and expects, of all Officers, and Soldiers, not engaged on actual duty, a punctual attendance on divine Service, to implore the blessings of heaven upon the means used for our safety and defense."[38]

Washington estimated the British strength to be 11,000; in reality, it was less than 7,000, or about half the size of the Continental Army. However, with enlistments running out at the end of the year, Washington's forces dropped well below 10,000 before building back up to 20,000 in mid-1776.

Cannon moved from Fort Ticonderoga. The British, who had taken Fort Ticonderoga on the south end of Lake Champlain during the French & Indian War, continued to occupy the fort. In May 1775, 100 Americans led by Ethan Allen and Benedict Arnold attacked and captured Fort Ticonderoga and its 48 British defenders, and in the process, gained possession of 43 cannon and 16 mortars, along with ammunition. Fort Ticonderoga, near the New York and Vermont border, is about 300 miles from Boston over hilly and wooded country.

Henry Knox, a 25-year old Boston bookseller, approached Washington with the idea of riding to Ticonderoga and hauling the cannon to Boston. Washington agreed, and on November 16, Knox and his 19-year old brother left for Ticonderoga with $1,000 to hire workers, oxen and sleds.[39] Knox procured 42 sleds and 80 teams of oxen and then hoped for snow. Three feet fell on Christmas Day; however, a thaw on New Year's Day threatened to melt the snow, thus making the trip impossible. Fortunately for Knox and the Americans, on January 7 the weather turned cold again, making it possible to haul the cannon across the Hudson River and on to Boston. In late January, the caravan arrived in Framingham and awaited further orders. "To those who rode out from Cambridge to Framingham to look over the guns, it was clear that the stalemate in Boston was about to change dramatically."[40]

Artillery on Dorchester Heights force British to evacuate Boston. Dorchester Heights was not occupied by either the British or colonial armies. During the night of March 4, 1776, Washington had 3,000 men set up fortifications on the heights, including moving in the Ticonderoga cannon. "The ground being frozen too hard for digging, the Americans brought their fortifications with them in wagons: bundles of sticks, three feet thick and four long, and also the heavy wooden frames in which the bundles were to be piled to make ramparts..."[41]

The next morning the British, realizing that the colonists had mounted cannon on the heights overlooking Boston, embarked several regiments for Dorchester Neck. However, "the sky blackened with what soldiers on both sides considered the most awesome storm they had ever seen," and the British withdrew to Boston. Within days, the British loaded up their ships and sailed out of Boston Harbor, headed for Halifax, Nova Scotia. When the British pulled out, Washington did not march through the streets "like a Caesar"; instead he went to church.[42] Abigail Adams saw "the hand of Providence in the departure" of the British from Boston.[43]

For an agricultural country short of artillery, gaining possession of the Ticonderoga cannon and mortars was a miracle. Then, the physical act of hauling these artillery pieces and ammunition to Boston was a heroic achievement. Furthermore, the American troops occupying the areas surrounding Boston were weak, and could have easily been defeated by a determined British assault. Under normal circumstances, the probability of Washington being able to chase the British out of Boston was remote. Washington and his small and inexperienced army viewed this whole series of events as evidence of divine providence.

In anticipation that the British would eventually return and land in New York City to take advantage of the city's excellent harbor, Washington and his army began to move to Manhattan and Long Island.

Franklin's Unique Role

Benjamin Franklin had lived in England for 15 out of the previous 17 years before returning to Philadelphia in May 1775, just in time to be named a delegate to the second Continental Congress. When he departed for England, and during much of his stay in London, Franklin was a loyal British subject and an admirer of King George III and the British Empire; when he returned he was a radical voice for independence. What happened? The so-called Hutchinson letters were a key turning point. "This affair was the most extraordinary and revealing incident in his political life. It effectively destroyed his position in England and made him a patriot."[44]

Between 1767 and 1769, well before the outbreak of hostilities in Boston, Governor Thomas Hutchinson of Massachusetts and his brother-in-law, Andrew Oliver (lieutenant governor), wrote a number of letters to royal officials in London. "The gist of the letters was that the troubles in America reflected no broad dissatisfaction but simply the political perversions of a minority." One of the letters called for an "abridgement" of English liberties for the colonists.[45] An unknown person delivered copies of these letters to Franklin, and as Massachusetts' agent to Britain, he forwarded the letters to friends in Boston. Enemies of Hutchinson and Oliver obtained copies of the letters and had them published. The letters created an uproar; they were interpreted as part of a British plot to enslave the colonies. "In England the letters provoked charges and countercharges as to who could have been so dishonorable as to steal and publish private correspondence."[46]

On January 29, 1774, just a few days after word of the Boston Tea Party reached London, Franklin was summoned before the Privy Council, which was considering a petition from Massachusetts to dismiss Governor Hutchinson. However, since Franklin had previously admitted sending the Hutchinson letters to friends in Boston, the hearing focused on him rather than Governor Hutchinson. Before a packed house (including Lord North, the prime minister; Lord Dartmouth, the American secretary; the Archbishop of Canterbury; and the Bishop of London) in what is referred to as the "cockpit," Solicitor General Alexander Wedderburn led a two-hour attack on Franklin. Wedderburn called Franklin "'...the first mover and prime conductor' of the conspiracy by the Massachusetts House against the honor and integrity of two fine servants of the king."[47]

Franklin remained silent and stoic throughout the entire proceeding. "The audience, including many of the lords, laughed and cheered at the solicitor's slashing assault on Franklin's behavior and character, but the object of the day's entertainment stood before his accuser betraying not the slightest emotion."

Franklin himself later compared it to a "bull-baiting," with him being the bull, chained to a post at the center of the arena.[48]

Within 48 hours of the hearing, Franklin was stripped of his job as deputy postmaster general for the colonies. Franklin's experience in the cockpit and his firing from the postal service job left him outraged. However, he remained in London for another year hoping for the opportunity to facilitate reconciliation between England and the colonies. After concluding that the cause was hopeless, Franklin boarded ship for Philadelphia and in May 1775 arrived home to a hero's welcome. The "shot heard round the world" at Lexington happened while Franklin was on board ship from London.

When he was elected to the Continental Congress, the disillusioned Franklin immediately became one of the most outspoken members favoring independence. His experience over the previous two years had convinced him that independence was the only viable alternative.

Why did Franklin change his views so dramatically? Franklin biographer Gordon Wood said, "In many respects Franklin seems the least likely of the Revolutionaries. Certainly his participation in the Revolution was not natural or inevitable; indeed, Franklin came very close to remaining, as his son did, a loyal member of the British Empire. On the face of it, it is not easy to understand why Franklin took up the Revolutionary cause at all."[49] But, much to the benefit of America, he did become a strong advocate of independence.

The Canadian Fiascos

In 1775 there was hope among American leaders that Canada, owned by the British since the end of the French & Indian War, but populated mainly by descendents of early French traders and settlers, would join the 13 colonies in seeking independence from England. This led Congress to attempt a two-prong approach—the first involved attacks into Canada, and the second was a diplomatic mission that included Benjamin Franklin. Both ended in failure.

Invasions of Montreal and Quebec City. In the fall 1775, assured by spies that Canada was lightly defended, Congress ordered General Phillip Schuyler to lead an invasion of that country. Schuyler, who was in ill health, obtained a brigadier general's commission for Richard Montgomery and ordered Montgomery to lead the offensive movement, initially to Montreal. Benedict Arnold and Daniel Morgan, along with handpicked troops, were to march north through Newburyport, up the Kennebec River valley (in present-day Maine) and join Montgomery at Quebec City.

At the outset, the combined forces of Montgomery and Arnold (including Morgan's three companies of riflemen) were slightly more than 2,000 men. However, more than 300 of Arnold's troops turned back during their difficult march up the Kennebec River Valley into Quebec. Montgomery took Montreal without resistance, and his troops then set out to meet those of Arnold and Morgan at Quebec City. However, when the Montgomery and Arnold/Morgan units joined on December 2, their total force had dwindled to 1,125 men facing a British force of 1,800 (including British regulars, French civilians and American loyalists).

"At midnight on December 31, 1775, in a howling blizzard, Montgomery and Arnold assaulted Quebec. They divided their little army into two columns, Montgomery attacked from the south, Arnold from the north."[50] However, a sentry spotted Arnold's men; bells rang and cannon boomed. Montgomery was killed by a blast from a cannon as he led his army up a narrow road, and his army fled. Arnold was wounded in the leg and turned over command to Morgan. After a hard fight, Morgan and 371 of his men surrendered.

The siege of Quebec and the retreat down Lake Champlain. With the 500 men who remained, Arnold (even though bedridden) directed a siege of Quebec City. However, British ships carrying several thousand troops arrived in the spring; they immediately attacked the Americans, breaking the siege and driving Arnold and his remnant of the army out of Canada.

Even with additional colonial troops—the Continental Congress ordered Washington to send six regiments to Canada, and promoted John Thomas, a physician, to major general to take charge of the campaign—the resistance collapsed. As the American troops retreated from Canada down Lake Champlain toward Fort Ticonderoga, the 2,500 soldiers suffered grievously from a major outbreak of smallpox (one-third came down with the disease and hundreds died, including General Thomas) and military pressure from the British and their Indian allies.[51]

Chaplains worked to maintain the spirits of the troops. For example, Reverend Ammi Robbins of Connecticut preached to dozens of officers and over 1,000 troops near Fort Ticonderoga (site of several makeshift hospitals) on a Sunday afternoon. "Many people came up to the minister afterwards and congratulated him on a powerful sermon. Robbins shrugged off the praise, telling them, 'May I be more concerned to please God and less to please men.'"[52]

After returning to Fort Ticonderoga for his third tour of duty in early September (he had been sent home twice to recuperate from serious illnesses), Reverend Robbins presided over a large prayer meeting. There were so many men in the crowd that those in the rear could not see him. "Holding his Bible with great care, he then carefully climbed up the wall of drums to the top of the platform and there, with all able to see him, both his feet planted gingerly on the wooden platform, he preached the word of the Lord, his voice loud and vibrant, his figure illuminated by the dozens of burning torches against the star-filled sky."[53]

Arnold's navy—an important delaying action. Benedict Arnold assembled a small fleet to control Lake Champlain. He began with three former British ships acquired when he and Ethan Allen captured Fort Ticonderoga in May 1775 and through a concentrated effort, increased his fleet to 15 small ships. In the summer of 1776 he believed that the Americans had control of the lake. However, unbeknownst to Arnold, the British had disassembled a number of their ships that had sailed up the St. Lawrence River earlier in the year, transported them over land to Lake Champlain, and reassembled them; the British had 34 vessels. In a series of skirmishes near Valcour Island, and a miraculous escape, Arnold and 300 men eventually abandoned their remaining ships and marched to Fort Ticonderoga.

Following the initial fighting at Valcour Island, and the nighttime withdrawal, Arnold said, "On the whole I think we have had a Very fortunate escape, & have great reason to return, our humble, & hearty thanks to Almighty God for preserving, & delivering so many of us from, our more than Savage Enemies."[54]

Despite the overwhelming defeats in Canada and on Lake Champlain, Arnold's small navy chalked up a major accomplishment—delaying the British long enough that they decided to withdraw to Canada for the winter. This delay gave the Americans an opportunity to beef up Fort Ticonderoga's defenses, and add thousands of troops further south near Saratoga. One Vermont historian observed that without the delaying action of Arnold and his small navy, there would have been no victory at Saratoga. Was this an example of divine providence? Although it wasn't viewed this way at the time, in retrospect it appears that way.

The diplomatic mission. About the same time as the disastrous military campaigns, Congress sent a delegation to Canada to negotiate that country's entry into the American effort to achieve independence. The group included Benjamin Franklin; Samuel Chase of Maryland; Charles Carroll, another Marylander; and his brother John Carroll, a Catholic priest. The thinking was that the two American Catholics would be able to influence the predominantly French Catholic population of Canada. The mission failed and "the exhausting midwinter trip almost killed the seventy-year-old Franklin. He and his fellow ambassadors advised the Congress to give up on making the Canadians into defenders of liberty."[55]

The bottom line was that the efforts of the Continental Congress, both militarily and politically, failed to convert Canada to the American cause. Of the several thousand troops involved in the Canadian campaign, more than 5,000 were lost—killed in battle or by smallpox, disease and fever, or captured.[56]

The Link between Christianity and Liberty

The evidence presented in this chapter supports the viewpoint that religion and freedom leaned on each other in America prior to and during the Revolutionary War.

Evidence supporting a connection. During the peak of the Great Awakening, revivalists had begun to employ words like "liberty," "faction," and "virtue" in defining man's spiritual condition. Moreover, beginning about 1750, sermons by American preachers and those individuals who were thinking about freedom and independence from England began to merge: There was a growing convergence between Christianity and freedom. The concept of the freedoms associated with self-government, or republicanism, began to take hold.[57]

Mark Noll described how this all came together in America: "In the thirteen colonies that became the United States, republican and Protestant convictions merged as they did nowhere else in the world. That merger was not a random happenstance. Rather, from the mid-1740s (in the midst of the Great Awakening) Protestant believers actively embraced republican ideals, emphases, habits of thought, and linguistic conventions, and they did so by folding them into their traditional theologies."[58] Noll added: "Historians have long recognized the Christian republicanism of American Congregationalists and Presbyterians, the denominations that ardently favored the Revolution and that furnished the most visible spokesmen after the war to explain the religious meaning of what had transpired."[59]

Dr. Benjamin Rush, a leading Philadelphia physician and a signer of the Declaration of Independence, was trained and influenced by revivalistic New Side Presbyterians. Rush wrote to John Adams saying, "The precepts of the Gospel and the maxims of republics in many instances agree with each other." In 1800, Rush wrote to Thomas Jefferson with greater emphasis: "I have always considered Christianity as the strong ground of republicanism."[60]

George Whitefield was primarily a preacher of spiritual liberty in Christ. As an Englishman, he wasn't anticipating a break between Great Britain and the colonies; his focus was on the salvation of souls regardless of where they lived. However, as Nathaniel Whitaker, a Presbyterian minister who had been Whitefield's assistant during a lengthy tour in Britain, wrote, "He was a warm friend to religious liberty," but "he was no less a friend to the civil liberties of mankind."[61]

John Adams concluded that the Revolution "connected, in one indissoluble bond, the principles of civil government with the principles of Christianity."[62]

Ministers supported independence. As pressure for the war for independence began to build, Christian churches and their ministers promoted it: "A few British officers understood that. General William Howe's aide, Serle, warned the Colonial office in London of religious passion in the states. He reminded them that hundreds of ministers in New York, delivering sermons on street corners and in parks as well as in churches, spoke out against the Crown and that 'the preachers look upon the war very much as a religious one.' A British visitor to America that year wrote in his diary that 'the Presbyterians are the chief instigators and supporters' of the rebellion."[63]

Historian James Hutson noted that other than a few Anglican pastors, preachers of every denomination supported the Revolution. "That ministers should have played a role in the Revolution is not surprising, for it was customary, in most colonies, for clergymen to interest themselves in politics. Although tradition forbade them, in most places, to hold public office, in New England and elsewhere ministers regularly delivered sermons to newly elected legislators in which they commented, openly or obliquely, on the issues of the day."[64]

Additional Evidence of God's Blessings Leading to Declaration of Independence

Historian Walter McDougall identified the hand of providence in the events preceding the Declaration of Independence: "The American cause was profoundly religious for Protestants and Deists alike because both identified America's future with a Providential design..."[65] Here are examples of providential design during this period:

- The coming together of the various colonies to support Massachusetts, and the willingness of their representatives to sign the Declaration of Independence knowing they would be hung as traitors, was miraculous.
- The British assault on Breed's Hill, which was ultimately successful, led to such high casualties that British generals were more conservative in future conflicts. Later in the war, the British often opted for a cautious approach, which on several occasions allowed the Continental Army to escape (e.g., Brooklyn Heights, second battle of Trenton).
- Henry Knox's success in hauling cannon 300 miles from Fort Ticonderoga to Boston was a miracle. This feat proved to be the key factor in freeing Boston and kept the British from ending the war with a decisive victory over a fragile American army.
- The colonial army, which in a single night had placed cannon behind wooden barricades on the frozen ground on Dorchester Heights, was aided by a terrible storm. The British had moved troops to the foot of the heights and were preparing for an assault. While British casualties would have been high, the charge by the redcoats would in all likelihood have been successful against the lightly fortified and inexperienced colonial troops.
- Benedict Arnold's success in delaying the British and Hessians in their attack on Lake Champlain and down the Hudson River made possible the victory at Saratoga nine months later.

- Franklin's transformation from an admirer of England (he was planning to retire there) to an ardent advocate of independence was unexpected. Even though a generation older than most of the other Founding Fathers, he went on to play key roles during the 1775 and 1776 sessions of the Continental Congress, as a negotiator in France during the war, as part of the team that negotiated the peace treaty with England, and during the Constitutional Convention.

- John Adams noted the "coincidence of circumstances" that set the stage for independence and self-government. He observed—accurately—that no other people in the world had experienced a similar opportunity.

The next chapter covers a decisive 16-month period—the disastrous fighting on Long Island and Manhattan in the fall 1776, the totally unexpected American victories at Trenton and Princeton, survival during the winter camp at Morristown, through victory at Saratoga.

CHAPTER 5

▼

The Revolutionary War—The First Months

Almighty God has created the mind free... Truth is great and will prevail if left to herself...
—Thomas Jefferson in James Hutson, *Religion and the Founding of the American Republic*, 74.

General William Howe replaced General Gage as the British commander in Boston; he and his troops, who had been out of sight for four months, finally re-appeared in early July, the same time the Declaration of Independence was being signed. The British and Hessian armies disembarked on Staten Island. They came 32,000 strong, including 11,000 Hessians, on 400 troop carriers plus 10 ships of the line (battleships of the day) and 20 frigates. This represented two-thirds of the total British army and half its navy.[1]

After a month of preparation, the British moved most of their troops to Long Island, about eight miles east of the small village of Brooklyn. Washington had split his army of 20,000, with 10,000 on Long Island near Brooklyn and the remainder in Manhattan. The British navy had control of the New York harbor, including the East River, which separated Brooklyn from Manhattan.

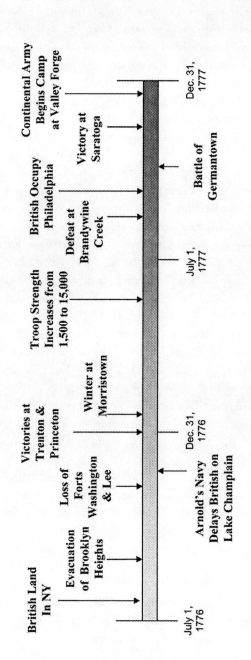

On August 27 the inexperienced and outmanned Continental Army was badly mauled by the British and Hessians. There were 1,400 killed, wounded or captured, including many officers. Those who were not casualties fled to the earthwork fortifications that had been dug at Brooklyn Heights. The British and Hessians paraded in front of the American fortifications just out of musket range. However, instead of pressing the attack immediately, General Howe decided on an artillery barrage—a siege—to break the back of the Continental Army and thus minimize British casualties; he wanted to avoid another Bunker Hill.

Evacuation from Brooklyn Heights. As the Continental Army was digging in and preparing to meet the expected British assault, rain flooded the trenches and dampened gunpowder; however, strong winds kept the British fleet from coming up the East River that separated Washington's two forces. One historian put it this way: "Nine thousand (or more) disheartened solders, the last hope of their country, were penned up, with the sea (East River) behind them and a triumphant enemy in front, shelterless and famished on a square mile of open ground swept by fierce and cold northeasterly gale..."[2]

On August 30, based on the recommendation of his staff and contrary to his own predilections to stay and fight, Washington reluctantly ordered a withdrawal across the East River to lower Manhattan. The evacuation began at nightfall; however, because of bad weather and confusion of orders, the retreat was not completed by dawn. "But again the 'elements interceded,' this time in the form of pea-soup fog." As daylight came, the fog obscured the evacuation. By 7:00 a.m., when the fog lifted, "the British saw to their astonishment that the Americans had vanished."[3]

"But what a very close call it had been. How readily it could have all gone wrong—had there been no northeast wind to hold the British fleet in check through the day the Battle of Long Island was fought, not to say the days immediately afterward. Or had the wind not turned southwest the night of August 29. Or had there been no fortuitous fog as a final safeguard when day broke."[4]

The "fortuitous fog" and the three-day British delay of the assault on the fortifications at Brooklyn Heights saved Washington and the Continental Army. One New Yorker said that such a fog in this season "had not been known for twenty or thirty years."[5]

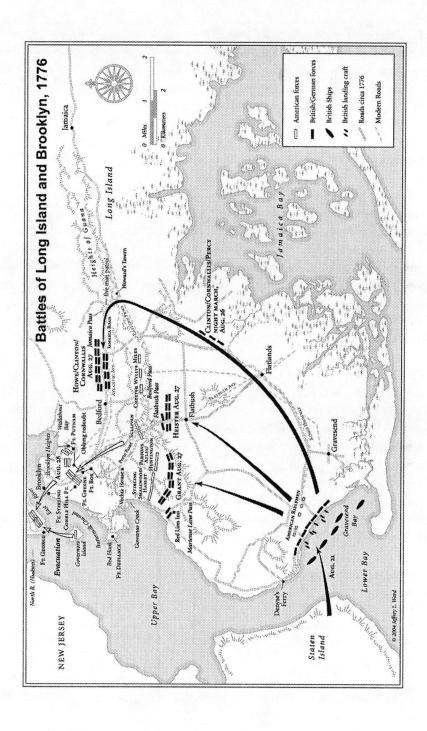

Fighting shifts to Manhattan Island. The evacuation from Brooklyn Heights was not the end of the problems facing General Washington and his untested army. As the British prepared to move into Manhattan, elements of the Continental Army moved north to forts Lee and Washington where they planned to make a stand. Another 5,000 were stationed in lower Manhattan to slow the British advance.

On September 15, two weeks after the Brooklyn evacuation, the British landed troops in lower Manhattan; the Continental Army's rear guard fled in terror. Two fresh brigades came up to stop the British, but when 60 to 70 British troops appeared, the Americans fled in panic. Washington came riding up but was unsuccessful in stopping the mass confusion and retreat. "Unwilling to follow the retreat, Washington soon loomed on horseback alone. Some fifty of the enemy dashed towards him. He watched them without moving. Had not aides galloped up and pulled him away, he would have been killed or captured."[6]

In mid-November, Washington again divided his forces, this time between Fort Washington on the Manhattan side of the Hudson River and Fort Lee on the New Jersey side. Since Fort Washington was heavily fortified, both Washington and General Nathaniel Greene assumed their troops would be able to hold out against a direct British assault. They were wrong: "Watching from across the river at Fort Lee, Washington saw the widely spread American ramparts prove almost useless against professionally expert assault. His anguish was so poignant that he made no effort, until it was too late, to organize some way to get at least some of the troops down from the cliffs and across the river. Having absolutely no means of escape as a superior British force bore down upon them, thousands of American troops milled helplessly around the main fort, which was too small to hold them. They had only two choices: annihilation or surrender. By nightfall, they had surrendered."[7]

Most of these troops—there were more than 3,000—later died of starvation and disease aboard British prison ships anchored in New York Harbor. From 20,000 troops in August, the Continental Army was down to fewer than 5,000 as it retreated across New Jersey to eastern Pennsylvania; by mid-December, the army had almost disintegrated.

Despite the desperate situation faced by the Continental Army, Washington was like a rock: "The General hopes the justice of the great cause in which they are engaged, the necessity and importance of defending this Country, preserving its Liberties, and warding off the destruction meditated against it, will inspire every man with Firmness and Resolution in time of action, which is now approaching—Ever remembering that upon the blessing of Heaven, and the bravery of the men, our Country only can be saved."[8]

Battles of Trenton and Princeton

Following his devastating defeats in New York and the retreat across New Jersey, Washington gathered his remaining troops on the Pennsylvania side of the Delaware River, seven miles north of Trenton. It was two days before Christmas 1776 when he formulated a daring plan: a surprise attack on the 1,200 Hessians at Trenton. Facing the expiration of enlistments of many of his troops on January 1, and a desperate need for a victory to encourage public support for the war, Washington and his staff decided to take the risk.

The attack was planned as a pincer movement. Troops under Washington would cross the river and march south to Trenton. Two other units, James Ewing's brigade of 800 militia and John Cadwalader's group of about 1,800, would cross the Delaware south of Trenton and march north to meet Washington's main force. However, because of heavy ice flows on the lower Delaware, these 2,600 men were not able to cross the river in time to participate in the first battle of Trenton.[9]

Crossing the Delaware. The famous painting of Washington crossing the Delaware on Christmas night 1776, though controversial, accurately reflects the blizzard conditions and ice flows on the river. Because the British and Hessians were not accustomed to fighting under unfavorable conditions, Washington believed that bad weather worked in favor of the Continental Army.

There were delays, but the Continental Army, including a few artillery pieces (most had been lost in New York), finally crossed the river before daylight on December 26. The army marched into Trenton without encountering resistance, and opened cannon and musket fire down the streets toward the Hessian barracks. In the attack, Colonel Johann Rall and 30 Hessians were killed; 900 surrendered, and another 200 escaped south. Washington's losses included two

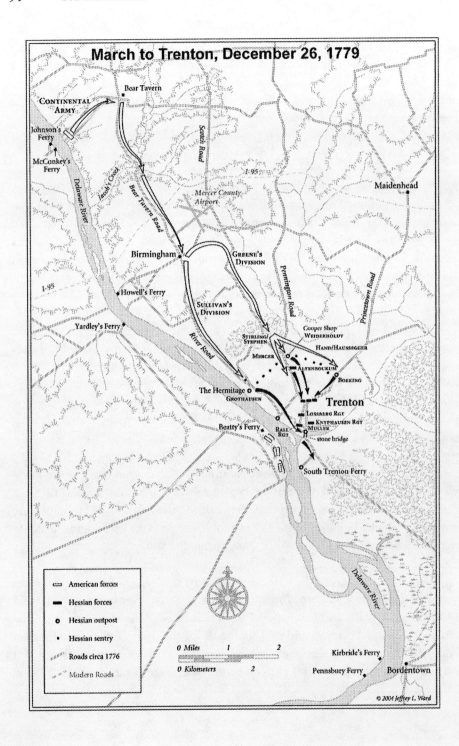

killed and two wounded; Lt. James Monroe, a future president, was one of those seriously wounded, taking a musket ball in the shoulder. Following the brief battle, Washington and his army, along with the captured Hessians, returned to the Pennsylvania side of the Delaware River. That night, Washington and his top officers rested, celebrated, and hosted a dinner for the defeated Hessian officers (a custom of the times to be repeated at Saratoga and Yorktown).

One of the interesting sidelights of this story is that a British loyalist had spotted the Continental Army preparing to move across the Delaware, and sent a written message to Colonel Rall alerting him of the possibility of attack. Rall, who was the officer in charge of the Hessian troops that had bayoneted 500 surrendering Americans on Long Island a few weeks earlier, either ignored the message or did not believe it. He was later criticized for not posting sentries. The truth of the matter was that neither the British nor Hessians thought the Continental Army capable of mounting an attack.

In describing the first Trenton battle, General Henry Knox, the artillery commander, said, "Providence seemed to have smiled upon every part of this enterprise."[10] Given that Colonel Rall had been warned, and the Continental Army was in poor condition, it would be hard to argue with Knox. Historian David Fischer said that as the news of Trenton spread, "…many people received it as a vindication of the Cause. They deeply believed that the battle of Trenton was a Sign of God's redeeming Providence, and proof that the Continental army was the instrument. This idea of God's all-powerful Providence gave them a sense of agency in the world, as a part of divine purpose."[11]

A second crossing. A day later, on December 27, Washington received word that Cadwalader's 1,800 troops had finally crossed the Delaware south of Trenton and were heading north. Late that night Washington and his key officers conferred and made another bold decision: They would strike New Jersey a second time.

On December 29 and 30 the Continental Army again crossed the Delaware. To his surprise, Washington received a report that several thousand British troops, under the command of General Charles Cornwallis, were passing through Princeton, 12 miles northeast, and marching toward Trenton. This could have been a fatal intelligence breakdown and a deadly mistake for the Continental Army.

On the same day Washington was leading his troops into Trenton, Benjamin Franklin embarked on the *USS Reprisal* bound for France with instructions to persuade the French to become America's ally in the war for liberty. The day before he sailed, Franklin wrote to a friend: "I hope our people will keep up their courage. I have no doubt of their finally succeeding by the blessing of God, nor have I any doubt that so good a cause will fail of that blessing."[12]

Second battle of Trenton. As Cornwallis and his army moved toward Trenton from the northeast, Washington and his outnumbered troops set up a battle line behind Assunpink Creek near what is now downtown Trenton. Washington's army had its back to the Delaware River and there was no way to escape in that direction. (The boats that had ferried them across the Delaware were several miles upstream.) In the meantime, the weather turned warm and it began to rain; the roads were knee-deep in mud. Because of the poor condition of the roads, it took three days for Cornwallis to move his troops from Princeton into position north of Assunpink Creek. When the British finally arrived, Washington was exposed to heavy fire at the bridge as he directed the withdrawal of the Continental Army.

After heavy skirmishes at the creek in the late afternoon of January 2, 1777, both armies withdrew to set up camp for the night. Cornwallis knew he had the Continental Army cornered, and that his force was numerically superior, and better trained. He was in no rush to finish off Washington and the Americans that night; he told his men that they would "bag the old fox (Washington) in the morning."[13]

The miraculous evacuation and victory at Princeton. As a farmer and a careful observer of the weather, Washington believed that a northwest wind that had come up late in the day would freeze the ground later that night, making it possible to quickly move his army toward Princeton and then on to Morristown, where he planned to spend the winter. He instructed several men to tear down fences and build large bonfires so that the British would believe the American army was camping for the night and preparing for battle the next day.

About 11:00 p.m. the weather turned colder, and a few hours later, as Washington had anticipated, the muddy roads froze solid. Washington instructed his troops to wrap rags around the wheels of wagons and artillery pieces to cut down on the noise, and the entire army began to move out. By dawn, they had covered the 12 miles to the western edge of Princeton and escaped certain annihilation from Cornwallis and his army. That same morning, British reinforcements were leaving Princeton heading for Trenton when Generals Hugh Mercer and Washington saw them. In a fierce battle lasting 45 minutes, 300 British troops were killed and an equal number were captured.

The battle began badly for the Americans. General Mercer, a physician and commander of a group of Americans, was on the ground and his troops fled in terror. (He later died of eleven bayonet wounds.) However, when Washington saw that Mercer was seriously wounded and his troops were retreating, he came forward and led them in a charge. Washington was no more than 30 yards from the British lines during the peak of the fighting, and emerged unscathed. Many of his troops considered this a miracle.

The combination of the first Trenton victory and the success against elite British troops at Princeton represented a huge morale boost for the Continental Army, Congress and the American people. The numbers of troops and casualties involved were not large, but the psychological lift—and the blow to British prestige—were vitally important. For example, following these two victories, the American press, which had been divided in its endorsement of the revolution, almost unanimously supported the war. When word reached Paris, the French, although not ready to declare war on England, immediately sent several shiploads of military supplies to the Continental Army.

Following these embarrassing defeats, the British government and military leadership in London engaged in finger pointing, blaming General Cornwallis, Colonel Rall and a variety of officers for letting their guard down and being "out-generaled." In America, Washington was a hero.

Surviving the First Winter at Morristown

There were several reasons why Washington selected Morristown as the site for the Continental Army's winter quarters for 1777:

- Several New Jersey patriots and state leaders lived in Morristown.
- The area had a 700-man militia and a light horse company.
- An earlier encampment by General Lee had found the people hospitable.

- Morristown was the home of an ironworks industry that could make shot and cannon.
- Morristown and nearby hamlets were Christian communities, which Washington believed important, since most ministers supported the war.[14]

Local ironworks industry makes cannon. Washington and General Henry Knox set a goal of producing several hundred cannon that winter. Although they did not meet their objectives, the local ironworks produced dozens of badly needed cannon to replace those lost in the evacuation from New York a few months earlier. One of the interesting aspects of this story is that hundreds of the Hessian prisoners captured at Trenton were put to work in the ironworks and the supporting mines. Several of these firms were owned by Americans of German ancestry; it was a natural fit.

Smallpox outbreak. Upon his arrival in Morristown, Washington learned of a smallpox outbreak among both civilians and soldiers. He made an immediate decision to have his soldiers inoculated, and encouraged civilians in the Morristown area to undergo this medical procedure. Washington's decision was risky on two counts. First, since inoculated soldiers were usually sick for several days, or even weeks, he did not want the British to find out that the fighting ability of his force of 3,000 had been further diminished. Secondly, the traditional medical practice for inoculation required several days of special diet and other preparations. He ordered inoculation to proceed immediately with none of the normal precautionary measures.

His order went beyond the troops wintering at Morristown to soldiers in Philadelphia and other locations. The result was a resounding success; only a handful of the troops in Morristown died, and none of the 1,000 troops in Philadelphia perished. By contrast, 20 percent of the civilians living in the Morristown area who chose not to be inoculated died that winter. Historian Bruce Chadwick sums up the importance of Washington's quick action this way: "The British never attacked the weakened army. A medical historian later wrote that Washington's efforts to save the army and populace from smallpox was as important a factor in winning the war as victory in any battle."[15]

Support of Morristown ministers and churches. The Morristown Presbyterian Church was a product of the Great Awakening. Washington became friendly with the minister, Reverend Timothy Johnnes, and attended services every Sunday during the winter. These services were usually held out of doors since the church building had been converted to a hospital. Washington ordered all soldiers not on sick call to attend weekly worship services and hired as many chaplains as possible.

"Johnnes and the other Presbyterians, and their guest speakers, preached just what Washington wanted his men to hear—that God encouraged people to not only embrace new religious views, but the Revolution as well."[16] Reverend Gano, a Baptist, enlisted in the army as a chaplain and the church elders turned their building over to the army as a hospital.

Washington was grateful for the support received from local Morristown churches and clergy, especially the Presbyterians and Baptists. As a result of these experiences, and others, Washington frequently acknowledged the critically important role that religion, specifically Christianity, played in America's love for freedom and in the Revolutionary War effort.

Washington's close brush with death. In late February, not long after the mass smallpox inoculations, Morristown was hit by a severe snowstorm. Washington, who personally supervised clearing the snow, developed a serious cold and sore throat, which soon became a throat infection accompanied by high fever. Local physicians tried all the usual tricks of the trade—bleeding, applying a glass cup to his head to draw out the bad sweat. Washington's condition was so grave that his officers planned his funeral and selected General Nathaniel Greene of Rhode Island to be his replacement.

However, in mid-March, Martha Washington arrived and immediately began treating her husband with a special formula of molasses and onions. Within a few days he was out of bed and had resumed his normal duties. (The British did not learn of his illness and brush with death; it was a closely held secret.)

Troop strength during the winter and spring 1777. The effective fighting force of the Continental Army shrank to about 1,500 at its lowest point during the winter at Morristown when enlistments ran out and many soldiers were recovering from smallpox inoculations. However, by May additional recruits plus the calling up of militia units swelled the ranks to 15,000.

Battles of Brandywine Creek and Germantown

Washington decided to make a stand against the British, who had left New York by ship and were coming north up the Chesapeake Bay toward Philadelphia. Washington's troops also engaged the British at Germantown, north of Philadelphia. These were the two major actions of Washington's portion of the Continental Army during the summer campaign of 1777. Of course, the Battle of Saratoga, described later in this chapter, was the most decisive action of the year.

Battle of Brandywine Creek, September 11, 1777. In mid-June, General Howe sent a force toward Morristown; it was beaten back. A few days later, he sent a second force, which was again pushed back. Both of these were feints to keep Washington's army bottled up.[17] Despite these attacks, Washington anticipated the real British objective—Philadelphia, the capital city.

On July 24, 170 British troop carriers left New York. Although Washington was almost certain the ships were headed out to sea with the intention of entering the Chesapeake Bay, he could not make a full commitment; there was the possibility that the British Army was sailing north up the Hudson River to link up with General Burgoyne. On August 22 Washington received a report confirming that the British were sailing up the Chesapeake with the obvious objective of taking Philadelphia.

Washington's troops marched through Philadelphia and took up positions at Brandywine Creek near the Pennsylvania/Delaware border facing the expected British line of march. However, General Howe fooled the Continental Army by making a sweep around its left flank. Fortunately for Washington and his army, many of the troops, including Marquis de Lafayette, who had come to Morristown that winter, fought a delaying action that allowed most of the Continental Army to escape. "Washington himself was fortunate not to be shot when he rode unawares into an enemy command post."[18] Continental Army casualties at Brandywine Creek were 1,300 killed, wounded or captured, twice the losses of the British.[19] The way to Philadelphia was wide open. The unhappy and disgraced Continental Congress quickly evacuated Philadelphia and headed for York, Pennsylvania.

Battle of Germantown, October 7, 1777. General Howe occupied Philadelphia with 3,000 troops and had another 7,000 to 8,000 soldiers stationed in Germantown on the Schuylkill River five miles north of the city. In early October, Washington saw the opportunity to pull another Trenton, this time on a larger scale. With 8,000 Continentals and 3,000 militia (one of the few times the Continental Army enjoyed a numerical advantage over the British), Washington decided to attack the English forces in Germantown. To achieve surprise, the Continental Army was to move out in four columns and march 15-19 miles from their camp north of Germantown, rejoining at dawn.

Unfortunately, the columns of American troops did not arrive in Germantown in a coordinated fashion. Fog and mist obscured visibility and contributed to poor communications and a lack of coordination. After an initial penetration of the British lines, and some success, Washington and his army were forced to withdraw to their camp, and then move to Valley Forge for the winter.

Meanwhile in the Hudson River Valley, Victory at Saratoga

After gathering his forces near Montreal, General Johnny Burgoyne sailed down Lake Champlain (about 110 miles) to prepare to attack Fort Ticonderoga. Approximately 2,500 Continental Army troops were defending the fort. When it became obvious that the British had taken artillery positions overlooking Fort Ticonderoga, General Arthur St. Clair, who reported to General Phillip Schuyler, ordered his army to evacuate under the cover of darkness and retreat south down the Hudson Valley.

Both St. Clair and Schuyler were disgraced (even Washington was critical of the decision to abandon Fort Ticonderoga) and relieved of their commands. Fortunately for early America, however, many of these same troops fought a delaying action down the Hudson Valley, and most (including the Polish engineer, Colonel Thadeus Kosciuszko) survived to take part in the pivotal battle of Saratoga. Historian Richard Ketchum said, "…had it not been for St. Clair's courageous decision to abandon Ticonderoga, there would have been no Saratoga."[20]

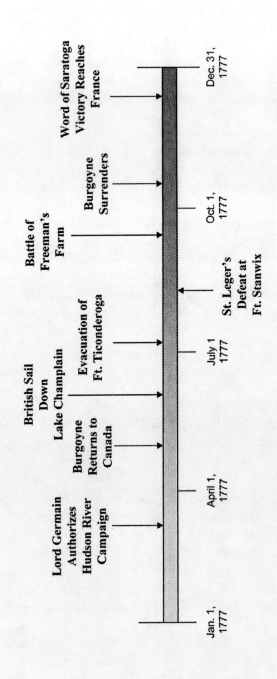

Burgoyne and his army chased the retreating American force past Lake George and down the Hudson Valley. However, as the Americans were able to slow the British advance by cutting trees and erecting barriers across the limited roads in the area, militia from surrounding states, including some from as far away as Virginia, began to assemble near Saratoga. The stage was set for a series of major battles. Key American leaders included General Horatio Gates, who was in command; General Benedict Arnold; Daniel Morgan and 400 expert riflemen; and Colonel Kosciuszko.

There were several important side battles as part of General Burgoyne's overall campaign, and two proved to be especially costly for the British:

- On August 11 a force of 800 Hessians led by Lt. Col. Friederich Baum attempted to capture the supply depot at Bennington, Vt. Bennington was defended by militia under the command of Brig. General John Stark, a hero of Bunker Hill. On August 15 the entire force of Hessians was annihilated. A relief column of British troops was also beaten. All told, the Bennington campaign cost Burgoyne 15 percent of his combat force.

- Another force of 1,000 British solders and 1,000 Indians, under the command of Lt. Col. Barry St. Leger, marched south and east from Canada with orders to capture Fort Stanwix (defended by 750 New Yorkers) and then join up with General Burgoyne at Albany. This was to be the third spear of the campaign. St. Leger began the siege on August 3; however, a reinforcement column of 800 New York militia under General Nicholas Herkemer forced the British to send a limited number of troops and most of the Indians to meet them. Following a bloody battle at Oriskany in which General Herkemer was killed, a relief column of 1,000 Americans under Benedict Arnold succeeded in forcing the British and their Indian allies to lift the siege of Fort Stanwix and retreat to Canada. The American troops were then free to return to the Saratoga area.

By the end of August, General Burgoyne's army had supply lines extending 200 miles from Canada, but he remained hopeful that General Howe's army

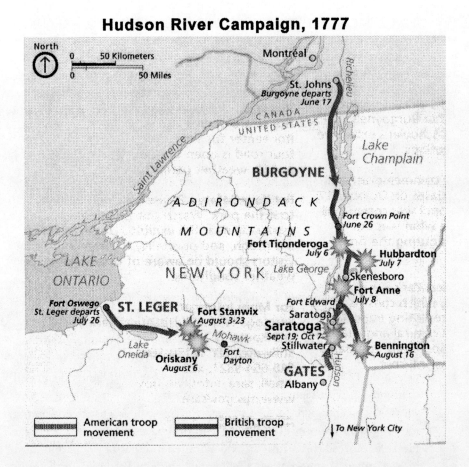

from New York would soon come up the Hudson River to attack the rear of the Continental Army. In effect, the two British armies would have had the Americans in a pincer. Of course, Burgoyne did not know that Howe had deployed most of his troops to Philadelphia.

After several serious skirmishes near Saratoga in late September (Freeman's Farm is the best known), Burgoyne retreated a short distance and dug in. Three weeks later, Burgoyne sent General Simon Fraser on a "reconnaissance-in-force" with 1,500 troops to envelope the American lines from the west; this didn't work (they were met by 12,000 Americans) and more than half of the British troops (including General Fraser) were killed, wounded or captured. Two major redoubts (fortress-like structures) were successfully attacked by Arnold and others, and the British and Hessians were forced to retreat to higher ground that they had previously fortified. However, they were surrounded and their supplies cut off; American troops had returned to Ticonderoga and re-captured the fort from a small detachment of British troops. When General Howe failed to show up from the south, and with his army growing weaker by the day, General Burgoyne had no choice but to surrender; the date was October 17, 1777.

The soldiers who fought at Saratoga believed that God had blessed their efforts and given them victory. In letters home, they gave credit to divine providence. Dr. James Thatcher, who treated soldiers wounded at Saratoga, said, "We witness the incalculable reverse of fortune, and the extraordinary vicissitudes of military events, as ordained by Divine Providence..."[21] It was part of the cultural pattern of giving God the credit for saving lives or for military victories over the British or Hessians.

Related to this point, historian Robert Middlekauff summarized what motivated American soldiers during many of the Revolutionary War battles: "Belief in the Holy Spirit surely sustained some in the American army, perhaps more than in the enemy's. There are a good many references to the Divine or to Providence in the letters and diaries of ordinary soldiers. Often, however, these expressions are in the form of thanks to the Lord for permitting these soldiers to survive. There is little that suggests soldiers believed that faith rendered them invulnerable to the enemy's bullets. Many did consider the glorious cause to be sacred; their war, as the ministers who sent them off to kill never tired of reminding them, was just and providential."[22]

The ramifications of General Burgoyne's ill-fated plan, and General Howe's failure to mount an offensive up the Hudson River, changed the nature of the Revolutionary War. It was the first large-scale defeat of a British Army (close to 9,000 troops and camp followers had set out from Canada that spring). The British public and government were apoplectic. When word of Burgoyne's defeat reached Paris, it changed the tone of discussions between the American delegation (Benjamin Franklin, Silas Deane and Arthur Lee) and French diplomats. Shortly thereafter France declared war on England—they were impressed with the outcome at Saratoga and liked the Americans' chances of beating the British.

Lessons Learned by the Leaders of the Continental Army

The costly losses on Long Island and Manhattan taught Washington and his staff an important lesson—they could not afford to put the Continental Army at risk with a frontal assault against the better trained and equipped British and Hessian armies. From that point forward, the Continental Army (with notable exceptions like Trenton and Germantown) would limit itself to hit and run tactics, and avoid full-scale assaults; it would fight a war of attrition and thus make sure the army could escape to fight another day.

As discussed in subsequent chapters, implementing this strategy wasn't as easy and straightforward as it may sound. The Continental Army almost perished at Valley Forge, and the army was close to collapse during a second winter at Morristown. The lack of financial support from the Continental Congress, and from the states, runaway inflation, the vagaries of state militias (When would they show up and when would they fight?) combined with uncertainty about the role of the French, led to discouragement and outright despair on the part of Washington and his staff, and members of the Continental Congress.

Furthermore, Washington was under almost constant political pressure to engage and defeat the British Army. As noted in the next chapter, to keep the British off balance, Washington and his officers were excellent at "disinformation" relative to the size and combat readiness of the Continental Army. Unfortunately, this same propaganda gave Americans, including some members of Congress, an overly optimistic view of the Continental Army's ability to conduct offensive operations.

Evidence of Divine Providence

The 16 months covered by this chapter—July 1776 in New York and concluding in October 1777 at Saratoga—include many examples of what most Americans would have considered divine providence, one of three criteria for evaluating God's blessings on early America:

- *Fortuitous fog covering the evacuation of half of the Continental Army from Brooklyn.* The probabilities that a fog would cover the withdrawal of Washington and the army and keep the British Navy from cutting them off was remote. Related to this, the decision by General Howe to delay his attack on Continental Army fortifications at Brooklyn saved the army and Washington.

- *Washington escaped death on lower Manhattan.* As noted, he was on horseback alone after failing to stem a panicky retreat and within close range of British solders before his aides rushed him to safety.

- *Colonel Rall's failure to heed the warning of Washington's attack at Trenton.* Even though he was handed a note warning that the Continental Army was on the move, Colonel Rall did not post guards or take normal precautions to protect his garrison from attack. If Rall had heeded this warning, Washington's gamble would, in all probability, have failed.

- *Freezing of the ground between Trenton and Princeton.* Both the British and American armies were bogged down in mud at the end of the day's fighting at Assunpink Creek Bridge in Trenton. Cornwallis was relaxed knowing that he could finish off the Continental Army the next morning. However, the freezing temperatures allowed Washington and the Continental Army to not only escape, but also set the stage for another astounding victory over British troops just outside Princeton.

- *Washington's life preserved at Trenton and Princeton.* Washington survived a hail of bullets and cannon fire at Assunpink Creek Bridge during the second Trenton battle. After General Mercer went down and his troops retreated in disarray, Washington led them back—in fact he was between his own troops and the British riflemen when both sides exchanged volleys. He was unhurt.

- *Washington survived a life-threatening sickness at Morristown.* The throat infection that downed Washington was serious; his aides were planning his funeral. However, with the arrival of Martha, and in answer to many prayers, he was nursed back to health.

- *General St. Clair's unpopular decision to evacuate Fort Ticonderoga.* Generals St. Clair and Schuyler were accused of cowardice, and dismissed. However, the delaying action fought by St. Clair's troops and their presence at the Battle of Saratoga were key factors in what was, in retrospect, one of the most decisive victories of the war.

- *The failure of General Howe to move north to meet General Burgoyne.* General Howe decided that it was more important to take Philadelphia and embarrass the Americans by occupying their capital, and failed to complete his part of the move to sever New England from the rest of the colonies. This led to the biggest British defeat of the war—9,000 troops and supporting personnel were either killed, wounded or captured; New England remained physically connected with the other states.

In addressing the Continental Congress a month before the victory at Saratoga, John Jay described "...a revolution which, in the whole course of its rise and progress, is distinguished by so many marks of the Divine favor and interposition, that no doubt can remain of its being finally accomplished." Jay went on to say that history would find it extraordinary that 13 colonies, "...divided by a variety of governments and manners, should immediately become one people...unanimously determined to be free and, undaunted by the power of Britain, refer their cause to the Almighty and resolve to repel force by force."[23]

CHAPTER 6

▼

The Revolutionary War—Years of Survival

The man must be bad indeed, who can look upon the events of the American Revolution without feeling the warmest gratitude towards the great Author of the Universe whose divine interposition was so frequently manifested in our behalf.
—George Washington in James Hutson, *The Founders on Religion*, 19.

Between the winter at Valley Forge, which began in December 1777, and the final victory at Yorktown in October 1781, the challenges facing the fledging United States and its army did not get any easier. The army barely survived the winter in Valley Forge and two years later, Washington's troops almost perished in heavy snows in a second winter camp at Morristown. The Battle of Monmouth following Valley Forge was the major action in 1778. There were two serious battles near Springfield, New Jersey, in the summer of 1780. Most of the fighting in 1780 and 1781 had moved to the South.

There were many other problems during these years of stalemate in the northern and middle colonies. The economy was poor and inflation was rampant. Enthusiasm for the cause of independence had steadily eroded, and it became increasingly difficult to recruit and retain troops. Some of the states did not meet their financial commitments. The attitude among many Americans was: "Let's get this thing over with and get back to a normal life."

110 God Bless America

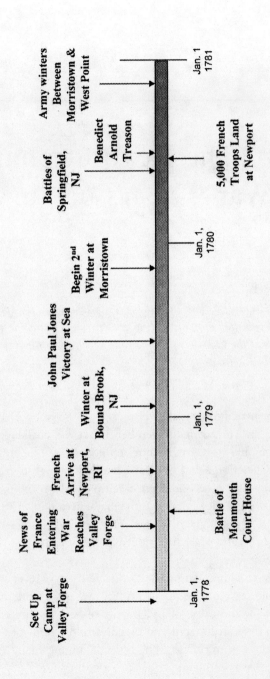

Winter at Valley Forge (1777-1778)

As a place to winter with his 9,000 troops, Washington was not impressed with Valley Forge, 20 miles west of Philadelphia. It was a political decision; when the Continental Congress moved to York, and the Pennsylvania Supreme Executive Council moved to Lancaster, both political bodies were anxious that Washington's army establish a barrier between them and the British in Philadelphia. They also thought that the presence of the army near Philadelphia would keep civilians from going over to the British side.

A positive aspect of the Valley Forge site was its defensive potential; it was a high plateau facing east. Although his position at Valley Forge was defensible, Washington worried about an attack from the 15,000 British troops in the Philadelphia area; no attack came.

Failure of the commissary department. Beginning in October, Washington had written to the Continental Congress and others expressing his concerns about food and clothing. Unfortunately, the United States did not have a well-developed textile industry; most clothing was imported from England. Washington had patrols scour the countryside to purchase clothing, but with little success.

When the army arrived at Valley Forge on December 19 they expected the commissary department of the Continental Congress to have stockpiled food and clothing. Three days after arriving, Washington was told that the last cow in the pens had been slaughtered and no more cattle could be found. Furthermore, nearly all the flour was gone and there was no wheat.

In addition to finding virtually no supplies, Washington learned that the top people in the commissary department had resigned. Henry Laurens, the president of the Continental Congress, wrote a friend: "Not only the Commissarial but other departments on which the salvation of the army equally depends are somewhat more than deranged; they are shattered and distracted."[1]

Washington was furious, but the three departments were outside his direct control, at least for the time being. Historian Thomas Fleming wrote: "Contrary to myth, Valley Forge was not an example of American poverty. The soldiers starved because the Congress had allowed the army's supply system to fall into chaos. Elsewhere in America people were feasting on one of the best harvests in memory. But no one seemed to know how to get food to the army. It was the beginning of an ominous decline in the relationship between the soldiers and the Congress."[2]

The soldiers were also upset with many of the Quakers living in the area, who avowed support for the revolution but because of their religious beliefs, would not fight. Furthermore, they would not sell their flour, grain and cattle to the army on credit.

When Gouverneur Morris visited the army at Valley Forge in January, 1778, he wrote to John Jay, who was chief justice of the supreme court of New York, that he found, "just a skeleton of an army," in a "naked, starving condition, out of health and out of spirits."[3] Washington finally gave up on Congress' ability to solve his supply problems and in mid-February appointed Nathaniel Greene to clean up the mess. It took about six weeks, but by early April, Greene and his staff had food moving to Valley Forge.

One of the solutions was to broaden the food supply network by reaching out to Massachusetts in the north and Maryland in the south where food was plentiful. There were "old west" type cattle drives to Valley Forge, and civilians were hired to drive wagons long distances to procure food. "The cattle drives, which involved hundreds of soldiers and civilians, succeeded beyond anyone's expectation," and a thousand head of cattle a week began to arrive at Valley Forge.[4]

The medical crisis. As soon as the army arrived at Valley Forge there was an immediate need for hospitals to treat several hundred soldiers who had been wounded at the battles of Brandywine Creek and Germantown. Some of these men were sent to hospitals in Reading and Bethlehem, filling them to capacity. Washington then authorized his officers to commandeer public buildings, barns, and churches, and convert them to hospitals. "One year before, in Morristown, the general had enjoyed the near-complete cooperation of ministers in Morris County and throughout New Jersey. Most of them were Presbyterians and fervent supporters of the Revolution. Now, though, he had to deal with religious leaders who were not so cooperative. Southeastern Pennsylvania was home to the large communities of Quakers and Moravians, plus smaller eclectic religious groups, such as a community of German mystics. These religious groups were all pacifists and opposed to all wars."[5]

Since there were few large communities within 70 miles, Washington needed every church and public building he could find. The Moravians reversed their position in opposition to the army and decided to help. "Moravians who ran another Brethren's House in the small town of Lititz also welcomed the army. The number of patients housed there soon topped 250, surpassing the total population of the community."[6] When other religious groups, even the German mystics and the Quakers, realized the seriousness of the situation, they also came around. Still, some groups resisted and their buildings were forcefully seized by the army.

All of the medical centers were hopelessly overcrowded. For example, "The Reading Hospital, which could hold 360 patients, was home to more than nine hundred. Brethren's House in Bethlehem had room for three hundred, but by January it housed more than four hundred sick soldiers, many in beds set up in the kitchen and narrow hallways."[7] In several of the hospitals, half or more of the patients died, as did most of the doctors and support staff. For example, more than 500 soldiers died in the Bethlehem Hospital. "Half of the 250 soldiers at Lititz died, along with a local doctor, Moravian pastor, and five aides."[8]

There was another outbreak of smallpox in Virginia, and Washington again had all soldiers inoculated. "The second mass-inoculation program prevented a much feared outbreak of smallpox in the army, and only 10 soldiers died. The halt of any smallpox in the army meant, too, that no one in Chester County (Pennsylvania) was infected by the soldiers and that, again, Washington's actions had saved thousands of lives."[9]

By April, the combination of favorable weather and more food helped ease the problems of sickness. Unfortunately, more than 2,000 of the 9,000 troops who had set up camp at Valley Forge died of their wounds or disease.

Gates and others try to overthrow Washington. In addition to the problems of keeping his army together, Washington faced a coup. Fresh from his success at Saratoga, General Gates had ambitions, and political support, for taking over as commanding general. Although Gates did not overtly campaign for the job, others did so on his behalf. Washington's staff members, who understood the situation, were furious. Part of Washington's problem was that in order to avoid attack by the British, he put out information (propaganda) indicating that his army was stronger than it really was. In so doing, he increased the expectations of the Continental Congress and American people. Not realizing how weak the army really was, Congress and the people could not understand why Washington did not take the initiative against the British Army, particularly as they occupied the nation's capital.

Criticism of Washington reached a crescendo during the early part of the winter at Valley Forge. By spring, however, the furor had died down and Washington remained in command of the Continental Army.

Von Steuben's arrival a shot in the arm. It was a blessing that Baron von Steuben came on the scene to institute military drills, and thus transform the army into a more disciplined, effective fighting force. Recruited by Franklin in Paris, Steuben was neither a baron nor a lieutenant general under Frederick the Great, as he claimed. His highest rank had been captain, but he knew how to train an army.

Steuben began by drilling 100 men, and when they reached a high state of training, he had others try to imitate them. There were two advantages for the army—Steuben's drills helped morale and they also made the army a more disciplined entity when it emerged in the early summer to challenge the British at Monmouth Court House. Furthermore, a British spy watched the Continental Army marching in precision and reported this to General Howe in Philadelphia; the British were duly impressed.

Celebration of France's recognition of the United States as an independent country. The agreement with France, following news of the American victory at Saratoga, was critical to success in winning the war. Benjamin Franklin, more than any other person, was responsible for bringing France into the war on the side of the United States. Franklin never doubted the success of what he called "a miracle in human affairs," and "the greatest revolution the world ever saw."[10]

Upon learning about the treaty in which France recognized the independence of the United States, no one at Valley Forge rejoiced more than Lafayette.[11] Washington was also thrilled and set aside May 6 as a day of celebration. "The day was one of the most festive of the war. Following a huge outdoor religious service attended by just about all the troops, a parade of all fifteen thousand soldiers and officers was held, with the men performing von Steuben's intricate maneuvers with perfection, looking as polished as any army on earth."[12]

Importance of worship services and personal prayer. Despite their hunger and lack of adequate clothing, Washington ordered all able-bodied men who were not on duty to participate in worship services. Of course, he and his officers also attended these services.

Here is one of Washington's written prayers during the winter at Valley Forge: "Almighty God, and most merciful Father, who didst command the children of Israel to offer a daily sacrifice to Thee, that thereby they might glorify and praise Thee for Thy protection both night and day; receive, O Lord, my morning sacrifice which I now offer up to Thee...I beseech Thee, my sins, remove them from Thy presence, as far as the east is from the west, and accept of me for the merits of Thy Son, Jesus Christ, that when I come into Thy temple, and compass Thine altar, my prayers may come before Thee as incense; and as Thou wouldst hear me calling upon Thee in Thy Word, that it may be wisdom, righteousness, reconciliation and peace to the saving of my Soul in the day of the Lord Jesus."[13]

Congress used ministers to build support for the country and the army. On May 8, 1778, as the encampment at Valley Forge was winding down, Congress ordered ministers to read an assessment of the situation immediately after divine services. The address was a characteristic congressional state paper that made repeated references to religion: "Our dependence was not upon man," Congress asserted, "it was upon Him who hath commanded us to love our enemies, and to render good for evil"; our success has been "so peculiarly marked, almost by direct interposition of Providence, that not to feel and acknowledge his protection would be the height of impious gratitude."[14]

Ready for action. Changes in the rules of recruiting (three-year tours of duty instead of three months) allowed Washington to break camp in the spring with an army of 15,000. One summary of the condition of the Continental Army that May read as follows: "They had survived the valley of death that Valley Forge had become, and finally had decent clothing to wear and nutritious meals to eat. Von Steuben had transformed them into a well-trained, aggressive fighting force...They had bonded together in that awful winter as soldiers and Americans."[15] This set the stage for the Battle of Monmouth Court House.

Battle of Monmouth, June 1778

Washington's intelligence sources, which were increasingly well developed, indicated that the British would leave Philadelphia and march north through New Jersey to lower Manhattan Island. Washington saw this as an opportunity to test his more disciplined and motivated army in a significant action, and a chance to deal the British another embarrassing defeat.

Return of General Lee. General Charles Lee had been captured by the British during the ignominious retreat from New York in late 1776; however, Washington negotiated his release as part of a prisoner exchange. General Lee reported back to Washington at Valley Forge. In subsequent staff meetings, Lee opposed attacking the British army; he saw nothing but defeat and ruin for the Continental Army.

On the advice of several officers, Washington agreed that the long British lines of 10,000 soldiers and 3,000 loyalist civilians, plus 1,500 supply wagons moving slowly toward New York, provided an opportunity to strike a blow. Furthermore, there was only one day left before the British would be clear of the open plains near Monmouth Court House and into the woods, which would cover their movements the rest of the way to New York. Washington assigned 2,500 men under Lafayette to attack the British column, and subsequently added another 1,000 troops; he kept several thousand troops in reserve. As second in command of the Continental Army, General Lee insisted that he be in charge of the enlarged attacking force, and Washington agreed.

Washington takes over. In the rear a few miles from where the first contact took place, Washington heard musket and cannon fire; then it died down. As he rode forward he saw elements of Lee's force retreating, and came upon General Lee and several of his officers. Lee offered a variety of excuses and Washington responded, "All this may be very true, sir, but you ought not to have undertaken it unless you intended to go through with it."[16] Washington dismissed Lee on the spot and took personal command of the force. Lee was later court-marshaled.

Washington then rushed forward to rally his fleeing troops. Once they were positioned in a line, the Continental riflemen cut down a unit of British cavalry and then stood its ground against a strong infantry assault. According to several observers, Washington's presence and Steuben's training saved the day for the

Continental Army. "Washington, atop one of his signature white horses, raced up and down the American lines, an easy target for the British, urging his troops to fight harder."[17]

Finally, after sporadic action and the coming of darkness, the British troops reached the woods and traveled on to New York; the Battle of Monmouth was over. Monmouth was a military standoff, but many Americans considered it a victory. They had attacked the British, retreated, and then attacked again, recovering all the lost ground. The standoff at Monmouth gave the troops confidence, renewed patriotic fervor swept the country and restored the sharply criticized Washington to the lofty position of unquestioned public trust he had held prior to the winter at Valley Forge.

Following the Battle of Monmouth, and after the British had withdrawn to lower Manhattan and were strengthening their ramparts there, Washington believed that God had blessed the Americans:

> It is not a little pleasing nor less wonderful to contemplate that after two years maneuvering and undergoing the strangest vicissitudes that perhaps ever attended one contest since the creation, both armies are brought back to the very point they set out from, and that which was the offending (offensive) party in the beginning is now reduced to the use of the spade and pickax for defense. The hand of Providence has been so conspicuous in all this that he must be worse than an infidel that lacks faith, and more than wicked that has not gratitude enough to acknowledge his obligations—but it will be time enough for me to turn preacher when my present appointment ceases, and therefore I shall add no more on the Doctrine of Providence.[18]

The Fiasco at Newport, August 1778

In July a strong French fleet, under the command of Admiral d'Estaing, a cousin of Lafayette, appeared off the American coast. Although the French had almost twice the firepower of the English fleet anchored in New York harbor, Admiral d'Estaing refused to attack, claiming that his ships drew too much water to maneuver in the waters around New York. Washington was disappointed and as an alternative proposed an attack on a 3,000-man British garrison at Newport, R.I., a deepwater harbor valued because it did not freeze. Admiral D'Estaing agreed to cooperate in a joint operation—4,000 Continentals, plus militia to be called up, and 4,000 French marines.

On August 9, 1778, the day after the American army had been ferried from the Rhode Island mainland to the north end of Newport's Aquidneck Island, the French discovered that the English fleet was sailing north out of New York. Admiral d'Estaing promptly sailed out to meet the British. However, a gale scattered and badly damaged both navies. The French fleet along with the marines promptly left for Boston for repairs leaving the American army to face the British on Aquidneck Island.

After vicious fighting on August 30, the battered Continental Army made it back to the mainland. This was fortunate; on September 1, General Clinton arrived from New York with an additional 5,000 troops. The net effect of the Newport fiasco was American disillusionment with the French. Lafayette was enormously depressed and asked for permission to lead another expedition into Canada; Washington refused and suggested that Lafayette return to France in an attempt to persuade the French to send more substantial aid than the d'Estaing "sail-by" fleet.[19]

Winter at Bound Brook, New Jersey (1778-1779)

Following the disastrous winter at Valley Forge, and the Battle of Monmouth, most of the army spent its next winter in Bound Brook, near Newburgh in central New Jersey, just outside lower Manhattan Island. The weather was good, and thanks to General Nathaniel Greene, who had taken over the Quartermaster and Commissary Departments during the previous winter, food and clothing were adequate. As a consequence, there was little sickness.

The British remained in New York and did not harass Washington's army. "Winter at Bound Brook was so uneventful that Washington was able to slip away to Philadelphia for two months to renew relationships with delegates to the Continental Congress."[20]

Since the British had shifted their focus to Charleston and the southern states, the only significant clashes in the north were with loyalists and Indians in western and upstate New York, and with the British at Stony Point on the Hudson River near New York City. In this latter clash, 700 British soldiers seized the American fort at Stony Point on May 28, 1779. "However, Washington retaliated six weeks later with a midnight attack, led by Major General Anthony Wayne, which killed or captured the entire 700-man British garrison."[21]

Second Winter Camp in Morristown (1779-80)

Although the Continental Army went into winter camp at Morristown in relatively good physical condition, the second Morristown encampment turned out to be a nightmare. The first snow of the winter, nine inches, fell on December 6. "Then on December 14, a cold front hit the greater New York area, a front that was to keep the east coast in a deep freeze for thirteen weeks." As a result, wagons filled with food destined for the troops in Morristown never arrived; they were stuck in eight-foot high snowdrifts. "The Atlantic seaboard would be pounded by 26 snowstorms, four of blizzard proportions, between December and April."[22]

Building huts in Jockey Hollow. During the earlier stay in Morristown following the Trenton and Princeton victories, most of Washington's 3,000 troops resided in private homes. However, with a force of 13,000 and new laws prohibiting the quartering of troops in homes, Washington ordered the army to build 12-man huts in Jockey Hollow, a wooded area just outside Morristown; the huts were similar to those constructed at Valley Forge. Washington and his staff were quartered in the Ford House, three miles east in Morristown.

Digging out. There was food available for the army, but the snow-covered roads made it impossible to transport it into Jockey Hollow. On January 9, more than 300 sleds and wagons belonging to residents of the area launched a gigantic effort to clear roads inundated with four to five feet of snow. Within 48 hours, all of the major roadways connecting Jockey Hollow to nearby towns—up to eight miles away—were passable. They had been plowed open by a "miracle of engineering and determination."[23] The farmers and merchants then loaded their sleds with straw, food and clothing, and herded cattle into Jockey Hollow. A crisis had been averted; by January 11, warehouses were full.

By the end of January, however, supplies had dwindled and another crisis developed. Some soldiers went out on their own stealing from residents of the area. Washington was embarrassed and livid. Several men were punished and one executed. Problems of lack of food and clothing persisted through April.

British fail to kidnap Washington. The British knew that if they could kidnap or assassinate Washington, their chances of winning the war would increase dramatically. Consequently, 500 mounted British troops descended on Morristown. Fortunately, Washington was tipped off and left the Ford House for quarters three miles away. Continental Army pickets killed several of the British soldiers and drove the rest off before they could get into Morristown.

Mutiny. Washington was concerned about desertions and mutiny among the troops. Matters came to head in late May following another week of meager food supplies: "Two Connecticut regiments, comprising eight hundred men, took their muskets and left their huts. They told other soldiers in Jockey Hollow that they were starving and had not been paid in more than five months. Any money they did possess, or their families had saved, had been rendered worthless by depreciation. The men had had enough."[24]

Several hundred officers and men from other units surrounded the Connecticut soldiers, who returned to their huts without a shot being fired. Washington understood why the men were upset and other than the leader, who was executed, he could not bring himself to have the troops punished.

Experiences of common soldiers. Although the National Park Service materials provided at Jockey Hollow make no mention of God, the video shown in the visitor center includes a touching scene indicative of what soldiers endured that winter. The film depicts a sick soldier, near death, lying on his bunk reading a letter from his wife. She tells him that she and his family are praying for him and trusting that God will bring him home safely. As he finishes reading the letter, he begins to recite the 23rd Psalm, and dies.

This brief and depressing scene suggests that letters of prayer support from loving families and home churches were not unusual. These are the sort of letters that are common in every war. The letters were personal and usually not publicized; however, they help understand how God interacted with the troops and their families during the difficult times of the Revolutionary War.

The Benedict Arnold Affair (1780)

General Benedict Arnold was the hero of Saratoga, where he was shot in the same leg that had been hit earlier in the unsuccessful attack on Quebec. Washington wanted to spare Arnold further combat and after the British had left Philadelphia in 1778, he assigned him the job of military governor of the city.

While in Philadelphia, Arnold was accused of using military shipping for personal reasons, and was court-martialed. The hearing, held in Morristown during the severe winter of 1779-1780, found Arnold guilty of one of several counts. Always a supporter of Arnold—one of the few according to Arnold—Washington minimized the reprimand by having it published in General Orders for April 6, 1780, between an ad for a man to clean horses and another for firewood. He then assigned Arnold to be military governor of West Point.

Arnold had been contacted by the British in May 1779, but had not responded. Following his court martial and assignment to West Point, Arnold got in touch with British Major John Andre. Arnold gave Andre a copy of the plans for the defense of West Point, a summary of the American forces there, and Washington's plans to visit the French in Hartford. Through an unusual series of events, Andre was subsequently apprehended by American soldiers and Arnold's treachery was uncovered.

Washington, who was riding through West Point on his return from his visit with the French, soon found out about Arnold's treason. While in West Point, he went by Arnold's house where he was surprised to find Arnold's young wife, who was six-months pregnant, weeping and wailing. "Instead of arresting her, Washington, upset by her dramatics, that others claimed were staged, let her go back to Philadelphia alone. He sent men out to find Arnold, but the traitor had too much of a head start."[25]

Since Major Andre was in civilian clothes and considered a spy, he was promptly executed. Arnold served without distinction in the British army in Virginia and after the war, he and his wife moved to England.

Two Battles of Springfield (1780)

Following the second winter at Morristown, the British and Hessians decided to come out of their New York base and strike a blow at Washington's army. Washington expected an attack, but didn't know whether it would be at West Point, Morristown or some point in between. He elected to spread his forces and defend all potential targets of attack. He made sure the signal fires between Morristown and West Point were ready and posted additional sentries. On June 2, he also had the governor call out the 5,000-strong New Jersey militia, and three days later they were on line between Elizabeth and Springfield.

On June 6 (only two weeks after Washington put down the mutiny of Connecticut troops), the British and Hessians transported 6,000 troops across a waterway and marched toward Morristown. The Americans fought well for three hours and then fell back. By the next morning, hundreds of New Jersey militia swarmed into Springfield to reinforce the regular troops. As the British and Hessians were pulling back, Washington's regular army division arrived. After several days of skirmishing the enemy troops withdrew to New York.

A few days later, General Clinton and his warships returned from their victory in Charleston, and he decided to launch another attack. Washington thought West Point would be their target and began to move 2,000 troops north; however, Clinton was after Morristown. By noon, 5,000 militia were back in the Springfield area linking up with 2,500 Continentals under General Nathanial Greene. Washington and his 2,000 troops then joined the battle, having marched back from near West Point. The second battle is another of several examples of Washington being exposed to close enemy fire and escaping unscathed.

"Clinton, his forces now stopped in two separate battles, decided to cut his losses and retreat back to New York."[26] Historian Bruce Chadwick concluded, "The battles at Springfield have been overlooked by most historians, but they were two of the more important engagements of the Revolutionary War."[27]

John Paul Jones Threatens England (1778-1779)

Although John Paul Jones did not, by himself, account for a large number of naval victories, he harassed the British coastal areas and created an atmosphere of fear. The impact of Jones and his crews was disproportionately important to the outcome of the Revolutionary War.

Ranger vs. HMS Drake. In 1778, commanding the *Ranger*, which was built under his personal supervision at Portsmouth, N.H., Jones and his crew of 110 sailed up the western coast of England conducting raids at Whitehaven and Kirkcudbright, and then defeated the *HMS Drake* off the coast of Ireland. The *Ranger* then sailed around the west coast of Ireland and escaped to France.

As a result of the attacks by the *Ranger*, the British admiralty was embarrassed and residents of several seaside villages were panic stricken. "In London, warnings and messages were flying about between Whitehall and the Admiralty. A letter from the Secretary of State's office to the Admiralty Lords declared that 'the rebel privateer which plundered Lord Selkirk's house has thrown the whole western coast into consternation.'"[28]

Bonhomme Richard vs. HMS Serapis. The following summer, this time commanding the larger but slower *Bonhomme Richard*, Jones sailed northwest of Ireland, around the northern tip of Scotland, down the east coast past Edinburgh, and as far south as Hull (directly east of Liverpool). The *Bonhomme Richard* was fitted with 40 guns, including 28 twelve pounders.[29]

In late September the *Bonhomme Richard* encountered the *HMS Serapis* and other British vessels escorting a squadron of cargo ships from the Baltics to ports in England. After a series of cannon and musket exchanges, which badly damaged the *Bonhomme Richard*, Jones was able to hook the *Serapis* and send a boarding party onto its deck.

Thinking that someone on the *Bonhomme Richard* had yelled "quarters," the captain of the *Serapis* yelled, "Have you struck? Do you call for Quarters?" Jones's answer was the classic, "I have not yet begun to fight."[30] A few minutes later, Captain Pearson of the *Serapis* called out, "Sir, I have struck. I ask for quarter."[31] The casualty rate for the two ships was over 50 percent.

Following the battle, a half dozen British sailors who had been prisoners aboard the *Bonhomme Richard* made it to shore in a small boat. "They described the incident of Jones throwing his pistol at the *Bonhomme Richard's* carpenter, as the frightened man was trying to strike the American flag. The tale was quickly and colorfully embellished by the newspapers..."[32] The legend of John Paul Jones was made!

Reliance on God During Middle Phases of the War

During the 1777-1781 period, there was plenty of prayerful concern about the future of the country and the status of the American troops. There were also several examples of divine providence.

Congressional proclamations. Both prior to and during the conflict, "The language of the congressional proclamations was unapologetically Christian. Congress specifically sought the intervention on the nation's behalf of Jesus Christ, praying God in 1776 'through the merits and mediation of Jesus Christ (to) obtain his pardon and forgiveness,' and in 1777 inviting its fellow Americans to 'join the penitent confession of their manifold sins...and their humble and earnest supplication that it may please God, through the merits of Jesus Christ, mercifully to forgive and blot them out of remembrance.'"[33]

Bibles for troops. During the middle years of the war, the Continental Congress became concerned about a shortage of Bibles for the troops. The issue had initially come up in 1777 because the war had interrupted the supply of Bibles from England, "...raising fears of a shortage of Scripture just when it was needed most." In 1780 the Congress moved that "the state be requested to procure one or more new and correct editions of the Old and New Testaments to be published." A Philadelphia printer, Robert Aitken, took on the assignment and in 1782 published what was referred to as Aitken's Bible. Congress satisfied itself of the accuracy of Mr. Aitken's Bible and recommended it to the inhabitants of the United States. "It was the first English language Bible published on the North American continent."[34]

Christianity at Valley Forge. Valley Forge may be the country's most visible symbol of the grit and determination of Washington and the Continental Army. In a visit to Valley Forge, we thought the tour guide and the film in the visitor center put a more positive spin on the troops' experience than was warranted. Of the original 9,000 who began the encampment in late 1777, more than 2,000 died, mostly in the spring of 1778. Also, neither the tour guide nor the film mentioned the church services held at Valley Forge during the winter and spring, and nothing was said about the large worship service held to celebrate the French decision to enter the war on the side of the United States following news of the American victory at Saratoga.

Examples of divine providence. There were several "miracles," or evidences of divine providence, during this period, especially at Valley Forge, Morristown, Monmouth Court House and Springfield.

- *The survival of the army at Valley Forge.* Given the lack of food and clothing, the disorganization of the commissary department, and the complete disaster on the medical front, survival was a truly miraculous achievement.

- *The arrival of Baron von Steuben.* Although his credentials were suspect and he could speak little English, Washington immediately formed a favorable impression of Steuben. The work Steuben did with the troops was vital, not only in preparing then for future combat, but in boosting their moral at a time when sickness and death were at their worst.
- *Continental Army survived leadership breakdown at Monmouth.* Washington was able to counteract General Lee's quick retreat. He rallied and formed the troops to successfully beat back a British assault, then counter-attacked regaining lost ground.
- *Washington survived Battle of Monmouth.* As at Princeton and Brandywine Creek, Washington rode back and forth in front of his troops during the heat of the battle and survived.
- *Survival of the army during second winter at Morristown even more miraculous than Valley Forge.* This was the coldest and snowiest winter ever recorded on the eastern United States.[35]
- *Washington also survived close combat at the Battle of Springfield.* He galloped ahead of his troops and was an easy target for British snipers.[36]
- *Washington considered the discovery of Benedict Arnold's treason to be a miracle.* "Happily the treason has been timely discovered to prevent the fatal misfortune. The providential train of circumstances which led to it affords the most convincing proof that the Liberties of America are the object of divine Protection." [37]

Of all the evidence of divine providence during the middle periods of the war, none was greater than France's decision to ally with the United States. Benjamin Franklin, more than 70 years of age, was an improbable diplomat. John Adams referred to Franklin as "too old, too infirm, too indolent and dissipated, to be sufficient for the Discharge of all the important Duties."[38] Most other Americans in France, including Arthur Lee and Ralph Izard, questioned Franklin's approach to diplomacy. Izard told Congress that "the political salvation of America depends upon the recalling of Dr. Franklin."[39] Fortunately, Congress did not recall Franklin who continued to offer valuable service to the American cause.

Was Franklin's success with the French evidence of divine providence? Franklin biographer Gordon Wood noted that "...without Franklin's presence it is hard to see how the alliance (with France) could have held together as it did, and without the alliance it is hard to see how the Americans could have sustained their revolution." Wood went on, "Probably only Franklin could have persuaded (French Foreign Minister) Vergennes to keep on supporting the American cause, and probably only Franklin could have negotiated so many loans from an increasingly impoverished French government."[40] All told, the war cost France over one billion livres and almost bankrupted the country.

During this difficult four-year period that was crucial to the survival of the main body of the Continental Army, there were many additional examples of divine providence and of the support of Christians for the war effort. Prayers by the soldiers and their families appear to have been heard and answered.

CHAPTER 7

The Southern Campaigns: Defeat, Then Victory at Yorktown

When the British invaded the South, "The surrender of another great British army was unimaginable...Such a debacle should have been impossible considering the combined strength of British ground and naval forces available to prevent it."

—Larkin Spivey, *Miracles of the American Revolution*, 214.

Based on the movie, *The Patriot*, many readers are familiar with the viciousness of the fighting in the southern states. This chapter reviews the history of the southern campaigns from 1778 to 1781 culminating in the defeat of British General Charles Cornwallis at Yorktown in October 1781. The amazing series of events (e.g., communicating with Admiral de Grasse in the Caribbean, weather delays affecting the British fleet in New York harbor) leading up to the final siege at Yorktown are discussed in some detail.

When France entered the war in June 1778, several months after the victory at Saratoga, the British were challenged by more than just the cooperation France promised the Continental Army. They were concerned about a possible invasion of England, and French aggression against British possessions in the West Indies. Because of the French threat, King George III, Lord North and Lord Amherst considered withdrawing all troops from the colonies; however, they decided instead to redirect their strategy to the South.

General William Howe, who had returned to England following his replacement by General Henry Clinton, demanded a Parliamentary hearing relative to his conduct of the war. In his testimony, Howe blamed British leaders and the difficult conditions of fighting in North America. Howe, who had originally believed that most Americans were loyal to the crown, argued that, "Against an enemy determined to fight a defensive war, reconnaissance was essential (and almost impossible), but in a country made for the defensive and inhabited by a distinctly unfriendly people, attack was difficult to prosecute."[1] The inquiry dragged on and even when it ended, the British press continued its criticism of the war effort.

Elements of the British press also questioned the high cost of the war; for example, body counts were published in newspapers. The June 1780 issue of *London Magazine*, read by many members of Parliament, reported that "…so far England had suffered 8,900 men killed, 11,000 wounded and 9,116 captured."[2]

Despite evidence to the contrary, King George III, Lord North, Lord Germaine and other British leaders believed that there were substantial numbers of loyalists in America; some estimates were as high as two-thirds of the population. This viewpoint was reinforced by the anecdotal evidence of loyalists who traveled to England and claimed that large numbers of Americans were ready to rise up and welcome the British Army: "…British ministers had persuaded themselves that their troubles in America were inspired by a conspiracy of the few, that most colonists loved Parliament and the king. Not even the fighting dislodged this conviction from many heads, including the king's own, and it no doubt was a comfort to discouraged ministers who shared the responsibility for military failure."[3]

British leaders believed that loyalist sentiments were particularly strong in the Carolinas and Georgia. As a result, General Clinton was instructed to focus his efforts on these states.

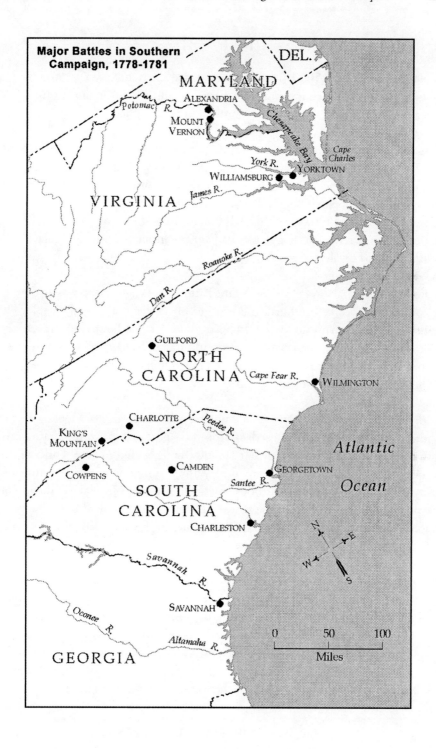

British Invade the South (1778)

In November 1778, 3,500 British troops boarded ships in New York and, with a column of rangers moving north from Florida, captured Savannah. Around 500 Americans were killed, wounded or captured in this conflict.

A year later, in an attempt to redeem his reputation from the fiasco at Newport, R.I. (described in the previous chapter), Admiral d'Estaing and an American force attacked the British garrison at Savannah. Admiral d'Estaing appeared off Savannah on September 4, 1779, and demanded the surrender of British General Augustine Prevost and his 3,200 men. In addition to the 4,000 French marines, General Benjamin Lincoln had 600 Continental Army regulars, 750 militia and 250 cavalry.

Following several days of siege warfare, Admiral d'Estaing, who was anxious to sail out of the area before hurricane weather hit, ordered a frontal assault. The British had built fortifications, and had cannon. In one hour, the French and Americans lost more than 1,000 men. Admiral d'Estaing, who was severely wounded, loaded his men on the ships and sailed home to France. What was left of the American army retreated to Charleston.

British victory at Charleston. The day after Christmas, 1779, General Henry Clinton withdrew the British garrison from Newport and sailed to Charlestown with 8,700 of his best troops. He left 10,000 troops behind in New York, a force he deemed more than adequate to deal with Washington's weak Continental Army. (The group of Hessian troops left behind, under General Willhelm von Knyphausen, were involved in the battles of Springfield described in the previous chapter.) In February, 1780 General Clinton and his force landed 30 miles south of Charleston and began a siege of the city.

General Lincoln wanted to withdraw from Charleston to save the army, but he bowed to political pressure to defend the city. In the meantime, British cavalry routed South Carolina militia defending the only escape route, and the Americans were trapped. Following several days of bombardment, and with their food supply down to five days, local politicians reversed themselves and approved a surrender. On May 12, 1780, Lincoln and his force of more than 5,500 capitulated. It was one of the worst losses of the war for the American army.[4]

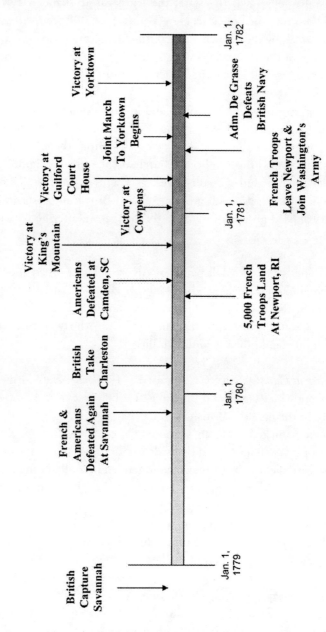

Timeline for Southern Campaigns and Yorktown Victory

With the fall of Charleston, the civil government of South Carolina collapsed. Governor Rutledge fled the state, the legislature disbanded and courts closed. General Clinton sailed back to New York with 4,000 troops (he was concerned about an attack by the French and Continental Army), leaving General Cornwallis in charge of the campaign in the South. The British fanned out across South Carolina and were successful in attracting a number of loyalists to their ranks.

Guerilla warfare. Despite British and loyalist domination, a number of South Carolinians refused to give up. "Many of them were Presbyterians who feared their freedom to worship would be taken away from them if the British won the war and established the Anglican Church as the official religion."[5] Several partisan bands were organized, some with as few as 50 men and none numbering more than 500. These small groups attacked British outposts and supply routes and also harassed groups of loyalists the British were trying to arm and enlist to their cause.

The hopes of these small bands of Americans rose when they heard that the Continental Congress was sending General Horatio Gates, the hero of Saratoga, to help fight the British. Washington reluctantly assigned 1,200 Maryland and Delaware Continental Army regulars to Gates, who was also able to summon 1,800 Virginia and North Carolina militia.

Disaster at Camden, S.C. On August 16, 1780, General Cornwallis and 2,500 British troops met Gates and his force of 3,000 just outside the small village of Camden. In the face of a British bayonet charge, the Virginia and North Carolina militiamen panicked and ran without firing a shot. The regular Continental Army troops were flanked and badly defeated. "The Americans did not withdraw from the battlefield in a manner recommended by military manuals. Rather they left in a crowd with no regiment retaining its integrity as a unit. Gates made no attempt to discipline or reorganize this herd, choosing rather to outdistance it astride a fast horse. That evening he reached Charlotte, sixty miles away, and by the 19th he was at Hillsboro, another 120 miles farther on."[6] It was a performance that destroyed the reputation of the hero of Saratoga.

American victory at King's Mountain. Three months later, rebel Americans, bolstered by several hundred "over the mountain boys" from Tennessee, destroyed a force of 1,000 loyalists (the equivalent of militia) at King's Mountain in North Carolina. The British learned the lesson that Washington had learned years earlier: unless militia were supported by regular army troops, they were usually ineffective as a fighting force.

Greene and Morgan enter the scene. Following General Gates' failure at Camden, Washington assigned General Nathaniel Greene, his most dependable general, to command the southern forces. "When Greene arrived in Charlotte...on December 2, 1780, he found little to encourage him. There were only 800 Continentals equipped and fit for duty in the American camp—and provisions for only three days."[7]

Because of Congress's failure to promote him, Daniel Morgan of Virginia, one of the heroes of Saratoga, had resigned from the army. However, he changed his mind and offered to assist Greene in the defense of the South. Greene assigned more than half of his regular troops to Morgan, who had been promoted to Brigadier General, and asked him to go into the backcountry and inspire the local militia to stay in the war.

Cowpens—a surprising victory. General Morgan, with 600 Continentals and 400 North and South Carolina militia, was tracked to Cowpens (a hilly plain in North Carolina) by the hated British Colonel Banastre Tarleton. "His unsavory reputation grew in 1780 after a series of victories that earned him the names 'Bloody Tarleton' and 'Butcher' for his savage attacks."[8]

Morgan knew that his militiamen would retreat when faced by the British and their bayonets. Therefore, he placed the militia in front of his regular troops, instructed them to get off two or three volleys, and then run for their lives. Even though Morgan's sharpshooters killed many British officers, Tarleton ordered a headlong charge after the militia; he was surprised to run into the Continental regulars in battle line. "With half their officers dead or wounded, Tarleton's exhausted regulars disintegrated. Most of them threw down their guns and surrendered; others took to the woods."[9] The British lost 110 men killed, including 39 officers, 229 wounded, and 550 captured. This represented about one-quarter of Cornwallis' army. Morgan's army lost only 12 killed and 60 wounded.[10] The American victory lifted the people of the Carolinas from almost total despair to hope.

Guilford Court House. Following his victory at Cowpens, illness forced Morgan to once again retire, and Nathaniel Greene took direct command. Greene's forces were small—about 2,000—and it was vitally important that they keep Cornwallis from joining Benedict Arnold and a second British force under General William Phillips that had been ransacking Richmond and other towns in Virginia. Furthermore, if Cornwallis was able to penetrate deep into Virginia—as far as Charlottesville—he would be able to release prisoners captured at Saratoga and Cowpens.

Using the same tactics that Morgan had employed at Cowpens, Greene met General Cornwallis at Guilford Court House and inflicted 532 casualties on his 1,600-man force. American casualties were also heavy. The British then moved to the North Carolina coast to be re-supplied.[11]

Following the battle at Guilford Court House, and with his army suffering from lack of provisions (following their loss at Cowpens, the British had destroyed their own supply train in order to increase their mobility and catch up with Morgan and Greene), Cornwallis then moved toward Virginia and the Chesapeake where his dwindling army could be more readily supplied.

Benedict Arnold raids Richmond. In March 1781, about the same time as the British loss at Cowpens, General Clinton dispatched Benedict Arnold and 2,000 troops to sail up the James River to raid Richmond. The few Virginia militia called out by Governor Thomas Jefferson were easily routed. Although there were almost 50,000 militia on the rolls in Virginia, only a handful took up arms during this emergency. The state constitution gave Virginia no power to force militia members to turn out.

In response to a plea from Jefferson, Washington ordered Marquis de Lafayette and 1,200 regulars to Virginia. Lafayette had been promised support from the French troops at Newport, but they were turned back by the British navy. Washington then ordered Lafayette, who was in Annapolis at the time, to proceed south even without the aid of the French forces.

Cornwallis' army joins forces with troops sent from New York. Combining his remaining forces with several thousand troops General Clinton had sent into Virginia under the leadership of Arnold (who was subsequently relieved of his command) and Phillips, Cornwallis had more than 7,000 men. Lafayette did not have enough troops to stop the British from penetrating into Virginia, including a brief occupation of Jefferson's home, Monticello, just outside Charlottesville.

Setting the Stage for Yorktown

Washington's position in early 1781 was desperate: "Not only were the people tired of the war; they were beginning to be apathetic about the eventual outcome, eager to have it over with on almost any terms so they could get back to some sort of normal life. The economy was in a shambles, the Congress was regarded as inept and incapable, and the future looked bleaker than ever."[12]

In our view, the amazing series of events that led up to the victory at Yorktown in October were nothing short of divine providence.

French troops land in Newport on July 11, 1780. Following the embarrassing defeat at Savannah in September 1779, the French landed 5,000 soldiers in Newport, R.I., which had been evacuated by General Clinton only a few months earlier (the British troops had been transferred to Charleston). The French troops were under the command of Count de Rochambeau. General Clinton was aware of the landing of the French soldiers and wanted to attack with 6,000 of his own troops; however, the British admiral in New York argued against it on the basis that French naval firepower would be too much.[13]

Washington, who had only 3,000 troops at his disposal, met with Rochambeau in Hartford, Conn., in September 1780, and while the meeting was a social success, the two generals could not agree on a strategy for the coming year. One of the uncertainties was whether the French would bring additional troops and ships to America.

Rochambeau's plea for help from France. About the same time he was meeting with Washington, General Rochambeau sent his son to Paris seeking help. However, the younger Rochambeau met with resistance from the French foreign minister, Comte de Vergennes. Vergennes said that the French had supported the Americans for four years and had no idea when the war would end. The French had had enough.

At this point Benjamin Franklin, in Paris, wrote a letter to Vergennes that helped persuade the king to send additional ships, troops and financial support to America. "Shrewdly, the old man reminded Vergennes that if the English were to recover their former colonies, an opportunity like the present one might not recur, while possession of the vast territory and resources of America would afford the English a broad basis for future greatness, ever expanding commerce, and a supply of seamen and soldiers that would make them 'the terror of Europe.'"[14]

On May 8, 1781, when the French frigate *Concorde* docked in Boston, the Americans received their long-awaited reply: "...M. de Grasse had left Brest March 22, with 26 ships of the line, 8 frigates, and 150 transports..." The destination was unknown but it was believed de Grasse would head for the West Indies. Of equal importance, the younger Rochambeau brought six million livres "to supply the needs and upkeep of the American army."[15]

Dispute between Generals Clinton and Cornwallis. Earlier in 1781, before word of additional help from France had reached Washington and Rochambeau, General Clinton disagreed with General Cornwallis' decision to move his army into Virginia; he thought that Cornwallis should have remained in the Carolinas. After letters flew back and forth, "Clinton finally ordered Cornwallis to retreat to the coast, send half his army to New York and occupy the tobacco port of Yorktown as a base for future operations in Virginia."[16] Cornwallis, however, informed Clinton that he would need all his troops to reinforce Yorktown and prepare for the winter.

Washington adopts backup plan. For months, Washington had believed that the Continental Army and the French at Newport should join in an attack on General Clinton's forces in New York City. However, "At a May conference...the French general resisted attacking New York. Even with the help of the French fleet from the West Indies, he doubted their two small armies were strong enough to crack the city's formidable defenses. Instead, he suggested a campaign in Virginia to help Lafayette, who he referred to as 'the poor Marquis.'"[17]

Washington agreed that the Virginia campaign would be an alternative to attacking the British in New York. The final decision would be based on Admiral de Grasse and his plans. "In the meantime, the conferees concluded, until word was received from de Grasse, the French army—minus several hundred left behind to guard the heavy artillery—would march to the Hudson and join the Americans in an operation against New York."[18]

The French left Newport for New York on June 10, on what would prove to be the first leg of a 756-mile journey ending at Yorktown. A month later, the American and French armies met for the first time near Dobbs Ferry. Shortly thereafter, there were several skirmishes with the British. Intelligence indicated that General Clinton had 14,000 troops in New York. At this point, no final decision had been made about moving toward Virginia; Washington and Rochambeau were awaiting word from Admiral de Grasse.

Communicating with Admiral de Grasse in the West Indies. Washington was determined to persuade de Grasse to sail for American waters—and soon. He dispatched Allen McLane, a cavalry officer whom he trusted, "...to see de Grasse and provide him with full details on the military situation in the states." This is an amazing story: "McLane, appearing as a marine captain on the privateer *Congress*, sailed for the islands (West Indies) hoping to meet with de Grasse. On the way they spoke (met) a French frigate, learned the location of de Grasse's fleet, and McLane was soon aboard the French admiral's flagship."[19]

At the time, de Grasse and his officers were considering an attack on the island of Jamaica, but interrupted their meeting to hear McLane's news from America. "Whether it was McLane's persuasiveness or the written recommendations de Grasse received from Rochambeau and Washington at this time, the die was cast. De Grasse would sail for America."[20]

Admiral de Grasse sends message that his fleet is headed for the Chesapeake. On August 14, 1781, while the French and Continental armies were continuing their probes of the British at New York City, a message arrived saying that Admiral de Grasse was coming to America from the French West Indies with 29 warships and 3,000 troops. "But he was heading for the Chesapeake, not New York."[21]

Despite his reservations about the Virginia campaign, Washington made an immediate decision to move both armies to Yorktown. He communicated this to Lafayette, and at the same time, he took several actions to deceive General Clinton in New York. He bought several flatboats with wheels to create the impression that he was readying for an amphibious landing on Staten Island. Washington sent a detachment to Stony Point to lead General Clinton to believe that the Americans and French were thinking of capturing the British fort there so that the French navy could enter New York harbor.

The difficulties ahead. The future of the American Revolution rested on a complex military operation that was fraught with uncertainties and potential problems: "First and foremost: what if the French naval squadron did not show up?

Allied cooperation had failed before: in 1778, in an abortive campaign at Newport; in 1779 at Savannah; and in 1780 when the French fleet had been cooped up by the British at Newport. Another possibility was that the French fleet might be driven off by the British, leaving the allied armies stranded between Clinton's forces in New York and Cornwallis and his army in Virginia. A further uncertainty had to do with (Admiral) Barras, who was then in Newport with his squadron. He had to be persuaded to abandon his proposed attack on Newfoundland in order to carry Rochambeau's heavy cannon to the Chesapeake, along with a large quantity of salt provisions Washington had laid aside for just such a purpose."[22]

Historian Richard Ketchum concluded, "It is hard to conceive the difficulties of timing inherent in the scheme. Here you had one (French) fleet sailing north from the West Indies and another coming south from Newport, both subject to the vagaries of wind, the possibility of severe storms, and the likelihood that they would be intercepted by British warships. And these two fleets were expected to meet on schedule." He added, "And—the all-important fact—these disparate allied forces had to come together at precisely the same moment. All things considered, it appeared that only a miracle could make it happen."[23]

Washington and Rochambeau leave New York. In August 2,500 American and 5,000 French troops began the march south. The French columns marched through Philadelphia where they received a heroes' welcome. When the armies reached Chester, Md., Washington received the welcome news that Admiral de Grasse was in the Chesapeake Bay and his 3,000 troops had already joined Lafayette.

Ketchum summed the situation facing Washington this way: "After six years of fighting and indescribable suffering, George Washington's Continental Army left the Northeast for the first time and headed south toward Yorktown, on a mission that would demand every ounce of the army's remaining stamina and resolve, plus a great dose of luck and timely assistance from the 'Providence' so often mentioned by the commander in chief."[24]

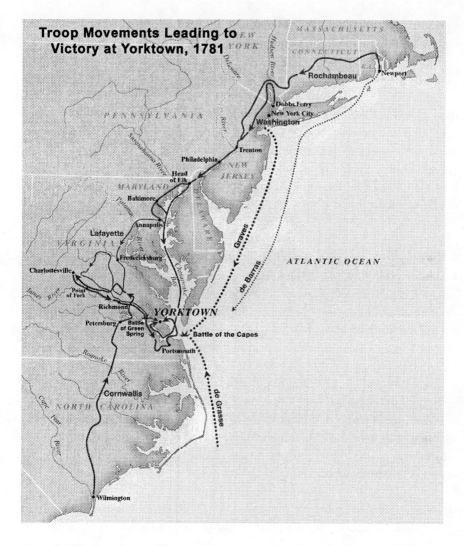

Joseph Ellis, another well-known historian, described the developing situation in Virginia in a similar vein: "Once Washington shifted his focus from New York to the south, he never looked back...And by early September there appeared on the southern horizon an unexpected convergence of forces that could only be described as providential. In August, Cornwallis had moved his entire army of more than seven thousand troops onto the Tidewater peninsula at Yorktown. On September 2, as Washington prepared to board ships at Head of Elk in the northern reaches of the Chesapeake, de Grasse and the main French fleet appeared off

Yorktown at Cape Henry. Washington could hardly believe the news or contain his excitement..."[25]

The naval maneuvers. After briefly visiting Mt. Vernon for the first time in six years, Washington received disturbing news: Admiral de Grasse had abandoned the blockade of the Chesapeake and sailed out to meet a British fleet under the command of Admiral Thomas Graves. The two navies clashed on September 5; the British, who were badly mauled, sailed away three days later, and Admiral de Grasse and his fleet, augmented by eight more line-of-battle ships, sailed back into the Chesapeake Bay to resume the blockade. This was the only victory over the British navy in the history of the French navy.[26] Was this evidence of divine favor?

In summarizing the naval battles off the coast of the Chesapeake Bay, Ketchum said: "Luck—or Providence—had been with the Americans in every instance that counted. First of all (Admiral) Graves never received (Admiral) Rodney's warning (about the presence of de Grasse's fleet). Then, inexplicably, the British under Graves failed to attack de Grasse's ships one by one as they emerged from Chesapeake Bay. Another stroke of luck was that the lethargic Graves—not the aggressive Rodney, who would not have let such a rare opportunity slip by—was commanding the British squadron."[27]

Washington reached Williamsburg in mid September and urged Admiral de Grasse to maintain the blockade through the end of October. Admiral de Grasse reluctantly agreed to this schedule; he was in a hurry to return to the French West Indies before bad weather set in.

British reinforcements from New York delayed. General Clinton notified General Cornwallis that he was sending 5,500 troops and a reinforced British fleet which would sail from New York on October 5. However, because of disputes between General Clinton and Admiral Graves, the fleet was not available to sail until October 13. On that day, "Terrific gusts of wind snapped the anchor cable on one of the ships of the line, smashing her into another ship and damaging both of them." [28] Admiral Graves then decided he could not leave New York until the damage had been repaired.

The siege of Yorktown. Following the advice of the French, the combined French and American armies proceeded with a siege. On the night of October 6 the armies began digging the first trench. By dawn, the British saw that the Americans and French had dug a trench in a wide arc that extended within 600 yards of the two most advanced British redoubts. "With a forest of French masts behind them on the water, Cornwallis's men knew they were trapped."[29]

Three days later, on October 9, heavy cannon, hauled by the French from Newport, were dragged into position in the newly dug trenches. "For the next six days the siege guns pounded the British fortifications day and night." One of the sidebars of this story is that Washington "...insisted on standing atop a parapet for a full fifteen minutes during an artillery attack, bullets and shrapnel flying all about him, defying aides who tried to pull him down before he had properly surveyed the field of action."[30]

On the night of October 14 Washington ordered the storming of redoubts 9 and 10, assigning one to the French and the other to Americans led by Colonel Alexander Hamilton. By morning, these redoubts were connected to the American and French lines and soon 100 big guns were pounding the British from close range.

Cornwallis's desperate gamble. There was a French and American outpost across the York River on the Gloucester Peninsula guarded by 750 French troops and a few militia. "...Cornwallis decided to ferry most of his army across the river on the night of October 16, and break out of the Gloucester lines at dawn." His plan was to defeat the small French and militia force in Gloucester and head north to New York.[31] Sixteen heavy boats took the first contingent across the York River, and around midnight, the boats returned for a second load. "About 10 minutes later a tremendous storm broke over the river. Within five minutes there was a full gale blowing, as violent, from the descriptions in various diaries, as the storm that had disrupted the fleet in New York...Not until 2 a.m. did the wind moderate. It was much too late to get the rest of the army across the river...About 7:00 a.m. Cornwallis; his second in command, Brigadier Charles O'Hara; and their staffs went to the forward trenches and morosely studied the sweep and scope of the allied bombardment. The commander of the artillery informed them that there were only 100 mortar shells left. The sick and wounded multiplied by the hour."[32]

Cornwallis surrenders. The surrender was signed three days later, on October 19, 1781. In the afternoon, the British—7,157 soldiers and 840 seamen—

marched out to stack their arms in a meadow about half a mile down the Williamsburg Road. Brigadier General O'Hara rode at the head of the column; General Cornwallis feigned sickness and skipped the surrender ceremony.

On the same day, a British fleet crammed with 6,000 soldiers left New York harbor headed toward Yorktown. However, just off the mouth of the Chesapeake Bay, loyalists sailed out to the fleet and informed General Clinton that Cornwallis had surrendered. The British turned back to New York where Clinton found a letter from Cornwallis confirming the loss of his entire army.

Victory celebrations and worship services. Washington dispatched his trusted aide, Tench Tilgham, to carry word of Yorktown to the Confederation Congress (the Articles of Confederation had finally been passed into law) meeting in Philadelphia. When Tilgham arrived with the news, Philadelphia erupted in celebration. After giving a detailed report to Congress, "At two o'clock that afternoon congressmen proceeded in a body to the Dutch Lutheran church to attend a service held by one of their chaplains, the Reverend Mr. Duffield..."[33]

Washington acknowledged divine providence in calling the troops to worship services following the victory at Yorktown: "Divine service is to be performed tomorrow in the several brigades or divisions. The Commander in Chief earnestly recommends that the troops not on duty should universally attend with that seriousness of Deportment and Gratitude of Heart which the recognition of such reiterated and astonishing interpositions of Providence demands of us."[34]

Dr. Ezra Stiles, president of Yale, wrote to Washington, "We rejoice that the Sovereign of the Universe hath hitherto supported you as the deliverer of your country..."[35] As the *New York Journal* reported, the remarkable capture of an entire British army was "...an event in which the hand of heaven has been visibly displayed—has been celebrated, in various expressions of thankfulness and joy, by almost every town and society in the thirteen United States."[36]

Elias Boudinot, president of the Confederation Congress in the years following Yorktown, summarized the role of divine providence in America's victory in the war: "I have been in the midst of the principle Scenes of Action during the whole contest. I have not been a bare Spectator. I have carefully and attentively watched and Compared the Steps of divine Providence thro' the whole; and as the result, I can assure you, that our Success has not been the effect of either our

Numbers, Power, Wisdom or Art. It has been manifestly the Effect (I was going to say the miraculous Effect) of the astonishing and unparalleled Interposition of a Holy God in our favor—of that God who speaketh and it is done—who commandeth and it cometh to pass."[37]

Continuing, Boudinot said that the American victory went against the wisdom of the experts; it beat the odds: "I do not mean in the least to derogate (denigrate) the bravery, wisdom, patience and perseverance of one of the most deserving armies that ever graced our country...My meaning is that in no instance has our numbers, power, wisdom or art been such, that in the judgment of rational, enlightened judges, success could have been reasonably depended on, independent of the special aid and overruling direction of heaven."[38]

After Yorktown, British Decide to Negotiate a Peace Treaty

When news of General Cornwallis's surrender at Yorktown reached London on November 25, Lord North said, "Oh God. It is all over. It is all over." However, when Parliament met the next day, King George III did not say a word about Yorktown.

Three months later, on February 22, 1782 the opposition in Parliament proposed a message to the king indicating the war should no longer be pursued. It lost by a single vote. A week later, a similar proposal passed 234 to 215. Lord North immediately attempted to resign, but the king would not accept his resignation. King George III threatened to abdicate the throne but was talked out of it by North and others. "Loathing every minute of it, the King let the opposition form a ministry and begin negotiating with the Americans."[39] Lord North's government collapsed in March 1782; he was succeeded by Lord Rockingham, who died three months later, to be replaced by Lord Shelburne.

In the meantime, Washington could not run the risk that the war was over. The British still had 14,000 troops in New York, and there was continued skirmishing in the South. Therefore, Washington kept the Continental Army intact and camped in the vicinity of New York.

The American negotiating commission. The United States peace commission, which had been appointed well before Yorktown, included Benjamin Franklin,

John Jay, John Adams and John Laurens, who along with Jay, was a former president of the Continental Congress. Franklin was the only member of the commission in Paris at the outset of negotiations.

One of the early issues was whether or not the United States could make a separate peace with England, or whether the peace accord had to include France and Spain. Franklin was loyal to the French; Adams and Jay were of the opinion that America's interests were of overriding importance. This issue clouded the negotiations for the next two years until the treaty was finally signed.

Franklin argued that the negotiations would not include independence since this was an accomplished fact given the Declaration of Independence and success in the Revolutionary War. Franklin told Thomas Grenville, the British agent, "...we do not consider ourselves as under any necessity of bargaining for such a thing that is our own and which we have bought at the expense of much blood and treasure."[40]

Franklin's initial proposal. In July Franklin offered a two-part peace proposal. The first part, which he called "necessary," included independence for America that was full and complete, removal of all British troops, secure boundaries (referring mainly to Canada) and fishing rights off the Canadian coast. The "advisable" category included payment for destruction caused in America, an acknowledgement of British guilt, a free trade agreement, and ceding of Canada to the United States.[41]

Shelburne's reaction was surprisingly favorable. He agreed that England would be willing to affirm America's independence as a preliminary to negotiations if the United States would drop the "advisable" provisions. Although it would take a few months, in essence that is what happened.[42]

Jay takes the leadership. Shortly after offering his proposal, Franklin was disabled by an attack of gout; John Jay, who had just arrived from Spain, took over as chief negotiator. After initial disagreement between Franklin and Jay on how to deal with both the British and the French, negotiations got back on track. "Oswald (the British representative) presented his formal new commission, and Jay presented a proposed treaty that was very similar to the one Franklin had informally offered in July. The only addition to Franklin's four 'necessary' points was a provision that was sure to please Britain, though not France or Spain: that both Britain and America would have free navigation rights on the Mississippi."[43]

Franklin and Jay were later joined by John Adams, who had been in Amsterdam negotiating loans from the Dutch. The fourth commissioner, John Laurens, was captured while crossing the Atlantic, spent several months in captivity in the Tower of London, was released to recuperate in Southern France, and finally joined the negotiating team a few weeks before the peace treaty was signed.

Resolving the issues. One of the important issues in the negotiations was the boundaries of the United States, especially north in the Great Lakes area along what is now the Canadian border, west toward the Mississippi River, between Maine and New Brunswick, and south toward Florida. In fact, much of the border with Canada that exists today was negotiated with Great Britain in 1783, and re-affirmed in the Jay Treaty in 1794 and the Treaty of Ghent in 1814. Another key issue was fishing rights in the North Atlantic, including the rights to dry cod on the shores of Newfoundland and Nova Scotia. American demands which were not granted included payment for damages caused by the British army, settlement of pre-war debts owed to English firms by Americans, and the stationing of troops in western areas (e.g., Niagara, Detroit) that had been held by the British at the end of the war.

The provisional treaty ending the war was signed on November 30, 1782. However, because of the need for England and France to agree on a peace treaty, it took 17 months for the treaty to become official. When the final peace treaty was signed by Franklin and Jay in Paris on May 12, 1784 Franklin reported to Congress: "the great and hazardous enterprise we have been engaged in is, God be praised, happily completed."[44]

Speaking in New York after his return to America following the successful conclusion of the peace treaty with England, John Jay referred to his heritage: "This being a land of light and liberty, I bless God that it is the land of my nativity. Here my forefathers sought and found freedom and toleration. I am bound to it by the strongest ties, and as its happiness has been the first object of my endeavors from early life, so the most fervent wishes for its prosperity shall be among those of my latest hours."[45]

Problems Within the Continental Army

During the months the peace treaty was being negotiated, and while the Continental Army was quartered in Newburgh, north of New York City, "...the embittered soldiers, still unpaid by the bankrupt Congress, brooded on their country's ingratitude." The officers had been voted pensions, but now the Congress could not deliver and the states were claiming that they had no obligations to cover federal promises.[46]

The leaders of the army circulated a mass letter calling for a meeting of officers. On March 13, 1783 Washington met with the officers. After giving a long speech that had little or no effect, Washington reached into his pocket for a letter from a congressman assuring the soldiers that the Congress was trying to respond to their complaints. He also pulled out a pair of glasses, and said, "Gentlemen, you will permit me to put on my spectacles, for I have not only grown gray but almost blind in your service." [47] The officers were swept with a wave of emotion; many wept openly. They voted their thanks to Washington and repudiated their demands to Congress. The crisis was over.

In November 2, 1783 Washington included these words in his farewell orders to the army: "A contemplation of the complete attainment...of the object for which we contended, against so formidable a power, cannot but inspire us with astonishment and gratitude. The disadvantageous circumstances on our part, under which the war was undertaken, can never be forgotten. The singular interpositions of Providence in our feeble condition, were such as could scarcely escape the attention of the most unobserving—while the unparalleled perseverance of the armies of the United States, through almost every possible suffering and discouragement, for the space of eight long years, was little short of a standing miracle..."[48]

Washington Surrenders His Commission

When the signed peace treaty reached America the British evacuated New York and sailed for England. Most of the officers and men of the Continental Army had already returned home. Washington and his few remaining officers rode into New York City the day the British left, and several days later they had an emotional farewell dinner at Fraunces Tavern.

Washington then rode south to Annapolis where the Confederation Congress was meeting. An angry mob of recent recruits demanding back pay had chased Congress out of Philadelphia. When Washington arrived at the Maryland State House around noon on December 23 only 20 members representing seven states were present. Washington then read a speech. "When he reached the passage in which he commended 'the interests of our dearest Country to the protection of Almighty God,' his voice dwindled and he had to struggle against an impulse to weep." Washington went on: "Having now finished the work assigned me, I retire from the great theatre of action, and bidding an affectionate farewell to this august body under whose orders I have so long acted, I here offer my commission and take my leave of all the employments of public life."[49] According to reports, all spectators and congressmen wept. Washington then left for Mt. Vernon arriving on Christmas Eve 1783, where he expected to resume his life as a farmer.

Evidence of Divine Providence

As the eight years of war came to an end, it is possible to reflect upon those individuals who stayed with the revolution to the end, and who maintained the strongest views about the close linkage between Christianity and freedom. George Washington certainly viewed his protection and leadership role as being directed by divine providence.

Benjamin Franklin thought that the American victory was due to divine providence: "I am too well acquainted with all the Springs and Levers of our Machine, not to see that our human means were unequal to our undertaking, and that, if it had not been for the Justice of our Cause, and the consequent Interposition of Providence, in which we had Faith, we must have been ruined. If I had ever before been an Atheist, I should now have been convinced of the Being and Government of a Deity!"[50]

Richard Ketchum, who devoted an entire book to the victory at Yorktown, referred to the complex naval and army operations involving forces from two nations that ended with Cornwallis' defeat as a series of miracles. Nothing even close to the complexity of this operation had been attempted previously in the Revolutionary War, and even less complicated missions had failed. Here are several examples from this brilliant success:

1. We find it extraordinary that an American cavalry officer, Allen McHale, could sail for the West Indies with messages for Admiral de

Grasse from Generals Washington and Rochambeau, find the French fleet and have a conference with de Grasse.

2. Furthermore, the letters and conference changed the admiral's plans; he agreed to sail immediately for the Chesapeake.

3. Heavy storms in the New York harbor prevented the British fleet from coming to the rescue of General Cornwallis. Also, General Cornwallis' attempt to cross the York River and fight his way up the Gloucester Peninsula to New York was foiled by bad weather.

4. The coming together of de Grasse's fleet and the French fleet from Newport, and the ability of Washington and Rochambeau to march and sail down the Chesapeake Bay to Yorktown and meet up with Lafayette at exactly the right time was a miracle. Historian Joseph Ellis called it providential, and that is the way Washington and other American leaders viewed it.

5. The French navy's defeat of the British off the coast of Virginia went against historical trends. This was the only major victory by the French navy in its long history of combat with the British.

6. For the eighth time in the Revolutionary War, Washington survived exposure to heavy fire during the early phases of the siege of Yorktown.

In terms of probabilities, if there was a 25 percent chance of McHale making contact with Admiral de Grasse (1 above), a 50/50 chance he could persuade de Grasse to sail for the Chesapeake (2 above), a 50/50 chance that de Grasse could defeat the British fleet (4), and a 10 percent chance of bad weather delaying the British from sailing from New York (2), the combined probability of success for Washington and the allies was less than one percent.

John Witherspoon, president of the College of New Jersey and a signer of the Declaration of Independence, summarized the workings of divine providence in winning independence: "Upon the whole nothing appears to me more manifest than that the separation of this country from Britain, has been of God; for every step the British took to prevent, served to accelerate it, which has generally been the case when men have undertaken to go in opposition to the course of Providence, and to make war with the nature of things."[51]

CHAPTER 8
▼

The Chaos of the Articles of Confederation and the Need for Change

What is so critical to understand is that they (the founders) really differed in a number of ways. They had tough, hard debates, jealousies and rivalries. But they came together, and the sum became greater than the individual parts.

—Jay Winik, *New York Times*, July 4, 2004.

When we walk around Philadelphia, the thought that comes to mind is synergy—the two plus two equals five effect. Philadelphia is where the Continental Congress met in 1774, 1775 and 1776 concluding with the Declaration of Independence. And, Philadelphia is where the Constitutional Convention met in the summer of 1787. Furthermore, the final two years of the Continental Congress and the Constitutional Convention met in the same room in what is now called Independence Hall. Some of the same Founding Fathers (Washington and Franklin are two of the most noteworthy) participated in both the Continental Congress and the Constitutional Convention.

One historian observed that many Americans came out of the Revolutionary War (and the Declaration of Independence) with a vision of a people and a country destined by divine providence for greatness: "The Americans in the 1780s still believed that they had been selected by Providence to do great deeds. They had been chosen, and their victory in the war and the achievement of independence demonstrated the worth of their calling. Undoubtedly some held this conviction more deeply than others did. It seems always to have existed in New England, especially among Congregationalists. It was a powerful feeling in Virginia even among planters who listened to bland sermons in the established church. Elsewhere it flourished among evangelicals and enthusiasts, among many Presbyterians and Baptists, for example."[1]

A number of serious issues led many of the Founding Fathers to recognize that the United States needed a new constitution. This chapter describes events leading to the call for a convention in Philadelphia, which concluded four months later with the signing of the Constitution. The fascinating story of the political process of ratification, including the role of *The Federalist* papers and the Bill of Rights, is discussed in the next chapter.

There are many excellent books on the development of the Constitution. Our purpose here is to highlight how this world-changing document came together, and to identify evidence of God's hand in the process.

The Need for a Constitutional Convention

The shortcomings of the Articles of Confederation, which was essentially the first constitution of the United States, were obvious to George Washington, Alexander Hamilton and James Madison. In a matter of a few short years, the three of them, along with several other leaders, decided to tackle the problem, first with a meeting in Annapolis in 1786, and then with a full-blown convention in Philadelphia the following summer.

Weaknesses in the Articles of Confederation. As we look back on how the United States functioned during the Revolutionary War (e.g., the lack of food and supplies during Valley Forge, months without paying the troops) and immediately after the signing of the peace treaty with England in 1783, it is amazing that the country survived.

During the Revolutionary War the United States operated informally under a draft of the Articles of Confederation with an elected Congress, but no president or what was then referred to as a "chief magistrate." Since there was no central government other than the Congress, the states held most of the power; this was part of the frustration felt by Washington and Hamilton as they, and others, tried to hold the Continental Army (really 13 armies) together as an effective fighting force. National requirements could be ignored by the states since the national government had no power to enforce its requests. Some readers might consider the fact that the United States was able to win the Revolutionary War under this sort of handicap to be a miracle!

Even before the war officially ended in 1783, the fledging United States was experiencing serious problems:

- Different states levying tariffs on goods passing across their border from a neighboring state.
- No tax base to support an army or navy.
- No responsibility for repaying the debt incurred during the war, no widely accepted currency and no central bank.
- Inability to set policy and manage the settlement of the western areas (called the Northwest Territories) that were rapidly being settled after the war.
- No coherent foreign policy reflecting the needs of the country as a whole. This was at a time when serious crises were developing between France and England, and between the United States and these two countries, plus Spain.
- Lack of interest of those serving in the Congress; attendance was sporadic and most of the tested leaders of the country did not participate.

Here is how one historian described the situation in America four years after the signing of the peace treaty with England: "These men (the Founding Fathers) inhabited a world alien to modern Americans, a world in which the United States was a fragile, uncertain experiment, a newcomer, and to some degree a beggar at the gates of power and prestige among nations. In 1787, our treasury was empty. Debts to foreign governments and debts to our own citizens could not be paid, and this was a blow to the nation's honor as well as to its future credit."[2] How could European nations deal with this rag-tag collection of states, each going its own way? The United States was certainly not "united" and could not truly be called a nation.

To many of the Founding Fathers, it was obvious that something had to be done—and fast. We marvel at how quickly several of these leaders were able to size up the situation. What is even more amazing is that when they saw a serious problem emerging, they didn't delay; they took immediate action!

The Annapolis Convention set the stage. In 1786, a year before the Constitutional Convention in Philadelphia, Washington, Hamilton, Madison and representatives from five states (the remaining eight states either declined to participate or simply failed to send representatives) met in Annapolis to discuss problems stemming from the Articles of Confederation, especially trade among the states.[3]

When Madison arrived in Annapolis for the meeting, he found the problems to be more serious than even he anticipated: "No money comes into the public treasury, trade is on a wretched footing, and the states are running mad after paper money."[4] Only two delegates were present when Madison arrived, and after a few days, it was obvious that several states had boycotted the meeting and there would not be a quorum. Since the convention could not complete its mission, a decision was made to issue a call for a convention in Philadelphia the following May.

In conclusion, "The Annapolis Convention accomplished nothing except the recommendation, drafted by Alexander Hamilton of New York, that the states should appoint commissioners to meet at Philadelphia the second Monday of the following May..."[5] The announced purpose of the Philadelphia convention was deliberately vague and the leaders and delegates of many states assumed they were being called to amend the Articles of Confederation, not to draft a constitution for a radically new form of government. (Even though we use the term "Constitutional Convention" in this chapter, that terminology was not used until after the convention had completed its work.)

Shays' Rebellion gave urgency to the need for a constitutional convention. When farmers in New England were threatened with the loss of their land to creditors, groups of men (including many veterans of the Revolutionary War) surrounded courthouses in Northampton, Worcester, Taunton and Great Barrington to block the entrance of lawyers and judges. The largest of these revolts took place in

Springfield where a former Continental Army officer, Daniel Shays, led 1,500 men in an assault on the courthouse.

Shortly after Shays' Rebellion, the Confederation Congress endorsed the proposed convention in Philadelphia. Virginia and New Jersey quickly agreed to send delegates, and Pennsylvania, North Carolina, Delaware and Georgia soon followed. "The Philadelphia Convention would have met even if the western farmland of Massachusetts had not been bathed in blood in the autumn of 1786. But Shays' Rebellion changed the environment in which the delegates would gather."[6]

The framers of the new Constitution. The 55 men participating in the convention represented a variety of religious backgrounds. The church membership of 54 of the framers was:

> Episcopalians (28)
> Presbyterians (8)
> Congregationalists (7)
> Lutherans (2)
> Dutch Reformed (2)
> Methodists (2)
> Roman Catholic (2)
> Deists (3)[7]

At least half of the attendees had had previous experience in drafting state constitutions. For example, Gouverneur (that was his name) Morris and John Jay had worked together drafting a constitution for New York.[8]

The framers came from every state except Rhode Island, which declined to send a delegation. The convention did not reach a quorum of at least seven states until May 25, almost two weeks after most of the Virginia delegation had arrived. The two delegates from New Hampshire did not make it to Philadelphia until late July, a week after the most contentious issue—small state representation—had been resolved through the Great Compromise.

What Was Philadelphia Like That Summer?

The sacrifices made by the men who spent most of the hot, humid summer of 1787 in Philadelphia living in boarding houses and cramped up in the Pennsylvania Statehouse for several hours each day represent an experience we sometimes forget. Furthermore, most of the delegates paid their own expenses.

The weather and personal hardships. "For anyone who knows Philadelphia summers…this is a city where the damp heat lies heavy on the spirit. Visitors from abroad despaired of it. 'A veritable torture during Philadelphia's hot season,' wrote a Frenchman, 'is the innumerable flies which constantly light on the face and hands, stinging everywhere and turning everything black because of the filth they leave wherever they light. Rooms must be kept closed unless one wishes to be tormented in his bed at the break of day, and this need of keeping everything shut makes the heat of the night even more unbearable and sleep more difficult.'"[9] "Close fitting wigs and woolen coats, close-buttoned; mosquitoes and bad water—delegates endured it all."[10]

Housing and hospitality. Other than Washington, who stayed with Robert Morris, his friend from Revolutionary War days, and Madison who stayed with Mrs. House, the rest of the Virginia delegation roomed at the Indian Queen Tavern. "By the middle of the summer so many delegates lodged at the Indian Queen that its common rooms were virtual convention annexes, and Madison so often visited them that travelers thought he lived there."[11]

Benjamin Franklin's large house and garden was a haven for delegates who often gathered to relax after a long, hot day of deliberation. The atmosphere, plus Franklin's sense of humor and hospitality, were important in healing wounds and building bonds of friendship. Here is one description of the fellowship at Franklin's house: "At his newly enlarged home on Market Street a block and a half from the House lodgings, he frequently entertained delegates in his courtyard, where he sat under a large mulberry tree surrounded by grass plots, gravel walks, and flowing shrubs." At a dinner for 20 or so delegates "…the company enjoyed a cask of London stout and ale which all declared 'the best porter they had ever tasted,' talk of government, the trials of revolution, and the prospects of nationhood filled the room."[12]

Madison's Role Prior to and During the Convention

James Madison is often called the "Father of the Constitution." Small in stature and soft spoken, Madison came to Philadelphia prepared to offer a plan for a new constitution. Furthermore, he was instrumental in convincing George Washington to participate as a delegate from Virginia.

The Virginia Plan. Although most of the Virginia delegates arrived in Philadelphia at the appointed Friday in mid May, Madison had arrived 11 days earlier. While awaiting other delegations to make up a quorum the Virginians developed what was called the Virginia Plan. The 15-point plan called for a national legislature, a chief executive, and a federal judiciary to take over the work done (or undone) by the Confederation Congress. Once the convention began its deliberations in late May, Governor Edmund Randolph introduced the Virginia Plan. (In the end, much to Madison's chagrin, Randolph refused to sign the Constitution. However, once Randolph returned to Virginia, he campaigned for ratification.)

Madison's insights. Early in the deliberations, there was concern that the United States covered too large a geographic area (and this was before the Louisiana Purchase!) to be governable as a single country, and that its vast size would create serious problems of competing regional interests and lack of communications. Considering that many delegates were knowledgeable about Europe, and the multitude of countries in a relatively small area, this is understandable. However, Madison saw this large size of the United States as an advantage. He thought it would keep any single state or region from dominating national affairs, and force states to work together. In our view, this was one of the most important insights that guided the framers; it had the hallmarks of providential "nudging."

Madison also saw the fragmentation of religious denominations in America as an advantage in that there was no chance of a single religious group partnering with the government as in England and in many European countries at the time. No denomination (or sect, as they were called) included more than one-fifth of the country's population. He also "...applauded the new federal constitution for its contribution to religious life in the new republic. To him, it safeguarded religious freedom for all citizens by eliminating the government's voice in ecclesiastical matters." [13]

Madison sat in the front row and took meticulous notes of the proceedings. He did this on his own initiative; there was no designated official secretary or recorder. Considering that there was no one to take dictation, and no tape recorders, his record is amazingly detailed. Furthermore, he did not miss a single session. Madison's notes provide a valuable record for those interested in the "intent" of the framers of the Constitution.

Alexander Hamilton's Plan Ignored

Although Alexander Hamilton played a key role in the Annapolis meeting leading to a call for a convention, and wrote over half of *The Federalist* papers in support of the Constitution, his role during the convention was inexplicable and somewhat divisive. His attendance was sporadic, although he was the only delegate from New York still in Philadelphia when the final draft was presented, and he signed the Constitution.

His proposal, which he presented on June 18 in a five- to six-hour speech three weeks after the start of the convention, was radical, and to some delegates, it came across as arrogant. He said that he was declaring himself unfriendly to the Virginia plan.[14] Hamilton's proposal included these statements:

- The British government was "the best in the world; and that he doubted much whether any thing short of it would do for America."[15]
- As an admirer of the British House of Lords, he thought that senators should be elected for life.[16]
- He also thought the president should be elected for life and he held up the British monarchy as an example of good government.
- The president would have power to veto any laws that had been passed by the Senate and the House of Representatives. There would be no provision for overriding the president's vetoes.
- No powers for the states except over local affairs.

"Hamilton's proposals, so energetic, so Hamiltonian, were supported by no other delegate, and were not even discussed."[17] Hamilton's proposal went down in flames, and in many respects, he never recovered from this speech. He lived with accusations of favoring England and the monarchy for the rest of his life.

The Process

As the best known and most respected man in America, George Washington was the unanimous choice to be presiding officer. He accepted this role and attended every session during the nearly four months of deliberations. Judging from Madison's notes of the speeches, Washington was a tolerant moderator; some speeches lasted for an entire day, and longer, and were often boring! Having Washington as the presiding officer was more than fortuitous; his fairness and integrity were indispensable in holding the delegates together in pursuit of a somewhat ambiguous goal.

Washington himself did not deliver a speech or participate in the debates until late in the process when he spoke in favor of reducing the population for each elected member of the House of Representatives from 40,000 to 30,000. He recommended a smaller base so that people would feel closer to their elected representative. The delegates unanimously agreed with him.

Confidentiality. On the second day it was agreed that the discussions would be held in confidence. The delegates even went so far as to board up the windows of Independence Hall (not a pleasant thing to do in Philadelphia in the summer!), and placed armed guards at the door. There was a desire that delegates be able to speak honestly and not be subjected to criticism—or political pressure—from their home states, many of which had strong vested interests in the outcome of the discussions. Madison and the other leaders wanted delegates to be free to change their minds as additional evidence was introduced and considered. They wanted to avoid political posturing and encourage a spirit of openness and compromise.

The idea of having important national discussions held behind closed doors would be almost unheard in the United States today. However, at the time, the delegates, the press and the public accepted these limitations. It is amazing that very little (if any) information leaked to the press over the four-month period; the delegates swore an oath of confidentiality and for the most part, they kept it. There was speculation in the press from time to time, and rumors, but little factual information was leaked.

A framework for discussion. The process of developing the Constitution was structured and logical, which was unheard of prior to these deliberations:
- The Virginia delegation's 15-point plan served as a starting point for discussion and debate. The delegates recognized that the convention would make more progress if there were concrete proposals on the table rather than delegates throwing out their ideas without a framework for discussion.

- For the first two months, most of the debate was structured around the Virginia Plan; as indicated, others, including Alexander Hamilton and William Paterson of New Jersey, introduced entirely different proposals, but none of these was seriously considered.
- At the end of two months, the convention took a break while a five-person committee considered the comments and compromises agreed upon, and came back with a 23-point proposal.
- After five more weeks of discussion on the committee's draft, the convention turned it over to another committee, which took four days to prepare a final draft.
- With a minimum amount of additional debate, and few word changes, 39 delegates signed the Constitution; four delegates refused to sign and the remainder had returned home.

The committee on detail. In late July, the convention took a 10-day recess while a committee of five "…arranged and systemized…the materials which that honorable body have collected."[18] During the break, Washington went fishing, and on his brief vacation, visited the site of the winter encampment of the Continental Army at Valley Forge.

The committee offered its report on August 6. The next phase could be characterized as more tedious than difficult. The delegates put themselves on a six to seven-hour day, six days a week. After studying and debating the committee's report for five weeks, the delegates were ready for a final draft.

The committee on arrangement and style. This committee entrusted the actual writing to Gouverneur Morris. "Morris reduced twenty-three unwieldy articles to three, with sections and subsections defining the great departments of government, plus four additional, and more miscellaneous, articles."[19] This was a miraculous achievement.

Important Compromises

As would be expected, there were serious compromises required in order to gain agreement among different delegates and states. These involved small state representation, counting of slaves for purposes of members of the House of Representatives, and the role and tenure of the president.

The Great Compromise. The Connecticut Compromise introduced by Roger Sherman, later referred to as the Great Compromise, was aimed at giving large and small states equal representation in the Senate. The compromise was initially voted down by a coalition of larger states and southern states.

As evidence of the seriousness of the issue to representatives of small states, Gunning Bedford of Delaware said to representatives of the large states, "I do not, gentlemen, trust you."[20] As a delegate from Virginia, the largest state, it is difficult to imagine what went through George Washington's mind when he heard that comment!

When the contentious issue of the number of senators from each state was finally resolved, the tone of the convention changed dramatically. Representatives of the smaller states were more flexible and interested in achieving a strong federal government. In retrospect, the Great Compromise appears to have been the tipping point, both for gaining agreement on a constitution, and for ratification.

Slaves and the three-fifths rule. To keep delegates from the southern states from walking out of the convention, it was agreed that slaves would count as a fraction of a free person. "The negotiated agreement decreed that each slave held in the United States would count as three-fifths of a person—the so-called federal ratio—for establishing the representation of a state in the House of Representatives (and consequently in the Electoral College, which was based on the House and Senate numbers for each state in Congress.)"[21] As a result, "The slave states always had one-third more seats in Congress than their free population warranted—forty-seven seats instead of thirty-three in 1793, seventy-six instead of fifty-nine in 1812, and ninety-eight instead of seventy-three in 1833."[22]

Rufus King and Gouverneur Morris were particularly outspoken against the three-fifths rule. Both of them gave blistering speeches to the effect that they would never concur in upholding domestic slavery. Morris argued "Upon what principle is it that the slaves shall be computed in the representation? Are they men? Then make them citizens and let them vote. Are they property? Why then is no other property included?"[23]

For those interested in how God has blessed America and its form of government, the federal ratio is disquieting. However, if the northern opponents of slavery had not yielded on the three-fifths rule, delegates from North and South Carolina, and Georgia, would have pulled out leaving the convention without a quorum. As noted earlier, Rhode Island did not send representatives, the delegation from New Hampshire was nine weeks late, and the New York delegation was down to one person—Alexander Hamilton. By not agreeing to this type of compromise, the convention would have dissolved, with repercussions that are difficult to comprehend. With respect to the three-fifths rule, James Madison concluded, "Great as the evil is, a dismemberment of the union would be worse."[24] Most white Americans agreed with him.

Defining the presidency. After deciding what to do about small states and slaves, the convention moved on to the issue of how the president would be selected. It took more than 60 ballots to agree on the question of how to select or elect a president. "Five times the Convention voted in favor of having the President appointed by Congress. Once they voted against that, once for electors chosen by the state legislators, twice against that, and then voted again and again to reconsider the whole business."[25] Other controversial issues related to impeachment of the president, his title, length of his term, use of the cabinet, and presidential power and privilege. Based on rumors, some newspapers reported that the convention was considering a king for America!

Religion and the Constitution. Article VI requires an oath from federal and state officers to support the Constitution, "...but no religious Test shall ever be required as a Qualification to any Office or public trust under the United States."[26] The Constitution was signed "in the year of our Lord 1787" indicating that the drafters acknowledged God. Other than these two references, the Constitution is silent on the subject of religion.

Historian James Hutson viewed the matter this way: "The Convention knew that its proposals to strengthen the national government would be controversial enough, without adding religious reforms to the mix. It wanted the Constitution to be what present-day legislators call a 'clean bill,' a measure stripped of as many provocative provisions as possible to make it as broadly palatable as possible."[27] The political acumen of the delegates was unique for the time; it was almost as if a strong power had drawn them together and guided their discussions and willingness to bend to the national interest.

Gouverneur Morris Makes Important Contributions

Gouverneur Morris, who was widely respected by his colleagues, was part of the five-person committee charged with taking the work of the various committees and coming up with a draft of the Constitution. He was selected to write the first draft and did it in four days! Although he was a lawyer, "...he avoided as much as he could the legalistic repetitions that his profession loves. The effect of his changes is to make for clarity, simplicity, and speed."[28] Most of what Morris wrote had already been agreed upon and was in rough draft form, but it was much longer and more cumbersome. For example, "the several states" became "the land," "the acts of the Legislature" became "the laws."[29]

Morris' best job was in the preamble, which he wrote from scratch: "We, the people of the United States, in order to form a more perfect union, to establish justice, insure domestic tranquility, provide for the common defence, promote the general welfare, and secure the blessings of liberty to ourselves and our posterity, do ordain and establish this Constitution of the United States of America."[30]

Morris' statement of "'We the *people*' instead of 'the states'" was viewed by some as a momentous shift, and one of the points Patrick Henry of Virginia focused on in his opposition to the ratification of the Constitution. Henry was concerned about the loss of power of Virginia and other states. Historian Richard Brookhiser wrote that Morris's phrase, "We the people," may be his greatest legacy.[31]

After a few minor adjustments, Morris' draft was approved on September 15, 1787. It was agreed that the Constitution would be submitted to special state ratification conventions and that it would be considered on a take-it-or-leave-it basis. The possibility of state conventions inserting changes and then ratifying the document would have complicated the process and might very well have killed the chances of ever reaching agreement on the Constitution.

The framers gave considerable thought about how to release the Constitution to the public, and how the state ratification conventions would be organized and convened. Madison was convinced that the state legislatures were "incompetent to make the proposed changes," from the Articles of Confederation to the new Constitution.[32] Nor did the framers want the Confederation Congress, with its vested interests, making the final decision. The plan to submit the Constitution to the public and to state ratification conventions proved to be providential.

Following the close of the convention and a briefing of the Confederation Congress in New York, Madison met with John Jay (who was not part of the Constitutional Convention) and Alexander Hamilton to map out strategies for dealing with the state conventions, and to plan a series of essays—which ended up being *The Federalist* papers—to be published in newspapers.

Virtuous People Needed for Success

As background for a country seeking self-government, the Founding Fathers were convinced that a republic wouldn't work without a virtuous people. Historian Hutson said: "Virtue was a concept of classical antiquity that shared so many characteristics with Christianity—selfless service, honesty, simplicity—that the revolutionary generation regularly conflated it with Christian morality and assumed that it was best promoted by Christianity."[33]

In the minds of the Founders, religion promoted virtue; virtue promoted republicanism; religion promoted, and was indispensable for, republicanism. Alexis de Tocqueville noted that the Christian religion of many Americans translated into good manners (he was talking about virtue).

"Mankind," claimed a writer in the *Virginia Independent Chronicle* in 1784, "have, generally speaking, enacted laws to restrain and punish enormities, to countenance virtue and discourage vice: yet the most approved and wisest legislators in all ages, in order to give efficacy to their civil institutions, have found it necessary to call in the aid of religion; and in no form of government whatever has the influence of religious principles been found so requisite as in that of a republic."[34]

Expressing a similar view, Massachusetts Supreme Court Justice Joseph Story later wrote that the "promulgation of the great doctrines of religion, the being, and attributes, and providence of one Almighty God; the responsibility to him for all our actions, founded upon moral freedom and accountability; a future state of rewards and punishments; the cultivation of all the personal, social, and benevolent virtues—these can never be matters of indifference in any well-ordered community. It is, indeed, difficult to conceive how any civilized society can well exist without them."[35]

Much more could be written about this theme—Christianity promotes virtuous citizens, and this is a necessary ingredient for republican government—but we stop here. The thinking of the Founding Fathers and other leaders on this subject should give us all pause.

Evidence of Divine Providence in Drafting the Constitution

As indicated earlier, many Americans believed that God had blessed their efforts in winning the Revolutionary War and achieving independence. They thought that America had benefited from divine providence. We agree that America has also been blessed by the Constitution developed that hot summer in Philadelphia.

There was also a keen sense among many early Americans, going back to the years preceding the Revolutionary War, of the importance of the Constitution. Writing in 1777 one pamphleteer offered this sobering assessment: "Men entrusted with the formation of civil constitutions should remember they are painting for eternity: that the smallest defect or redundancy in the system they frame may prove the destruction of millions."[36]

International events and timing of the convention. At the time the delegates were meeting, representative government around the world was on the wane. Portugal, Spain, Denmark, Germany and Hungary had all tried some form of representative government and all had failed. The delegates in Philadelphia were swimming against the tide.[37]

In retrospect, the timing of the convention was perfect. The states would not have been ready five years earlier, close on the heels of the end of the Revolutionary War. "Five years later and the French Revolution, with its violence and blood, would have slowed the states into caution, dividing them (as it indeed divided them) into opposing ideological camps."[38]

Washington's hopes and despair. In addition to perfect timing, George Washington's participation was critical to the success of the convention. Was this an example of divine providence? It strikes us that way.

In early July, two months after commencing deliberations, it appeared that the entire effort would fail. One of Washington's French officers, de Maussion, visited him in Philadelphia. Maussion wrote home to his mother that Washington appeared very gloomy. "The look on his face...reminded of its expression during the terrible months we were in Valley Forge Camp." On July 10, Washington wrote Alexander Hamilton, who had been called back to New York: "I am sorry you went away. I wish you were back. The crisis is equally important and alarming." He said our councils, "...are now, if possible, in a worse train than ever; you will find but little ground on which the hope of a good establishment can be formed. In a word, I almost *despair* of seeing a favorable issue to the proceedings of the Convention, and do therefore repent having had any agency in the business."[39]

Although no formal record exists of Washington's opening speech as presiding officer, Gouverneur Morris attributed these remarks to Washington: "It is too probable that no plan we propose will be adopted. Perhaps another dreadful conflict is to be sustained. If to please the people, we offer what we ourselves disapprove, how can we afterwards defend our work? Let us raise a standard to which the wise and honest can repair. The event is in the hand of God."[40] This is an example of Washington's leadership; he was intent on doing the right thing and being in tune with divine providence.

If religion was important, why wasn't it mentioned in the Constitution? On this question, historian Walter McDougall said: "Do not be misled by the failure of the Federalists (the supporters of the new Constitution) to say much about religion or even make a polite reference to the Almighty in the Constitution. The reason was *not* that they were enlightened secularists who thought faith unimportant. On the contrary, a large majority of the Framers were confessing Christians and church officers, while even skeptics repeatedly named faith and morals indispensable props for self-government. But Americans were a people of many denominations; to favor one or punish one or another was sure to imperil the Union. So the Framers said nothing about religion because it was just *too* important; the only solution lay in forbidding federal restrictions on free exercise of religion and leaving it up to states to decide whether to have local religious establishments."[41]

McDougal went on: "Madison even endorsed religious liberty as the best means to *promote* sincere faith in people, and of course almost all of the Framers agreed with (John) Witherspoon (the president of Princeton) that civil and religious liberty leaned on each other."[42] This latter point relates to our second criterion for evaluating God's blessings—the link between Christianity and liberty.

In an article in *The Wall Street Journal*, Samuel Huntington, a Harvard Professor, wrote that although the Constitution includes no references to God, "...its framers firmly believed that the republican government they were creating could last only if it was rooted in morality and religion. 'A Republic can only be supported by pure religion or austere morals,' John Adams said. Washington agreed: 'Reason and experience both forbid us to expect that national morality can prevail in exclusion of religious principles.'"[43]

Franklin's call for prayer. At one point in the convention's deliberations, following a particularly rancorous debate, Franklin handed a note to Washington suggesting that each day's session should begin in prayer:

> The little progress we have made after four or five weeks close attendance and continual reasonings with each other—our different sentiments on almost every question...producing almost as many noes as ayes, is methinks a melancholy proof of the imperfection of the human understanding. We indeed seem to feel our own want of political wisdom, since we have been running about in search of it. We have gone back to ancient history for models of government, and examined the different forms of those republics, which, having been formed with the seeds of their own dissolution, now no longer exist. And we have viewed modern states all round Europe, but find none of their constitutions suitable to our circumstances. In this situation of this Assembly, groping as it were in the dark to find political truth, and scarce able to distinguish it when presented to us, how has it happened, Sir, that we have not hitherto once thought of humbly applying to the Father of lights to illuminate our understandings?[44]

Franklin then reminded the convention that at the beginning of the war with England, the Continental Congress had offered prayers for divine protection "...and in this very room. 'Our prayers, Sir, were heard, and they were graciously answered.'" Franklin concluded, "I have lived, Sir, a long time, and the longer I live, the more convincing proofs I see of this truth—*that God governs in the affairs of men.*"[45]

Franklin's comments were received sympathetically. However, to the embarrassment of many of the delegates, there were no funds available to hire a chaplain! (In those days, laymen did not typically lead a group in prayer; it required a "professional.") Even so, Franklin's "suggestion had been salutary, calling an assembly of doubting minds to a realization that destiny herself sat as guest and witness in this room."[46] This is what many would refer to as divine providence.

Influence of prayer on the outcome of the Constitutional Convention. Despite the delegates' unwillingness to fund a chaplain to open each session in prayer, we draw several conclusions from the historical record:

- Many of the delegates, including George Washington, regularly attended worship services during the summer of 1787. Although a member of the Anglican Church, Washington often attended Presbyterian services in Philadelphia.

- Even though the framers had been sworn to secrecy about their deliberations, the fact that a convention of high importance was taking place in Philadelphia was well known across the country. It seems certain that individuals, including family members of the delegates and churches of all denominations, were praying for success in the deliberations of this distinguished group of Americans.

- As noted earlier in this chapter, most of the delegates were Christians and members of various churches in their hometowns.

Divine providence. Titles of two books about the drafting of the Constitution strike us as shedding light on this question—Berkin's *A Brilliant Solution* and Bowen's *Miracle at Philadelphia*. The final result was brilliant; few people would disagree with that conclusion. It is a *miracle* that leaders from 12 colonies, who had widely differing views on the role of a central government and slavery, could come together and agree on a radically different form of federal government for the United States. To accomplish this in four months was also miraculous.

Here is how Madison summed up the results of the Constitutional Convention: "It is impossible for the man of pious reflection not to perceive in it (the convention) a finger of that Almighty hand which has been so frequently and signally extended to our relief in the critical stages of the revolution."[47] Madison saw divine providence at work; that is the way it seems to us.

In his opening remarks after being selected as presiding officer, Washington was fearful that the convention would not be able to produce a plan that would be acceptable, but he said the outcome was "in the hand of God." It does not appear that God failed the framers of the Constitution and the new country!

CHAPTER 9
▼

Managing Change—The Ratification of the New Constitution

...they (the Founding Fathers) comprised, by any informed and fair-minded standard, the greatest generation of political talent in American history. They created the American republic, then held it together throughout the volatile and vulnerable early years by sustaining their presence until national habits and customs took root.

—Joseph J. Ellis, *Founding Brothers,*13.

Why do the ratification of the Constitution, *The Federalist* papers and the Bill of Rights warrant a full chapter? Over a period of two years, these accomplishments, plus the election of George Washington as president, had long-lasting implications for the country. The amazing series of decisions made by the American people, as influenced by strong leaders like James Madison and Alexander Hamilton, represent something especially impressive in the history of early America. Our goal, of course, is to identify and analyze the evidence of God's hand in this process, especially His blessings.

If we think the political rhetoric of today is strong, here is what one opponent of the new Constitution wrote: "The federalists (supporters of the Constitution) were 'demagogues despising every sense of order and decency;' they were the 'meanest traitors that ever dishonoured the human character' and as 'the haughty lordlings of the convention,' they were engaged in a 'conspiracy against the freedom of America both deep and dangerous, a conspiracy that could only end in one *despotic monarchy*."[1]

One of the most skillful moves by the drafters of the Constitution was to call for special ratification conventions in each state. Because of the vested interests of the state legislatures and the Confederation Congress, the drafters knew that a document threatening the independent nature of the states would not be ratified.

Despite the fact that fully one-third of the drafters of the Constitution were members of the Confederation Congress, when it was presented to this body, it ignited a firestorm of dissent. On September 29, 1787, following three days of debate and without either approval or disapproval, the Confederation Congress agreed to refer the matter to the states. That is what the framers of the Constitution had hoped for and they turned their attention to the monumental task of ratification.

Highlights of *The Federalist* Papers

Based on our experience as researchers and public policy analysts, the preparation of *The Federalist* papers in support of ratification of the new Constitution stands out as a remarkable achievement. Historian Robert Middlekauff characterizes *The Federalist* as "the most powerful body of political thought ever produced in America."[2] Given the diverse backgrounds of Alexander Hamilton, James Madison and John Jay (all brilliant men in their own right), and the lack of real-world experience in terms of what it took for republics to function and survive, it is truly providential that they were able to prepare these 85 papers in such a short period of time.

The Federalist papers were a series of what today would be called "white papers" to appear in leading newspapers, especially in New York and Boston. Most of the papers were much longer than the typical "Op/Ed" pieces that appear in newspapers today.

Fear—the overriding concern of opponents to the Constitution. Bernard Bailyn, a history professor and an admirer of the national debate that took place around the ratification of the Constitution, noted that many of the one million registered voters were involved, as well as the 1,500 delegates to the 12 state ratifying conventions. According to Bailyn, the underlying theme of the debates was a *fear* that the new Constitution called for a stronger central government, and "that unconstrained power will destroy free states, which are fragile, and the liberties that free people enjoy."[3] Many Americans felt that they had just pulled themselves out from under an oppressive, strong central government and they feared it might happen again.

Bailyn summarized the strengths of *The Federalist* in this way: "The great achievement of the authors of *The Federalist* papers is not merely that they replied in detail to specific dangers that critics saw in the Constitution and explained in detail how the new government should, and would, work, but that they did so without repudiating the past, without rejecting the basic ideology of the Revolution… *The Federalist* sought to embrace the Revolutionary heritage, and then to update it in ways that would make it consistent with the inescapable necessity of creating an effective national power."[4]

John Jay's Christian worldview. Jay was the most openly religious of the writers of *The Federalist* papers. "He quoted from and paraphrased the Bible in his political papers; he served as a leader of his parish church and of the national church; and he was a president of the American Bible Society."[5] More often than Hamilton or Madison, Jay referred to providence and the prayers of people for unity. For example, he said that "…the prosperity of the people of America depended on their continuing firmly united, and the wishes, prayers, and efforts of our best and wisest citizens (referring to the Constitutional Convention) have been constantly directed to that object."[6]

Jay went on to describe the blessings experienced by the United States, the same blessings that are often referred to today: "Providence has in a particular manner blessed it (the United States) with a variety of soils and productions, and watered it with innumerable streams, for the delight and accommodation of its inhabitants. A succession of navigable waters forms a kind of chain round its borders, as if to bind it together; while the most noble rivers in the world, running at convenient distances, present them with highways for the easy communication of friendly aids, and the mutual transportation and exchange of their various commodities."[7]

The need for a strong union. The nine papers making up the first section of *The Federalist* present compelling arguments for the new Constitution. Jay wrote the first four, Hamilton the next four, and Madison the last one in this series. (Jay became ill after his initial contributions and was unable to draft additional papers.)

Jay made a strong case that if the ground occupied by the United States were to end up as 13 separate and independent countries, or three or four consolidated countries (e.g., New England, the South, Mississippi Valley), it would be disastrous for the future safety and well being of the people. He pointed to many examples in Europe and the ancient world. Thomas Paine made essentially the same point in *Common Sense*: "Europe is too thickly planted with kingdoms to be long at peace…"[8]

Jay described the common threads of the people of the United States: "With equal pleasure I have as often taken notice, that Providence has been pleased to give this one connected country to one united people—a people descended from the same ancestors, speaking the same language, professing the same religion, attached to the same principles of government, very similar in their manners and customs, and who, by their joint counsels, arms, and efforts, fighting side by side throughout a long and bloody war, have nobly established general liberty and independence."[9]

When Jay referred to "professing the same religion," he did not mean that Americans were members of a single denomination or sect. He was reflecting the dominant Christian heritage of the early settlers and the first Great Awakening, which resulted in a significant proportion of the population becoming Christians.

Jay referred to a band of brothers: "This country and this people seem to have been made for each other, and it appears as if it was the design of Providence, that an inheritance so proper and convenient for a band of brethren, united to each other by the strongest ties, should never be split into a number of unsocial, jealous, and alien sovereignties."[10]

In his second paper, Jay identified the causes of war among nations. He concluded that the probabilities of war among neighboring countries in the land now occupied by the United States would be substantially less under a single republic than with several different countries. With Shays' Rebellion in Massachusetts fresh on the minds of all Americans, he commented: "As to those just causes of war which proceed from direct and unlawful violence, it appears equally clear to me that one good national government affords vastly more security against dangers of that sort than can be derived from any other quarter."[11]

In his third paper arguing for a strong and united nation Jay warned about the reaction of foreign countries that find the United States: "…either destitute of an effectual government (each state doing right or wrong, as to its rulers may seem convenient), or split into three or four independent and probably discordant republics or confederacies, one inclining to Britain, another to France, and a third to Spain, and perhaps played off against each other by the three, what a poor, pitiful figure will America make in their eyes!"[12]

Our remaining summary of *The Federalist* focuses on specific papers that are indicative of how God blessed America during its formative years. We have elected not to summarize papers that deal with issues such as financing the new government, international relations, the presidency, and the roles of the courts and the two legislative branches. Readers interested in these topics can read the relevant *Federalist* papers for themselves.

Madison's viewpoint on the size of the country. The conventional wisdom of the Greek and Enlightenment philosophers was that a republican form of government would only work in small countries. One commentator identified the issues this way: "…how could such an immense nation possibly be represented in a single legislature of manageable size? Would not the great diversity of factions, private ambitions, and passionate causes, all of them entirely free to flourish in any way they could, lead to a chaotic struggle of all against all?"[13]

In response, Madison argued persuasively in number 10—perhaps the most famous of *The Federalist* papers—that the United States would be more likely to have stable and effective government, and avoid wars, if it were a large country encompassing a variety of economic and special interests. Madison's insight was that a group of people—a faction (we might call it a special interest group)—with an ax to grind (e.g., religious preferences, tax breaks, special treatment for a specific group of people or a type of property) could exert a substantial (perhaps majority) influence in a community or state. However, in a larger country, their interests would be diluted and represent a small fraction of the population; the leaders of the faction would have much less ability to impose their will or desire on the country as a whole. This would not mean that their interests would be ignored; however, it would mean that in order for a faction to achieve its goals, it would have to work through the legislative process where many other factions were also setting forth their own, often competing agendas. Madison viewed this tension as healthy, and likely to lead to the preservation of the union.

Here is the way Madison summarized the situation in *Federalist* number 10: "The influence of factious leaders may kindle a flame within their particular States, but will be unable to spread a general conflagration through the other States. A religious sect may degenerate into a political faction in a part of the Confederacy; but the variety of sects dispersed over the entire face of it must secure the national councils against any danger from that source."[14]

Complexity and tension needed. In *Common Sense*, Thomas Paine argued for simplicity in government. However, *The Federalist* took the opposite position: "For the simpler the structure of government, the more likely it was to be dominated by particular interests or individuals at the expense of others. Complexity not simplicity was needed to provide the institutional conditions for adversarial challenges, without which ambition could run free. Complexity and adversarial institutions were instances of something broader. Tension—networks of tensions—were the fundamental necessity for free states. The whole of the Constitution, *The Federalist* made clear, was a great web of tensions, a system poised in tense equilibrium…"[15]

Hamilton and Madison knew, however, that the mechanics of the Constitutional system of government would not be enough, that it would take a virtuous people to make it work. "Its success would depend in the end on the character of the people who managed it and who allowed themselves to be ruled by it—their reasonableness, their common sense, their capacity to rise above partisan passions to act for the common good and remain faithful to constitutional limits."[16] In other words, as Alexis de Tocqueville and others said, the "manners" or character of the people made the difference.

Professor Bailyn concluded with this timeless summary of the views of the authors of *The Federalist*: "Goodwill and a degree of impartiality would always be needed. If every compromise is taken as a defeat that must be overturned, and if no healing generosity is ever shown to defeated rivals, the best-contrived constitution in the world would not succeed."[17]

Need for a strong national defense. Papers 23 to 29 focused on the need for an effective army and navy. Based on his extensive experience as a member of Washington's staff during the Revolutionary War, Hamilton noted that the voluntary system of providing men and supplies that was part of the Articles of Confederation was inadequate. He went on, "Is not a want of cooperation the infallible consequence of such a system? And will not weakness, disorder, and undue distribution of the burdens and calamities of war, an unnecessary and intolerable increase of expense, be its natural and inevitable concomitants? Have we not had unequivocal experience of its effects in the course of the revolution which we have just achieved?"[18]

In response to those who argued that state militias were adequate for defense, Hamilton sharply disagreed. He noted that reliance on militias almost cost the country the Revolutionary War. "The steady operations of war against a regular and disciplined army can only be successfully conducted by a force of the same kind." He complimented the militia for their valor and contributions, but concluded, "War, like most other things, is a science to be acquired and perfected by diligence, by perseverance, by time, and by practice."[19]

Separation of powers. In papers 47 to 51, Hamilton and Madison argued that the proposed constitution adequately provided for separation of the legislative, executive and judicial branches, and did so better than most of the state constitutions then in effect. It appears that history has proven Hamilton and Madison to be correct.

Absence of a bill of rights. In *Federalist* number 84, Hamilton explained why the new Constitution did not have, and in his opinion, did not need a bill of rights. The power of government under the Constitution of the United States comes from the people and is not handed down by a monarchy. He recited the preamble to the Constitution: "WE, THE PEOPLE of the United States, to secure the blessings of liberty to ourselves and our posterity, do *ordain* and *establish* this Constitution for the United States of America." He went on, "This is a better recognition of popular rights, than volumes of those aphorisms which make the principal figure in several of our State bills of rights, and which would sound much better in a treatise on ethics than in a constitution of government."[20]

Not perfect but good. Hamilton's last paper, number 85, argued that where flaws appear in the Constitution, which are inevitable with the passage of time, it can be amended, and that it is far easier to amend than to start over. Benjamin Franklin expressed a similar viewpoint, and a sense of humility, in his last speech before the Constitutional Convention: "I confess there are several parts of this Constitution which I do not at present approve, but I am not sure I will ever approve them...The older I grow, the more I am apt to doubt my own judgment, and to pay more respect to the judgment of others. Most men indeed as well as most sects in Religion, think themselves in possession of all truth, and wherever others differ from them it is so far error...I agree to this Constitution with all its faults, if they are such...because I think a general government necessary for us, and there is no form of Government but what may be a blessing to the people if well administered."[21]

Historical perspective on The Federalist. "In the 210 years between the (Supreme) Court's first session and January 2000, there are records of 291 citations (of *The Federalist* papers) in the Court's opinions...Analysis of the citations shows their uses by both liberal and conservative justices and litigants on a remarkably broad range of issues, from banking and taxation to the prohibition of alcohol, from term limits to piracy, and from slavery to presidential election laws."[22]

Ratification

If we think watching election results on election eve is exciting, think about the drama that unfolded in late 1787 through June 1788 as the state conventions met to consider ratifying the new Constitution.

Madison and others concede the need for a bill of rights. Thomas Jefferson, still in France, was among many political leaders who thought that the new Constitution needed a bill of rights. Madison, Gouverneur Morris and others who had played key roles in drafting the Constitution did not initially agree that such protections were necessary; they believed the Constitution itself, with its built-in checks and balances, and with power derived from the people, adequately protected the rights of individuals and minority groups.

In late March 1788, on his way home from New York, Madison stopped to visit an influential Baptist preacher, John Leland. Reverend Leland told Madison that he could not support the new Constitution unless it guaranteed freedom of religion. "The meeting was cordial, since the fiery preacher and the soft-spoken politician had worked together in Richmond in 1784 and 1785 to defeat Patrick Henry's plan for state support of religious instruction. Furthermore, as a leader of the great Baptist revival in Virginia that had accompanied the revolution, Leland knew very well of Madison's early and continuing support of religious liberty. Since the two men agreed completely in principle, they needed only to reach an understanding on how best to secure the maximum protection for freedom of conscience."[23]

Madison pointed out the difficulties of modifying the Constitution while it was in the ratification process. "In response to Leland's promise to withdraw his objections, Madison reaffirmed what he and other federalists had increasingly agreed to: they would support a bill of rights, including a firm article on religious freedom, as amendments to the Constitution *after* its ratification."[24]

Eleven states ratify. Here are the order of the states ratifying the Constitution, and the voting margins in each convention:

State	Vote Count	Date Ratified
1. Delaware	Unanimous	December 3, 1787
2. Pennsylvania	46-23	December 12, 1787
3. New Jersey	39-0	December 18, 1787
4. Georgia	28-0	January 2, 1788
5. Connecticut	128-40	January 9, 1788
6. Massachusetts	187-168	February 6, 1788
7. Maryland	63-11	April 28, 1788
8. South Carolina	149-73	May 23, 1788
9. New Hampshire	57-47	June 21, 1788
10. Virginia	89-79	June 25, 1788
11. New York	30-27	July 26, 1788

In August 1788, North Carolina rejected the new Constitution, but by November 1789, the state had reversed itself and voted 195-77 to become part of the union. Rhode Island "grudgingly" (34-32) ratified the Constitution in March 1790, a year after Washington became president.[25]

Virginia. By the time the Virginia convention had convened in early June, 1788, nine states had ratified the Constitution. Still, Madison and other backers of the Constitution recognized that without the support of the two largest states, Virginia and New York, it would be a hollow victory and a precarious basis for proceeding with the formation of a new national government.

Even though he strongly supported the Constitution, Washington did not attend the Virginia convention. This left Madison, Governor Randolph (who had been part of the Constitutional convention but had not signed the document), and John Marshall to argue for ratification. Their principle opponent was the respected and outstanding orator Patrick Henry. Opponents also invoked the views of Jefferson, who was in France.

Although Madison attempted to refute Henry's arguments, Madison was not a strong orator. Marshall, an accomplished young Richmond attorney who later became chief justice of the Supreme Court, listened closely to Madison's arguments and then took on Henry. He focused on Henry's main objection; the Constitution was an invitation for monarchy. "Marshall's tone was conciliatory. He did not speak apocalyptically of dire results that would inevitably follow if the delegates rejected the Constitution. There might be 'small defects,' he conceded, but if the other delegates were convinced, as he was, 'that the good greatly preponderates,' then they should vote for ratification."[26] In the end, the delegates sided with Marshall, Madison and Randolph and ratified the Constitution by a slim margin. That left New York.

New York. Newspaper readers in New York were the target for most of *The Federalist* papers, and this is where *The Federalist* had its greatest impact. Hamilton played a key role in getting New York to ratify the Constitution, going so far as to suggest that New York City might separate from the state. Fearing the worst, the anti-Federalist majority bent to the will of the minority and voted 30-27 to join the union. A crisis had been averted.[27]

First Session of Congress and the Bill of Rights

Madison was elected to the new Congress, and was present at the opening session in March 1789. One of his first actions was to open discussions on amending the Constitution. There were initially 18 proposed amendments, and that number was eventually reduced to 12. When the Senate considered the amendments, it further reduced the number to 10, now referred to as the Bill of Rights. The Bill of Rights passed in September 1789 and was sent to the states for their approval.

The First Amendment. When Madison was participating in the deliberations of the Virginia Ratifying Convention in July 1788, one of the possible amendments to the Constitution stipulated that "…no particular religious sect or society ought to be favored or established by Law in preference to others."[28] This phrasing expressed the concerns of the country's leaders at that time.

In the draft Madison introduced to Congress on June 8, 1789, the wording indicated that no "national" religion was to be established. The adjective "national" was dropped during Congressional deliberations. Historian Hutson elaborated: "To Madison and his colleagues the establishment clause of the First Amendment meant that Congress could not pick out one denomination and promote it to the status of an official national religion by favoring it—and it alone—with tax support and coercive authority."[29]

Another early draft of what eventually became the First Amendment said, "Congress shall make no law establishing religion, or prohibiting the free exercise thereof, nor shall the rights of conscience be infringed."[30] When finally enacted, the First Amendment was slightly different: "Congress shall make no law respecting an establishment of religion, or prohibiting the free exercise thereof."

In discussing the intent of the Founders relative to the First Amendment, Mark Noll wrote: "The founders held that the establishment of religion—official government support and funding for one form of Christianity—had been a blight on Europe. The establishment of religion had led to oppression and the denial of liberties that were part of natural rights. State-supported bishops, ecclesiastical courts, and religious tests for public office had all subverted the rights of life, liberty, property, and the pursuit of happiness."[31]

He went on: "The conviction that found expression in the First Amendment rested on several more general principles. Most of the men who wrote the Constitution welcomed the influence of religion on public life, but they wanted that influence to remain implicit, to be an indirect force in guiding public policy rather than an institutionalized agency participating directly in public affairs."[32]

Additional viewpoints. The First Amendment was designed to protect freedom of religion, not freedom from religion. One author said, "Any serious look at the Founding Fathers and their behavior would reveal how much they believed in freedom *of* religion and how deeply they would have opposed government trying to create freedom *from* religion…Jefferson was opposed to an official national religion but he was supportive of religion. The key was the term 'Establishment of Religion.' The secular Left looks to Jefferson's letter to the Danbury Baptists (January 1, 1802) in which he said there should be 'a wall of separation between church and state.' They then ignore the fact that two days later he went to the United States House of Representatives to attend church services.'"[33]

Paul Johnson said this about the First Amendment: "This guarantee has been widely, almost willfully, misunderstood in recent years, and interpreted as meaning that the federal government is forbidden by the Constitution to countenance or subsidize even indirectly the practice of religion. That would have astonished and angered the Founding Fathers. What the guarantee means is that Congress may not set up a state religion on the lines of the Church of England…In effect, the First Amendment forbade Congress to favor one church, or religious sect, over another." He added: "The House of Representatives passed the First Amendment on September 24, 1789. The next day it passed, by a two-to-one majority, a resolution calling for a day of national prayer and thanksgiving."[34]

Writing in *U. S. News & World Report*, Jay Tolson observed, "But Madison and the other founders never imagined they were banishing religion from the public sphere. In the words they spoke, the symbols they embraced, the rituals they established—from days of thanksgiving to prayers at the start of Congress—the founders made clear that acknowledgement of divine providence was not only acceptable but essential."[35]

The Dissolution of State-Supported Religion

Through the time of the first Great Awakening, and beyond, it was common for colonial governments to provide funding for churches and ministers. For example, the salary of Jonathan Edwards, America's greatest 18th century theologian and pastor of a Congregational Church, was set by the town board. "The Northampton town meeting specifically agreed that 'he should have an honorable and suitable maintenance according to the dignity of his office.' In addition he was given sufficient funds to purchase a home..."[36]

At the time the First Amendment was ratified, five states continued to provide tax support for ministers, and those five, plus six others, retained religious tests for state office. "Only Virginia and Rhode Island enjoyed the sort of 'separation of church and state' that Americans now take for granted—government providing no tax money for churches and posing no religious conditions for participation in public life."[37]

Within two decades of the conclusion of the Revolutionary War, religion was handed over to the people and to market forces. "In such an environment forms of evangelicalism not dependent on state-church support spread like wildfire. Baptists had never asked for government help, but in the old country they had been hemmed in by the Church of England, the establishmentarian restrictions of Parliamentary legislation...By contrast, in America after the War, Baptists in the middle and Southern regions found no state church, they were completely free to organize as they chose, and they were committed first of all to the gospel message they proclaimed."[38]

International Impacts

At the time of the formation of the United States, there were no republican commonwealths anywhere in the world. "Indeed, virtually every republic, whether in antiquity or in mid-17th century England, had been short lived."[39] The prevailing viewpoint was that republics were fragile and unsustainable over the long haul.

In the years immediately following the drafting of the Constitution, its ratification, and the addition of the Bill of Rights, the founding documents of America were widely translated, distributed and read around the world. These documents included Paine's *Common Sense*, the Declaration of Independence, state constitutions, the Articles of Confederation, and *The Federalist* papers. European countries where interest was greatest included France, England, Germany, Holland, Italy, Switzerland, and Norway. Leaders and scholars in many Central and South American countries, especially Brazil and Argentina, studied these documents and sought ways the principles could be applied.

Professor Bailyn said: "Thus awareness of provincial America, its successful revolution and constitutional creations, had quickly become part of the consciousness of officialdom and the clerisy (clergy or educated class) in both cosmopolitan Europe and its colonial dependencies. But with what consequence? The *general* effect of the American Revolution throughout the Atlantic world is well known: its creation of the sense that a new era was beginning, its amplification and embodiment of the ideas of liberty and equality, its legitimation of criticism of existing powers."[40]

Bailyn posed this question: "How can one assess the specific role that American constitutionalism played in the seismic transformation of power relations that took place throughout the Atlantic world in the age of revolution?" His response: "Provincial America, removed from the layered complexities of European life and the intricate racial structuring of Latin American society and having experimented with modes of enlightened constitutionalism, provided living examples: of what might be done, of the dangers that might be avoided, of alternatives that might be explored. American constitutionalism was not a theory to be debated or a model to be imitated but a reserve of experience…that could be drawn on when needed…"[41]

The London Corresponding Society, "…pointed to America to show that constitutional reform would ease the people's suffering as well as guarantee their liberties." English reformers, "…found within America's constitutionalism a deeper purpose that inspired the march toward radical social reforms."[42]

A Swiss scholar wrote: "The constitution of the United States of America is a great work of art which the human mind created according to the eternal laws of its divine nature…It is a model and a pattern for the organization of the public life of republics in general, in which the whole and the parts shall both be free and equal…The problem has been solved by the new world for all peoples, states and countries."[43]

All of this strikes us as evidence that God has blessed—and continues to bless—other countries through America's bold experiment in freedom and self-government. This would have greatly pleased many of the initial immigrants to America, especially John Winthrop and the Puritans who settled New England. They always thought that North America was a special place—"A city on a hill."

A Recap of *The Federalist*, Ratification of the Constitution, and the Bill of Rights

The process of ratification and the preparation of *The Federalist* papers are part of the country's heritage and culture. As noted, *The Federalist* continues to be referred to by the nation's highest courts in clarifying the intent of the framers of the Constitution.

Even though *The Federalist* says little about religion, several papers, particularly those written by John Jay, place a high value on unity of the country as a whole. Part of maintaining this unity is respect and tolerance for the religious opinions and practices of all people. On the other side of the coin, recognition of the common Christian heritage of the country, going back to the first immigrants and the Great Awakening, would, according to Jay, enhance unity and respect.

The Constitution and the First Amendment benefited Christianity by giving Americans freedom of choice. By 1833, there were no state- or town-supported churches or publicly-paid preachers, and no religious litmus tests for government jobs. This is generally considered to be a key factor promoting the rapid expansion of Christianity (the Second Great Awakening) that took place following the ratification of the Constitution. Madison and Jefferson agreed that God blessed America by eliminating state-supported religion.

Reflecting on the process of adopting the Constitution, Mark Noll said that the fact the "...Constitution comported well with Christian beliefs is not to claim that a special divine miracle lay behind its ratification. It is rather to say that the path from the Revolution to the Constitution, a journey that involved both the expansion of revolutionary principles and their restriction, led Americans, both believers and many influential leaders who were not Christians in a conventional sense, to a Constitution that conformed roughly to general Christian principles."[44]

While agreeing with Noll that the Constitution conforms with Christian principles, we believe that ratification was a miracle. In the critical large states—Massachusetts, Virginia and New York—ratification passed by narrow margins. If ratification had failed in any one of these states, it would have been a disaster of monumental proportions. We agree with many of the Founders—they thought that ratification of the Constitution was evidence of divine providence.

The world has been blessed by the American experiment in independence and self-government that began over 200 years ago. Many Founding Fathers believed that this would be the case, that the United States would be an example for peoples around the world as they considered the form of their own representative government.

Chapter 10

The Second Great Awakening—Lasting Influences

The Second Great Awakening was the most influential revival of Christianity in the history of the United States.
—Mark Noll, *A History of Christianity in the U. S. and Canada*, 166.

What was the religious status of America coming out of the Revolutionary War? Here is how Thomas Askew and Richard Pierard described the situation: "It was a wintry season for the churches of the post-revolutionary period. A historian of the Episcopal Church characterized the era as one of suspended animation and as 'the lowest ebb-tide of vitality in the history of American Christianity.' Lyman Beecher (1775-1863), who was a student at Yale in 1795, described the religious conditions there in his autobiography:...Most of the students were skeptical, and rowdies were plenty. Intemperance, profanity, gambling, and licentiousness were common."[1]

Martin Marty agreed. "Around the turn of the new century, Americans first started to recover from the spiritual slump that followed the First Awakening and the distractions of the Revolution, to find that only a very small minority of the citizens were on the rolls of church membership."[2] The major concerns of people at that time were creating a new nation, moving west to obtain land, avoiding Indian attacks and steering clear of foreign entanglements.

Historian James Hutson disagreed with the idea that religion was in decline after the war; he maintained that despite damage to church buildings and the wartime disruption of many congregations, Christianity remained vigorous. He wrote that most of the negative comments about the religious status of America originated with leaders of established denominations, especially the Church of England (most of its ministers fled to England during the Revolutionary War) and Congregationalists, who were concerned that their particular sects were not thriving.

Regardless of the status of religious intensity after the war, spiritual renewal was in the wind. A series of revivals, later called the Second Great Awakening, drove church expansion to unprecedented levels. "The wave of popular religious movements that broke upon the United States in the half century after independence did more to Christianize American society than anything before or since."[3]

This revitalization, or revival, of religion began around 1790, or perhaps a few years earlier, about the time the new Constitution was being drafted, debated and ratified, and a new national government was being formed. Forty years later, when Alexis de Tocqueville visited America, his observations reflected the results of the Second Great Awakening: "Upon my arrival in the United States, the religious aspect of the country was the first thing that struck my attention; and the longer I stayed there the more did I perceive the great political consequences resulting from the state of things, to which I was unaccustomed. In France I had almost always seen the spirit of religion and the spirit of freedom pursuing courses diametrically opposed to each other; but in America I found they were intimately united, and that they reigned in common over the same country."[4]

This chapter compares the two Great Awakenings, describes key players and events that marked the second Awakening (e.g. growth of the Methodists and Baptists, the success of camp meetings), and focuses on the impact of religious revivals on an array of new types of benevolent societies. We conclude with a discussion of the status of religion in 1830, and its impact on the culture—or values—of America at that time.

Comparison of Two Awakenings

The first Great Awakening introduced evangelicalism to America—the pre-eminence of the Bible and the need for personal spiritual rebirth. Itinerant and field preaching were developed and widely used in the colonies during the earlier revivals. Three of the major impacts of the first Awakening were (a) raising the status of the lower and middle classes; (b) reducing the influence of traditional churches, their ministers, and other authority figures; and (c) helping unite what had been 13 generally autonomous colonies.

Although the first Great Awakening was instrumental in breaking down class distinctions and reducing the authority of the established clergy and churches—impact (b) above—the second Awakening finished the job.

The theology of the Second Great Awakening differed somewhat from that of the first series of revivals. George Whitefield, Jonathan Edwards, Gilbert Tennent and other leaders of the first Awakening were, for the most part, strong Calvinists (e.g., they believed in the sovereignty of God, and that only certain people—the elect—had been pre-ordained to receive the gift of salvation). However, many of the itinerant preachers of the second Awakening, especially the Methodists, believed that the Gospel was readily available to all for the asking. In other words, they lowered the bar for admission to God's kingdom.

While Whitefield, Edwards and the Tennents did not have a political agenda, the leaders of the second Awakening were more aggressive in promoting patriotism. "Nineteenth century evangelists...saw no contradiction between their roles as preachers and political activists. They were proud citizens of the new American republic and subscribed without reservation to the Founders' conviction that religion was necessary for the preservation of republican government."[5]

Although large, the crowds in the western frontier were no bigger than some that Whitefield and Tennent drew during the first Great Awakening. "But they looked different. First Great Awakening audiences usually came from towns and cities and convened on short notice. In Kentucky and in other frontier areas, audiences came from great distances by wagon, packed with provisions to sustain families for several days. When assembled, usually in clearings in the wilderness, these conventions of frontier farmers became camp meetings—a unique American contribution to religious history."[6]

In addition to strong evangelistic preaching, which was common in both Awakenings, the second Awakening spawned a number of benevolent societies (e.g., non-denominational organizations) to promote education, including Sunday schools and the distribution of Bibles, foreign missions, temperance and the abolition of slavery. As a result of the activities of these benevolent organizations, the impact of the second Awakening became more permanently etched on the face of America.

A final factor differentiating the second Awakening is that the country was much larger and growing more rapidly than during the earlier revivals. The population of the 13 colonies during the time frame of the first Great Awakening ranged from 750,000 in 1730 to 2.5 million by 1770. By the second Awakening, the population of the United States had tripled, from 4.0 million in 1790 (including 900,000 slaves) to 13.0 million (2.0 million of whom were slaves) by 1830. Furthermore, Americans were scattered over a much larger geographic area, mainly west of the Appalachian Mountains, during the second wave of revivals.

Methodists Led the Second Great Awakening

Prior to the Revolutionary War, most of the strength of Methodism, which was part of the Church of England until the early 1780s, was in Great Britain. Because of John Wesley's opposition to the American war for independence, Methodism was not highly regarded in the fledgling United States. Mark Noll observed that "It took many years for the American followers of Wesley to overcome the stigma of disloyalty. But overcome it they did, and with a vengeance."[7] Another author reinforces this finding: "Starting from scratch just prior to the Revolution, Methodism in America grew at a rate that terrified other more established denominations."[8]

A giant in the Methodist movement. When Francis Asbury arrived in America in 1771, four years before the outbreak of fighting in the Boston area, there were four Methodist missionaries caring for 300 people. These four missionaries returned to England and Asbury was banished to Delaware for refusing to sign a loyalty oath to the new state government in Maryland.

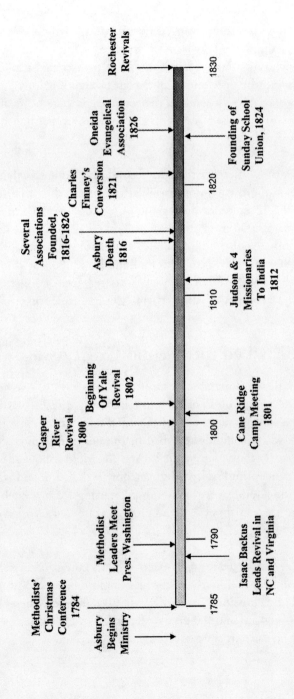

The turning point for the Methodists came during the "Christmas Conference" in Baltimore in 1784. At this meeting, Asbury and the Methodists set up an organization that bound eastern population centers to the western frontier. "Asbury used the Methodist pattern of organization—local classes, preaching circuits, and general conferences—to further the growth of the church and, in the process, to civilize the frontier."[9] One of the other important impacts of the Christmas Conference was the separation of North American Methodists from the direct control of John Wesley and his organization in England.

Asbury and the Methodists made a serious effort to repair their relationships with American revolutionaries. For example, in 1789, several Methodists "exchanged cordial greetings with the nation's new president. Washington pledged himself to the happiness of mankind, to liberty for the United States, and to vital religion."[10]

Asbury's leadership "…was based on personal piety, a determination to ask nothing of others that he would not do himself, and a pragmatic devotion to the spread of scriptural holiness across the land."[11] Asbury tried to visit every state at least once a year. Over his career, he visited New York more than 50 times, New Jersey 60 times, and Maryland 80 times. "Yet despite all his heroics, most Americans, Methodists or not, have never heard of Asbury. In his own day it was said that he was the best-known American outside the field of politics…"[12] When Asbury died in 1816, Methodism had 2,000 ministers in America.[13]

Importance of music. Methodists were pre-eminent in writing and singing hymns, which were originally intended to be prayers set to music. "It has long been recognized that the most distinctive, characteristic, and ubiquitous feature of the Methodist message, indeed the entire Methodist revival, was its transmission by means of hymns and hymn singing."[14] Charles Wesley composed an estimated 9,000 hymns and poems, some of which are classics. Almost every Methodist gathering began and ended with a hymn.

Itinerant preaching. This was the key to the explosion in Methodism in America. Millions of sermons were preached during the 1800s and 1900s by hundreds of itinerant preachers, mostly young, single men. Methodist itinerants were paid a small salary, and they all earned the same amount—$64 a year in 1796, increased to $80 in 1800 and $100 in 1816. These amounts, supplemented by reimbursement for some expenses, were one-fifth of what was earned by Congregational ministers and even less than the wages of unskilled laborers.[15]

Expanded role of women. There were consistently more women than men in Methodist congregations; a 60/40 ratio was typical. In his book on Methodism, David Hempton said, "Quite simply, as purveyors of hospitality, deaconesses, visitors, evangelists, prayers, exhorters, testifiers, class members and leaders, and preachers, women helped define the character of the Methodist movement."[16] He went on: "By dressing and speaking plainly, by sustaining 'islands of holiness,' in an otherwise raucous environment, and by building a grander Christian family out of their manifold and diverse families, women not only reshaped the American denominational order but also made a remarkable contribution to the shaping of the American republic."[17]

Martin Marty summed it this way: "Methodists, a relatively new sect in the national landscape (in the 1780s), vied with the Baptists for size and outdid them for influence throughout the century, North and South."[18] Noll added: "The emergence of the Methodists is one of the great stories of American history…"[19]

The More Subdued Eastern Seaboard Revivals Came First

Although sometimes referred to as the "western revival," the Second Great Awakening actually began on the Eastern Seaboard. "Almost imperceptibly, people began taking new interest in religion; fresh converts strengthened churches, and new congregations, especially in New York, Long Island, and New Jersey, were established."[20]

Virginia. Revival in Virginia began with college students. In 1787, the same year the Constitution was drafted, "…students at Hampden-Sydney College and Washington College, Presbyterian institutions in Virginia, experienced awakening; a number even decided to enter the ministry. The thirty or forty men who sought ordination eventually served Presbyterian churches on the frontier."[21]

Yale and Connecticut. Timothy Dwight, a grandson of Jonathan Edwards, was ordained in 1777 and served as a chaplain during the Revolutionary War. Following the war he was minister to a congregation in Connecticut. When he was called to be president of Yale in 1794, the struggling university had 110 students.

Upon arriving in New Haven, "Dwight found many of his students at least superficially attached to the deistical fashions of the French Enlightenment. To meet the challenges of 'infidelity,' Dwight launched a two-pronged effort. He labored by forthright argument to restore confidence in the Bible, and he began a four-year cycle of sermons designed to communicate the essentials of the faith."[22] Progress was slow, but in 1802, two students announced that they had received Christ, and shortly after that, another 50 were converted. The revival at Yale soon spread throughout Connecticut and up and down the Eastern Seaboard.[23]

In discussing Dwight's influence, one historian writes that Dwight "...had ample cause for good cheer. Under his tutelage, a remarkable coalition of talented leaders had developed and were now coming to maturity across New England."[24] More specifically, "Through his writings, his devoted students (which included Lyman Beecher) took up and carried on his work as well as his leadership of Connecticut Congregationalism. Timothy Dwight thus represents a watershed in the history of awakenings in America."[25]

Eastern revivals more subdued. The New England and Mid-Atlantic states that experienced the Second Great Awakening were the same ones most impacted by Whitefield, Edwards and the Tennents during the first Awakening. However, "The New England revival was conducted with a sobriety missing sixty years earlier; there were no wild-eyed itinerants, no split congregations, no massive, open-air meetings, and no carnivals of public emotion...Since these decorous proceedings were universally approved, they continued in some New England locations for decades."[26]

The Southern and Western Revivals

The most spectacular action of the Second Great Awakening took place west of the Appalachian Mountains and in the South. "Like the events in New England, the Kentucky revivals had a Great Awakening pedigree, for in their initial stages, they were led by Presbyterian ministers who had been trained in New Side schools sponsored by Gilbert Tennent and his associates and staffed by disciples and admirers of that redoubtable companion of Whitefield."[27]

James McGready and Gasper River. In the late 1790s, James McGready, a native of Pennsylvania, was preaching to three small congregations in North

Carolina—Red River, Gasper River and Muddy River. After an initial revival at Red River, McGready scheduled outdoor services at Gasper River. When word of the meeting spread, people came in wagons from as far as 100 miles with the intention of staying for several days. Gasper River was the first of many camp meetings that characterized the Second Great Awakening.[28]

Cane Ridge camp meeting. While in law school, Barton Stone had heard James McGready preach; however, at that time McGready's strong evangelical sermons turned him off. Stone was later converted and in 1796, the Presbyterians licensed him to preach. While in Kentucky as pastor of two small churches, he attended a McGready camp meeting; he was impressed.

In August 1801, a year after the Gasper River revival, a great camp meeting convened at Cane Ridge, near one of Stone's churches. "Thousands streamed to this gathering, as many preachers—black and white, Presbyterians, Baptists, and Methodists—fervently proclaimed the Good News…The results at Cane Ridge were electrifying."[29] It is estimated that 25,000 people attended the Cane Ridge camp meeting.

What did the people do at Cane Ridge and subsequent camp meetings? "The organizers of the camps awoke the faithful before dawn each day with a blare of trumpets, signaling that private prayer should begin and that breakfast would soon be served. After the first meal of the day, the trumpets would sound again, announcing the beginning of public prayer, followed by two hours of preaching. After lunch, which was normally served in each tent, the afternoon would be consumed by more prayer and sermonizing until early supper. Organizers scheduled another four hours, from six to ten, mainly for prayer, so that at ten o'clock everyone could retire after a long day."[30]

Relative to the non-denominational character of camp meetings, George Whitefield had preached that conversion was more important than membership in a particular denomination. "There was nothing really new, then, in the declarations by preachers like McGready that 'in that awful day, when the universe assembled, must appear before the quick and the dead, the question brethren, will not be, were you a Presbyterian—Seceder—Covenanter—a Baptist—or a Methodist; but, did you experience a new birth?'"[31]

Baptists. "The renewed interest in the faith touched at Cane Ridge and similar camp meetings led to a rapid growth of Presbyterian churches in the South. By comparison, however, Presbyterian efforts paled beside the accomplishments of the Methodists and Baptists...By the 1830s, these groups had replaced the Congregationalists and Presbyterians as the largest denominations, not only in the South but in the whole United States."[32]

"Baptist membership multiplied tenfold in the three decades after the Revolution; the number of churches increased from five hundred to over twenty-five hundred."[33] "By 1812, there were close to 200,000 Baptists in the United States, with half of them in the states of Virginia, North and South Carolina, Georgia and Kentucky. By 1850, the total exceeded 1,000,000."[34]

The Baptists were "localists" in that they believed in the authority of local congregations to select their pastors and govern their own affairs. At the same time, local congregations often joined together to support missionary activities. "As early as 1802 the Massachusetts Baptist Missionary Society was sending missionaries to plant churches on the frontier of the upper Midwest."[35]

Although the Baptists did not have leaders of the stature of Francis Asbury or Charles Finney, they made up for it with their vigor. "Their aggressive strategies for outreach, their combination of determined congregationalism and institutional association, and their traditional Calvinism adjusted to the American environment made Baptists a powerful force in the South and on the frontier."[36]

Later Eastern Revivals Also Part of Second Awakening

Charles Finney experienced a dramatic new birth in 1821 and was ordained in 1824. Finney, who was practicing law at the time of his conversion, banded together with leading New York ministers to create the Oneida Evangelical Association. In addition to members of the association, a number of other preachers formed a circle around Finney, called the "Holy Band." After meeting with Lyman Beecher and representatives of Massachusetts' churches, Finney emerged, at age 36, as the leader of the Presbyterian-Congregationalist campaign for spiritual awakening in America.

Finney then led a series of revivals in Wilmington, Philadelphia, New York City, Providence and Boston. However, it was, "a great revival in Rochester over the winter of 1830-31 (that) catapulted him to national renown."[37] A few years later, in 1835, Finney entered a new phase of his career becoming professor of theology and later president of Oberlin Collegiate Institute in Ohio. By then the Second Great Awakening had largely run its course.

Finney succeeded in joining evangelical religion and social reform. Finney was also an effective promoter of benevolence, an abolitionist, a pioneer of coeducation at Oberlin College, and a reformer in many areas of life: "Because of his dominant role in the revival tradition, and the dominant place that revivalism assumed in the antebellum period, a good case can be made that Finney should be ranked with Andrew Jackson, Abraham Lincoln, and Andrew Carnegie (or some other representative industrialist) as one of the most important public figures in nineteenth-century America. Beyond doubt, he stands by himself as *the* crucial figure in white American evangelism after Jonathan Edwards."[38]

Growth of Sunday Schools, Missions and Benevolent Societies

As noted earlier, one of the areas where the second Awakening differed from the first series of revivals, and had longer-term impacts, was in the formation of Sunday schools, missionary organizations and benevolent societies (including temperance and abolition of slavery).

Sunday school movement. The Sunday school movement in the United States flowed out of efforts in England prior to the Revolutionary War aimed at providing literacy and religious training to children. In 1804, a Sunday school society was formed in Philadelphia to provide education for poor female children. Other cities soon followed suit. In 1824, the American Sunday School Union was founded to provide lesson materials for these classes. In addition to educating children, the Sunday school movement advanced the cause of American women. Women taught the classes, and took more important roles in local churches.

Growth in missions. Enthusiasm for missions began at Williams College in Massachusetts and spilled over to students at Andover Theological Seminary (founded in 1807). Samuel Mills, a student at Williams College, along with several fellow students went on to Andover Seminary where in 1810 they formed a missionary organization, the American Board of Commissioners for Foreign Missions. "Among the first contingent of five that went to India in 1812 under the

American Board was Adoniram Judson, who later became a greatly revered figure among American Protestants."[39]

Some historians believe that the most important missionary activity of the early 19th century took place in the United States: "As significant as the overseas work became, however, the great achievement of missions in the nineteenth century was the conversion of American and Canadian citizens. The vision of Asbury, Finney, Baptist farmer-preachers, and like-minded individuals inspired North Americans to take the gospel abroad, but the work done by those who stayed at home to evangelize and civilize America was *the* truly great missionary story of the century."[40]

Benevolent societies. The benevolent societies established between 1816 and 1826 included the American Bible Society, American Tract Society, American Educational Society, American Society for the Promotion of Temperance, and the American Missionary Society. The Methodists founded the Missionary Society of the Methodist Episcopal Church in 1820, giving American Methodists an international perspective. Lyman Beecher, a student of Timothy Dwight at Yale when revival broke out there, was particularly active in founding benevolent societies.

Expiration of state-funded religion. "It is no coincidence that the years 1810-1830, in which the benevolent societies were founded and generated their maximum energy, also witnessed the expiration of government financial support for religion in America. The New England states, where the practice persisted, gradually abolished it during the first decades of the nineteenth century. Massachusetts held out until 1833, when its voters terminated tax support for religion, signaling the disappearance in the United States of the ancient concept of the state as 'nursing father' of the church."[41]

Impact on Culture, Women, Blacks and Slavery

One of the most notable impacts of the Second Great Awakening was improving the culture (morals, virtue) of Americans. Women and blacks were two groups that were affected by itinerant evangelists who were part of the second Awakening. In fact, "The Second Great Awakening has been called the 'central and defining event in the development of Afro-Christianity.'"[42]

Christianity and a more virtuous people. In the view of national leaders, one of the most important benefits of the second Awakening was an improvement in the virtue of people, especially those living on the frontier. As discussed in earlier chapters, the conventional wisdom of the time was that the country, which had just embarked on a republican form of government, was doomed without a strong base of virtuous people, and that Christianity promoted virtue.

Women. The revivals "brought women to the visible forefront of the churches, and even, to some extent, to the forefront of public life in general...A more fluid social setting on the seaboard as well as in the thinly populated regions newly opened to settlement and the rhetoric of democracy from the Revolution both served to advance women in the public practice of religion. In many areas of the country it soon became conventional to look upon women as the prime support for the nation's republican spirit."[43]

Christianity among blacks. By the time of the American Revolution, a few slaves and a number of free blacks had been exposed to the preaching of George Whitefield and had accepted the Christian faith. Samuel Davies, a Presbyterian evangelist, is credited with being one of the first to offer religious instruction to slaves.

The rapid rise of the Methodists and Baptists, who presented the gospel in easily understandable terms, broadened the appeal of Christianity among blacks. "In the wake of revivals led by itinerant preachers from these denominations and of increased preaching blacks to blacks, the number of African Americans adhering to churches rose dramatically from the 1770s to the 1830s."[44] Richard Allen, who came out of slavery and was exposed to Christianity by Methodist circuit riding preachers, was the patriarch of the strongest early Negro denomination. He said, "I was confident that there was no religious sect or denomination that would suit the capacity of the colored people as well as the Methodist."[45]

Following a snub during worship at Saint George's in Philadelphia (blacks were asked to vacate seats up front and move to the back pews), he and others founded their own church, which they named Bethel. By 1816, there were five fledgling congregations, and they formed the first Methodist General Conference for free blacks. "Bishop Allen faithfully and autocratically made the rounds and carried on oversight of the first 6,748 Methodists under his care around Philadelphia, Baltimore, and Charleston."[46]

In the South, where there were fewer opportunities to organize black churches, "Some masters encouraged their slaves to attend worship services with them. Others permitted supervised religious meetings on the plantations. Still others gave grudging approval to the work of white missionaries among the slaves..."[47]

Baptists also appealed to blacks. "Attracted to Baptist calls for a full religious liberty and happy to affiliate with a denomination that did not place white bishops or superintendents above them, African Americans cast their lot with the Baptists in astounding numbers."[48]

"No group stood as far outside America's dominant patterns of religion between the Revolution and the Civil War as the slaves. It is a testimony to their resilience as well as to the transforming power of Christianity that a religion used so often to support the slave system could become a means of counteracting its inhuman influence."[49]

Impact on abolition of slavery. The religious revivals contributed to the abolition of slavery in America. Historian Paul Johnson said, "Hence the Second Great Awakening, with its huge intensification of religious passion, sounded the death-knell of American slavery just as the First Awakening had sounded the death-knell of British colonization."[50]

In one specific example, Robert Carter, an Anglican turned Baptist and one of the wealthiest plantation owners in Virginia prior to the Revolutionary War, freed his 442 slaves. This was the largest single action of this type, which began in 1789. Carter wrote, "I have for some time past been convinced that to retain them in Slavery is contrary to the true Principles of Religion and Justice, and that therefore it was my Duty to manumit them."[51]

On a broader basis, between 1782 and 1861, white slave owners in Virginia freed more than 100,000 slaves without compensation and without the support of public consensus.[52] In our view, this is at least partially a reflection of the Second Great Awakening and its impact on Americans' moral and ethical standards.

Impact of Christianity on American Universities

The second Awakening and its aftermath led to the establishment of large numbers of colleges, many of which developed into prestigious universities with graduate training and large research programs. The Methodists and Presbyterians were especially active:

- As the denomination that grew most rapidly during the second Awakening, Methodists were leaders in establishing new colleges, including Boston University, Duke, Emory, Northwestern, Southern Methodist, Syracuse and Vanderbilt.
- Colleges and universities started by Presbyterians included Hampden-Sydney in Virginia, and the University of North Carolina.[53]

Even the University of California–Berkeley had its roots in the Christian-based College of California, sponsored by New Light Presbyterians and Congregationalists. The school was named after Bishop George Berkeley. The University of Chicago, heavily endowed by John D. Rockefeller, was one of the major institutions established by Baptists. Seven of the original 12 trustees at Johns Hopkins were Quakers. Daniel Gilman, the first president, thought there should be a spirit of "enlightened Christianity" at the university.

In nearly every case, as colleges and universities grew and expanded their educational offerings, they attracted faculty and students who did not share the beliefs of the founding religious denominations or governing boards. In a few cases, such as Princeton and Harvard, seminaries or divinity schools were established to provide theological education somewhat independent of the main university. Even though none of the colleges and universities identified above would be considered "Christian" or "denominational" today, their founding and early history represents a distinctive part of America's Christian heritage.[54]

Indicators of Growth and Shifts Among Denominations

During the Second Great Awakening, the growth in the number of Christians in America was impressive. Historian Sean Wilentz noted that the "...sheer scale of religious conversions was astounding, in every part of the nation...By the 1840s, the preponderance of Americans—as many as eight in ten—were churched, chiefly as evangelizing Methodists or Baptists (in the south) or as so-called New School revivalist Presbyterians or Congregationalists (in the North)."[55] The number of Christian preachers increased from 1,800 in 1775 on the eve of the Revolutionary War to 40,000 in 1845. During these same years, the number of preachers per capita tripled.

In another comparison, by 1834 states on the Eastern Seaboard had many more ministers and churches per capita than Scotland, which was considered the most thoroughly churched region of the British Isles at the time. For example, Edinburgh, with 150,000 residents had 70 ministers and 65 churches; by comparison, Philadelphia's 200,000 residents had 137 ministers and 83 churches.[56]

By 1830, the American Bible Society was printing 300,000 copies of Scripture per year. The American Tract Society reported five million items in circulation. Religious titles as a percentage of all nongovernmental publications were as high as 67 percent in 1740 at the peak of the first Great Awakening. By 1800, that percentage had dropped to 12 percent. However, by 1830, following 40 years of nearly continuous revival, the percentage had climbed back to 28 percent.[57]

Historian James Hutson noted that, "The accelerating activity of Presbyterians, Baptists, and Methodists during and after the American Revolution changed the country's religious landscape, for by the early decades of the nineteenth century these were the three largest denominations in the United States. How different the scene in 1740 when Anglicans, Quakers, and Congregationalists were the big three of American religion. These groups were eclipsed because they were either outright opponents of the Great Awakening (the Anglicans and the Quakers) or because they were divided by it (the Congregationalists)."[58]

There is evidence of a major shift in denominational membership between 1776 and 1850 (we do not have data for 1830):

- As measured by church membership, Methodists grew from 2.5 percent in 1776 to 34.2 percent in 1850, and Baptists increased from 16.9 percent to 20.5 percent during the same period. Presbyterians declined as a percentage of the country but remained above 11 percent in 1850.
- In 1776, 20.4 percent of religious adherents in the United States were Congregationalists; by 1850, this proportion had shrunk to 4 percent.

During this same period, the proportion of Episcopalians (formerly Church of England) dropped from 15.7 percent to 3.5 percent.

- Largely because of immigration, Roman Catholics grew from 1.8 percent to 13.9 percent during this 75-year period.[59]

Summary of the Impact of the Second Great Awakening

As noted earlier, one historian said that the revivals did more to Christianize America than anything before or since. He went on to argue that "...the transitional period between 1780 and 1830 left as indelible an imprint upon the structures of American Christianity as it did upon those of American political life."[59] Were the two—the religious and political structures—related?

Mark Noll argued that they were. He wrote that the hundred years from 1740 to 1840, which covered both the first and second Awakenings, were the most important period in American life, both in terms of religion and politics. In terms of numbers, another historian said, "Between 1800 and 1835, while the national population tripled, church membership increased five times over."[61]

There is plenty of evidence of the growing link between Christianity and patriotism during the second Awakening. Many saw religion as the cement that held civil society together. Hutson said, "In the first decades of the nineteenth century, evangelical America regarded itself (and was accepted by the nation's political establishment) as a voluntary partner of a weak national government, operating in an area that was constitutionally off limits—the formation of a national character sufficiently virtuous to sustain republican government—and in an area where the federal government was politically hamstrung—the creation of national unity."[62]

Christian heritage. America continues to be known as a "very religious country" with an emphasis on Christianity. Both the first and second Awakenings contributed to this feature of America, with the second Awakening having the most permanent effect. This is part of the Christian heritage of the United States that continued through the revivals and preaching of more recent evangelists, such as Dwight L. Moody during and after the Civil War, Billy Sunday in the early 1900s, and Billy Graham in the 1950s through the end of the 20th century and into the 21st century. In many respects, the large outdoor non-denominational revivals that characterize evangelism in America had their beginnings in George Whitefield's field preaching, and the camp meetings at Gasper River in North Carolina and Cane Ridge in Kentucky.

With their emphasis on evangelical Christianity, both the first and second Awakenings led to a decline in the importance of large, centrally controlled denominations (e.g., Church of England, Congregationalists) and encouraged the formation of new, less centralized groups, such as the Baptists. At the same time, the benevolent societies encouraged people of different, often competing denominations to work together.

Impact of the second Awakening on lifestyle, morality and a virtuous people. The second Awakening provides evidence of a link between Christianity and a virtuous people, something very important to the Founding Fathers. These religious revivals had a profound impact on the lifestyles of millions of Americans, especially those living in the rapidly growing western parts of the country. "The sins that McGready, Stone, the McGees, and others scourged—drunkenness, profanity, gambling, horse racing, cock-fighting, dueling, fornication, and adultery—dramatically declined."[63]

Charles Finney believed that Christianity and morality were linked. One of the distinguishing features of his efforts was social reform, and the creation of benevolent organizations opposed to slavery and in favor of temperance. In terms of the importance of living a more virtuous life, "Finney told disciples that wallowing in sin once a Christian would be an offense against *America*, an offense that risked its Providential destiny."[64] Alexis de Tocqueville credited the pervasive Christianity he observed as having a huge positive impact on the manners of the American people.

Christianity and political liberation. The leaders of evangelistic efforts in America in the 1790s through the first decades of the 19th century—mainly Methodists, Baptists and Presbyterians—recognized the connection between spiritual and political liberation: "The leaders of these movements almost always had experienced a life-redirecting experience of conversion, a surprisingly large number of them had been touched by the ministry of George Whitefield, most had received little formal education but often exerted prodigious self-discipline in mastering the Bible, and most also recognized a natural synergy between the evangelical message of spiritual liberation and the era's many movements of political liberation."[65]

Referring to the evangelists of the second Awakening, historian Walter McDougall said: "They preached popular sovereignty, democracy, community, liberty, opportunity...Far from exhorting the virtues of poverty and submission, they taught that God poured out his blessings on reformed individuals: 'Seek ye first the kingdom of God and all this shall be added unto you.'"[66]

Hutson referred to the massive revivals that began prior to 1800 as deserving to be called the true "republican religion" of the new nation. He also contended that the Second Great Awakening was made possible by the strong base of Christianity that existed in the years following the first Awakening that continued through the Revolutionary War.[66]

Divine providence. The Second Great Awakening—the pouring out of God's Spirit, particularly on blacks, women and people living in the western territories—represents especially strong evidence of divine providence. From all reports, the morals and ethics of Americans on the frontier were at rock bottom prior to these religious revivals. The Methodist circuit riders and organizations such as the American Bible Society and the American Sunday School Union played key roles in encouraging rural Americans to pursue higher standards of education and behavior.

We know from our analysis of the impact of the first Great Awakening on the Declaration of Independence and winning the Revolutionary War that the earlier series of revivals were critically important. The same is true of the second Awakening—the revivals began to pick up momentum during the time of the Constitutional Convention, ratification of the Constitution, and the establishment of the presidencies of George Washington and John Adams (discussed in the next chapter), and those of Thomas Jefferson, James Madison, James Monroe and John Quincy Adams.

Chapter 11

▼

Nation Building— Challenges and Triumphs of the First 12 Years

No people can be found to acknowledge and adore the invisible hand, which conducts the affairs of men more than the people of the United States. Every step by which they have advanced to the character of an independent nation seems to have been distinguished by some token of providential agency.

—George Washington in Hutson, *The Founders on Religion*, 182.

Following the drafting and ratification of the Constitution, and during Washington's first term, Alexander Hamilton observed that the country had overcome the "degraded and ruinous state of our affairs under the old confederation." In its place, "a respectable and prosperous nation" had emerged, and one that would never again be the sport of European powers.[1]

Our study of the period following the signing of the peace treaty with England that ended the Revolutionary War, and the drafting and ratification of the Constitution, suggests that Hamilton may have been overly optimistic. The future of the new country was precarious; it was hanging by a shoestring. Historian Walter

McDougall observed "The name 'United States' was more wish than reality before the 1790s."[2]

The crucial 12-year period covered by this chapter includes the inauguration of President Washington, important precedents in the new national government, Hamilton's efforts to put the country on a sound financial footing, coping with the growing tensions between France and England, the Jay Treaty, Washington's Farewell Address, and President Adams' success in avoiding war with France.

Washington Sets the Tone for the New Government

George Washington did not seek the office of president; indeed, he thought he had earned the right to retire to Mount Vernon and spend his remaining days as a farmer. Alexander Hamilton, Gouverneur Morris and others urged him to accept this public responsibility, and most of the members of the state constitutional ratifying conventions assumed that he would be the first "chief magistrate." Morris wrote Washington, "No constitution is the same on paper and in life. The exercise of authority depends on personal character. Your cool, steady temper is indispensably necessary to give firm and manly tone to the new government."[3] Without campaigning, Washington was unanimously elected to the nation's highest office.

The first inauguration. On the morning of April 30, 1789, a few days after Washington arrived in New York, church bells tolled to celebrate the inauguration of the nation's first president. Churches in New York were filled with people offering prayers for the new nation. At his inauguration, Washington put his right hand on the Bible, and after taking the oath, added the words, "So help me God." He then kissed the Bible.[4]

In his inaugural address Washington said: "…it would be peculiarly improper to omit in this first official act, my fervent supplications to that Almighty being who rules over the universe—who presides in the councils of nations—and whose providential aids can supply every human defect, that his benediction may consecrate to the liberties and happiness of the people of the United States, a government instituted by themselves for their essential purposes, and may enable every instrument employed in its administration, to execute with success, the functions allotted to his charge—in tendering this homage to the Great Author of every public and private good."[5] According to the record, "The President, the

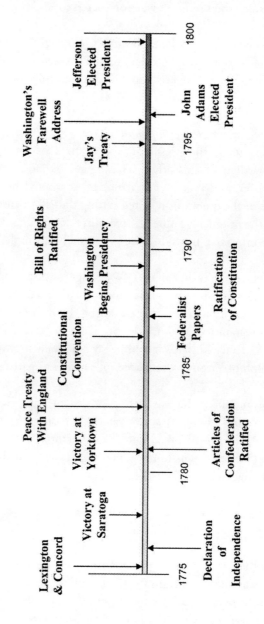

Vice President, the Senate and House of Representatives, etc. then proceeded to St. Paul's chapel, where divine service was performed by the chaplain of Congress, after which the President was conducted to his house…"[6]

In his Thanksgiving Proclamation that October, Washington declared "…it is the duty of all Nations to acknowledge the Providence of Almighty God, to obey His will, to be grateful for His benefits, and humbly to implore His protection and favor."[7]

Presidential power, leadership and precedents. When it came to conferring strong powers upon the president, the drafters of the Constitution assumed Washington would fill this office. They knew he had a track record of wisdom and moderation, and that he could not be corrupted by the love of power or money. One of the questions debated during the Constitutional Convention was what to call the president. Some wanted him referred to as His Excellency. Washington settled the issue by asking people to call him simply "Mr. President."

Historians generally agree that Washington possessed superb instincts in selecting people for military command and high office. As president, he relied on the people he had known and trusted during the Revolutionary War—Alexander Hamilton as secretary of treasury, Henry Knox as secretary of the army, Thomas Jefferson as secretary of state, and John Jay as chief justice of the Supreme Court. John Randolph of Virginia was placed on retainer as part-time attorney general.

Washington realized he was setting precedent with every action. "I walk on untrodden ground. There is scarcely any part of my conduct which may not thereafter be drawn into precedent."[8] For example, Washington met with the Senate for a detailed discussion of a possible treaty with the Creek Indians. The "inconsequential bickering" upset him; he concluded that such discussions were a colossal waste of time. Henceforth, Washington's approach—and that of subsequent presidents—was to submit a signed treaty to the Senate for its "advice and consent" as required by the Constitution.

Whether the heads of the large departments were to report to the president or to Congress was not specified in the Constitution. In fact, the initial proposal was that since department heads were to be approved by the Senate that these individuals should report to that body. James Madison played a key role by persuading the House of Representatives that department heads should report to the president. In the Senate, however, there was a tie on this question with Vice President John Adams casting the deciding vote. "Who can doubt that, had the President been less popular and trusted than Washington, the decision would have gone the other way, changing the whole direction of American government."[9] Washington then began the precedent of using his principal department secretaries as a means of consultation, the beginning of the president's "Cabinet."[10]

During the debate on the Jay Treaty (discussed later), the House of Representatives requested that Washington provide all documents related to the treaty. He rejected the request as "a dangerous precedent." This was the first example of what came to be called "executive privilege," the concept that internal papers concerning policy development at the presidential level were privileged and need not be surrendered to Congress. Other precedents included his "non-monarchial" means of interacting with citizens, his concern about responsible management of the public debt, and the art of spreading presidential appointments geographically, thus bringing disparate elements into the national government.[11]

Presidential travels. After six months in office, and with Congress in recess, Washington traveled to Massachusetts, Connecticut and New Hampshire. He skirted Rhode Island since that state had not yet joined the union. Signs in New Hampshire touting Washington's 1789 tour indicate that he and his group attended church during their visit, sometimes as many as three services per day. He made a second New England trip in late 1790 for the specific purpose of visiting Rhode Island, which by then had joined the rest of the states in ratifying the Constitution.

In April 1791 Washington embarked on a two-month visit to North and South Carolina and Georgia. "In these days of redundant communication, it is hard to credit that, owing to a confusion of roads and mails, the President was completely out of touch with his government for two months."[12]

Social life in the capital. Washington was initially inundated by people looking for jobs or expressing their opinions on controversial issues. After Martha arrived, she and the president developed three types of social affairs. Washington met with men only every Tuesday from three to four (called a levee); Martha's tea parties for men and women were held on Friday evenings; and official dinners were staged on Thursdays beginning at four in the afternoon. Washington's levees were open without invitation to any respectably dressed male.

Hamilton's important role. As secretary of the treasury, Alexander Hamilton was the strongest individual in Washington's cabinet. In the second year of Washington's first term, Hamilton proposed that the federal government assume all state debts incurred fighting the Revolutionary War. "Assumption" was controversial in that many soldiers had sold their IOUs to private investors. This meant that when these notes were redeemed the financial benefits would accrue to the moneymen in New York and other cities, and not the soldiers themselves. "Hamilton prophesied that the nation would topple into a bottomless financial crash if assumption failed, while the debtor states that hoped to be got off the hook—Massachusetts was joined by South Carolina—threatened to secede from the Union if the other states left them dangling."[13]

Hamilton's proposals on assumption of state debt could not have been carried out without Washington's support. "Every proposal was matured by the cool judgment of the President...The foreign and domestic debt was funded at par; the former was entirely paid off by the end of 1795..."[14] The result was that the United States soon had a credit rating "...such as few nations in Europe enjoyed."[15]

Bank of the United States. In late 1790, Hamilton proposed the formation of a bank to service the national debt, make loans to the government, and create bills of indebtedness, which would circulate as the basic currency of the country. The bank would also serve several of the functions of the present-day Federal Reserve System by controlling inflation and regulating local banks.

Although the bill authorizing the Bank of the United States passed the Senate easily, Madison opposed it as being unconstitutional. When it eventually passed both houses, Washington was perplexed about whether to sign the legislation and asked his cabinet for advice. Randolph and Jefferson agreed with Madison and opposed the formation of the bank. Hamilton prepared a rebuttal; his reasoning was so compelling that Washington signed the legislation.

The Whiskey Rebellion as affirmation of national sovereignty. In 1794, an excise tax on whiskey, which had been originally enacted in 1790, led to violence in four western Pennsylvania counties. A small detachment of soldiers trying to enforce the law had surrendered, and one man was killed. Any distiller who paid the excise tax had his still wrecked; government representatives were seared with hot irons.

After repeatedly failing to negotiate a settlement, the president activated the Pennsylvania militia, plus militia from three other states, and was prepared to march west if his final proclamation to the rebellious distillers was not obeyed. Washington himself took command of the force being assisted by Alexander Hamilton and Governor Henry Lee of Virginia. Before making contact with the distillers, Washington was forced to return to Philadelphia for important business. The army, under Hamilton, continued its march into western Pennsylvania where two ringleaders were arrested; the rebellion faded away.

Relations with Indians, Great Britain and Spain. The French Revolution was in its early phases during Washington's first term, and although it had an emotional impact on him (he was encouraged when people in other countries sought freedom), it required no special handling. Washington's major concerns were Indian attacks on frontier settlements, building commerce with England, and improving relationships with Spain, which had gained possession of New Orleans and Louisiana.

The advent of political parties. Not long after Washington took office, it became obvious that there were two widely differing views on the future direction, and strategic alliances, of the new country. Jefferson and Madison, and many in Virginia and the South, favored the French and admired their revolution (at least in its early days); Washington, Hamilton, Adams, and most New Englanders and New Yorkers, favored the British as trading partners.

Furthermore, Washington and Hamilton argued for a "more energetic" federal government (including a central bank and a strong army and navy), while Jefferson, Madison and Monroe favored states rights, a weaker central government and a balanced budget. These differing views, plus conflicting attitudes toward France and England, led to the formation of the first political parties—the Republicans (Jefferson was the leader) who tended to favor states rights and France, and the Federalists who favored a stronger central government and trade with England (Hamilton and John Adams were key players). Washington was not aligned with either party—in fact, he was opposed to political parties—but he was obviously more in tune with the views of the Federalists.

Major issues in Washington's second term. Although Washington seriously considered retirement after his first term, he was talked out of it and unanimously elected to a second term. Shortly after his inauguration, Washington received word that King Louis XVI had been guillotined. By April 1793, England and France were again at war. Washington was convinced that the United States should stay neutral at almost any cost. However, neutrality was complicated by the fact that both France and England relied on ocean commerce for food and war materials. England had the more powerful navy and was able to keep the sea-lanes open. England made it a practice of seizing American ships bound for French possessions and ports.[16] Jefferson and the Republicans favored the French interpretation of open seas—"free ships made free goods."

British impressment of American sailors was a sore point: "Most of the common sailors in the Royal Navy had been brutally forced into service and were brutally treated. At foreign ports, they scurried across wharves at midnight and enlisted on American merchantmen where, because of the similarity of language, they were indistinguishable from native sailors. No one denied that when an American ship was stopped on the high seas, the British had the right to take their own deserters back. The difficulty was that British captains, who admittedly suffered from the confusion, took advantage of it and impressed at gunpoint squads of American citizens."[17]

The Jay Treaty

John Jay was serving as chief justice of the Supreme Court when Washington asked him to travel to England to negotiate a treaty on the impressment of American merchant sailors, the removal of British troops from the Northwest Territories (present-day Detroit), continuing border disputes in present-day Maine and the Great Lakes region including Minnesota, and conflicting interpretations of financial obligations remaining from the Revolutionary War. If unsettled, these issues threatened armed conflict with Great Britain.

In selecting a person to represent the United States, Washington considered Alexander Hamilton and John Jay. Hamilton told Washington that Jay was better qualified. However, Jay was reluctant to leave his family for what he recognized would be an extended trip to England. He knew that from a public perspective, the mission could help prevent "the effusion of blood, and other evils and miseries incident to war." After praying about the matter and mulling it over in his mind, he said he would be inclined to accept if it would "please God to make me instrumental to the continuance of peace."[18] Once a decision had been made, Jay, his son Peter (a recent college graduate) and John Trumbull (the famous painter), sailed for England, arriving in London at an extraordinary moment in world history—mid-summer 1794 when 1,400 people were tried and guillotined in Paris.

Key elements of the treaty. The treaty with England following the Revolutionary War specified that the northern boundary of the United States would run from the Lake of the Woods (northern Minnesota) due west until it hit the Mississippi River. However, such a line does not intersect the Mississippi. A related issue was navigation of the Mississippi River; the British argued that to exercise these rights they needed to own the northern portion of the river. Jay countered and "By insisting on a more northerly boundary, Jay secured for the United States the northern plains..."[19] Other elements of Jay's Treaty included British evacuation of its forts in the northwest, the opening of West Indies trade for American vessels, and "most favored nation" status for American trade with England. The treaty was unsuccessful in stopping impressment of American sailors.

When he returned to the United States, Jay was not surprised to find that the treaty he had negotiated was highly controversial; the Federalists (including Hamilton) generally supported it and the Republicans, led by Jefferson, Madison and Monroe, were vehemently opposed, mainly because they viewed it as favoring England over France. After prolonged and heated debate, the Senate passed the Jay Treaty and Washington signed it into law.

Results of the Jay Treaty. One historian summarized the long-term implications of Jay's Treaty this way: "The key point, lost perhaps in the review of specific provisions, is that Jay preserved peace and postponed war. Without the treaty, the United States might have had to fight Britain in 1794, rather than in 1812, with no navy, with essentially no army, and with its backcountry laced with British forts supported by Indian allies. How such a war would have ended is impossible to say, but in all likelihood it would have ended badly for the United States, and it is quite possible that Britain would have demanded some American territory at the peace table. Jay was right to fear such a war and to make concessions to avoid it...Viewed in this way, his work on the treaty was a clear success, indeed one of his key contributions to early American history."[20]

Historian Joseph Ellis agreed: "Jay's Treaty was a landmark in the shaping of American foreign policy. While the specific terms of the treaty were decidedly one-sided in England's favor, the consensus reached by most historians who have studied the subject is that Jay's Treaty was a shrewd bargain for the United States. It bet, in effect, on England rather than France as the hegemonic European power of the future, which proved prophetic."[21]

From a British perspective, Lord Shelburne (the prime minister) observed that the Jay Treaty represented "...a strong foundation...for eternal amity between England and America...General Washington's conduct is above all praise. He has left a noble example to sovereigns and nations, present and to come."[22]

Opposition to President Washington was mild during his first term; however, this changed during his second four years, especially during debate over the Jay Treaty. For the first time, Washington was openly criticized—and ridiculed—for his policies and leadership style; some of his opponents spread word that he was senile. Thomas Jefferson, who had served as secretary of state during Washington's first term (and had subsequently resigned), was behind much of this criticism. Although Jefferson did not criticize Washington directly, he hired a newspaper writer to do the job. Washington got wind of this, and following the completion of his presidency, avoided further personal contact with Jefferson.

Washington's Farewell Address

On September 19, 1796, an article addressed to "The PEOPLE of the United States" appeared on the inside pages of the *American Daily Advertiser*, Philadelphia's major newspaper. Over the next few days, the article was reprinted in almost every paper in America, and given the title "Washington's Farewell Address" by the *Courier of New Hampshire*. "Over a longer stretch of time, the Farewell Address achieved transcendental status, ranking alongside the Declaration of Independence and the Gettysburg Address as a seminal statement of America's abiding principles."[23]

Writing to Washington prior to the release of the Farewell Address, Hamilton proposed a number of ideas for inclusion in Washington's statement. Here are two paragraphs Hamilton suggested:

- To all those dispositions which promote political happiness, Religion and Morality are essential props. In vain does that man claim the praise of patriotism who labours to subvert or undermine these great pillars of human happiness these firmest foundations of the duties of men and citizens.

- Nor ought we to flatter ourselves that morality can be separated from religion. Concede as much as may be asked to the effect of refined education in minds of a peculiar structure—can we believe—can we in prudence suppose that national morality can be maintained in exclusion of religious principles?[24]

With slight modifications, both of Hamilton's suggestions were included in the final version of the Farewell Address. Other key points in the Address dealt with holding the union together and avoiding civil war, staying out of tight alliances with European countries, a warning against political parties, importance of paying debts, and (where possible) working with all nations. As a reflection of his humility, Washington's second to last paragraph included these sentences: "Though, in reviewing the incidents of my Administration, I am unconscious of intentional error, I am nevertheless too sensible of my defects not to think it probable that I may have committed many errors. Whatever they may be, I fervently beseech the Almighty to avert or mitigate the evils to which they may tend."[25]

John Adams' Presidency

Although he expected to succeed Washington, and would have been hurt had the office not been offered, Vice President John Adams did not overtly campaign for president. Adams narrowly won the 1796 election with 71 electoral votes compared with 68 for Thomas Jefferson. Charles C. Pinckney was third at 59.

The Alien and Sedition Acts. These acts, signed into law early in the Adams administration, were designed to crack down on the spread of false information, triple the immigrant residency requirement for citizenship and increase the voting age. The Sedition Acts, which were pushed by the ultra-Federalists, outlawed opposition to the federal government by deed or by "false, scandalous, or malicious writing."[26] Adams is often criticized for not opposing or vetoing these unpopular (and perhaps unconstitutional) acts.

The potential for war with France. Adams inherited serious problems with France. In the months before he became president, the French had captured 300

American ships, mainly in the Caribbean. "The 'Quasi-War' produced a bitter political argument between the pro-war Federalists, who opposed alienating Britain, and the Republicans, who viewed France as America's only European ally and the French revolution as a continuation of the American Revolution."27

In an effort to avoid all-out war, Adams sent John Marshall and Elbridge Gerry to France to join Charles Pinckney to discuss ways to improve relations between France and the United States. The American envoys expected to meet the new French foreign minister, Charles Maurice de Talleyrand, who had an American connection; he had lived in exile in Philadelphia for two years. However, during the summer of 1798, the situation in France changed dramatically. The armies of France, under Napoleon Bonaparte, swept across Italy and Austria, and were threatening England.

One year to the day of his inauguration, Adams received word that other than 15 minutes with Talleyrand, the government of France had refused to see his envoys. "The mission had failed. Furthermore, the Directory (the new French leadership) had decreed all French ports closed to neutral shipping and declared that any ship carrying anything produced in England was subject to French capture."28

The XYZ Affair. But, the situation was even worse; the United States was being asked to pay bribes to Talleyrand and the French. "The Foreign Minister was favorably disposed toward the United States, the American envoys were informed, but in order for negotiations to proceed, a *douceur* (a sweetener) would be necessary; a bribe of some $250,000 for Talleyrand personally. In addition, a loan of $10 million for the Republic of France was required as compensation for President Adams's 'insults' in his speech before Congress the previous May."29

The backlash from what has been called the "XYZ Affair" (before submitting the paperwork to Congress, Adams blacked out the names of the three French agents who had demanded bribes) put the American public in a belligerent frame of mind. Congress appropriated funds to arm private merchant ships and build an army. War fever was high.

National days of prayer and fasting. In the face of these disconcerting events, Adams proclaimed the first of two national days of fasting and prayer. This move was mocked by the Republican press, "...but on the day itself the churches were filled."[30] Here is part of President Adams' proclamation:

> I have therefore thought it fit to recommend that Wednesday, the 9th day of May next be observed throughout the United States, as a day of Solemn Humiliation, Fasting and Prayer; That the citizens of these states abstaining on that day from their customary worldly occupations, offer their devout addresses to the Father of Mercies, agreeably to those forms or methods which they have severally adopted as the most suitable and becoming: That all religious congregations do, with the deepest humility, acknowledge before GOD the manifold sins and transgressions with which we are justly chargeable as individuals and as a nation; beseeching him, at the same time, of his infinite Grace, through the Redeemer of the world, freely to remit all our offences, and to incline us, by his Holy Spirit, to that sincere repentance and reformation which may afford us reason to hope for his inestimable favor and heavenly benediction...[31]

The following spring, Adams declared a second national day of prayer. The proclamation "...asserted that there was no truth 'more clearly taught in the Volume of Inspiration, nor any more fully demonstrated by the experience of all ages, than that a deep sense and full acknowledgement of the governing providence of a Supreme Being and of the accountableness of men to Him as the searcher of hearts and the righteous distributor of rewards and punishments are conducive equally to the happiness and rectitude of individuals and the well-being of communities.'"[32]

France signals a desire for peace. The attitudes of the American public were such that if Adams had asked for a declaration of war against France, Congress would have obliged. However, John Marshall, who had just returned from France, assured Adams that war could be avoided. Eldridge Gerry, another of the three peace envoys who had remained in Paris for several months, finally arrived in Boston in early October 1798 and met with Adams. "The French wanted peace, Gerry reported...Talleyrand, Gerry assured him, was ready to treat seriously with the United States."[33] Adams' hopes for peace were further buoyed in late November when he learned that the British under Admiral Nelson had overwhelmed the French fleet off the coast of Egypt.

Peace with France finally achieved. A year later, Adams sent a second delegation to France. However, in early November 1799, Adams received a shock that affected the delegation's chances for success—"General Bonaparte had taken power as First Consul, which made him, at age thirty-three, sovereign ruler of France and much of Europe."[34] However, one year after sending the second delegation to France, and shortly after he had lost the presidential election to Jefferson, Adams finally heard from the envoys. "A treaty with France, the Convention of Mortefontaine, had been signed on October 3, 1800, at a chateau north of Paris...The news had come too late to affect the election, but peace had truly been achieved."[35] Adams later referred to the peace treaty with France as "the most splendid diamond in my crown."[36]

Three-fifths rule cost Adams the election. Adams had the dubious distinction of being the first sitting president to lose a bid for re-election. Jefferson and Burr tied with 73 electoral votes each compared with 65 for Adams and 64 for Charles Pinckney. The tie threw the election into the House of Representatives, and after 36 ballots, and some deal making, the House selected Jefferson as the next president. Adams' defeat could be attributed to the three-fifths rule (also called the federal ratio) in the Constitution—"Had slaves not been counted in the allocation of electoral college seats, Adams would have nosed out Jefferson by a sixty-three to sixty-one margin."[37]

Evidence of Divine Providence in Washington and Adams Presidencies

What is the evidence of divine providence during this 12-year period? First and foremost, the country was blessed by having someone of Washington's stature available and willing to serve as president. The first inauguration and Washington's subsequent decisions set important precedents. He took the oath of office with his hand on a Bible. There were church services preceding the inauguration, which was immediately followed by another worship service attended by Washington and other national leaders. In his Farewell Address, Washington "...called religion and morality the indispensable supports of political prosperity and argued that religion was always necessary for morality."[38]

George Washington was the indispensable man when it came to establishing the new national government. He set the precedent of separating the *person* of the president from that of the *office*. He was careful to treat the office of president with care and dignity. Washington recognized the need for a sound financial system to under-gird both domestic and international trade. He avoided war with

England, France and Spain, yet when faced with a domestic insurrection (the Whiskey Rebellion), he did not hesitate to call on the army to enforce national law. Having a man of Washington's talents and stature serving as president during the critical first years of the American Republic can be considered an act of providence.

While he was president, John Adams wrote in his diary: "One great advantage of the Christian religion is that it brings the great principle of the law of nature and nations, love your neighbor as yourself, and do to others as you would that others should do to you—to the knowledge, belief and veneration of the whole people."[39]

Near the end of his term, John Adams traveled to Washington for his first visit to the partially completed White House. At his desk the next morning, on a sheet of paper headed, "President's House, Washington City, Nov. 2, 1800, he wrote:...'I pray heaven to bestow the best of blessings on this house and all that shall hereafter inhabit. May none but honest and wise men ever rule under this roof.'"[40]

John Adams' success in avoiding what would have been a disastrous war with France strikes us as divine providence. Furthermore, if Adams had not resisted the public clamor for war, thereby forfeiting an almost sure bet to win a second term in office, the opportunity to purchase Louisiana in Jefferson's administration would have gone by the boards.

Chapter 12

Thomas Jefferson—A Change in Direction?

> *It is no exaggeration to say that, on Sundays in Washington during Thomas Jefferson's presidency, the state became the church.*
> —James Hutson, *Religion and the Founding of the American Republic*, 91.

The eight years of Thomas Jefferson's presidency were exciting and important times for the United States. His presidency included the Louisiana Purchase in 1803, the Lewis and Clark Expedition in 1804-1806, and deteriorating relationships with England which eventually led to the War of 1812 four years after he left office. Jefferson's conflicts with the Supreme Court, especially Chief Justice John Marshall, and with Vice President Aaron Burr, had historic implications. One of Jefferson's major accomplishments—the advancement of freedom of religion—is also discussed in this chapter.

Despite being labeled an atheist by opponents, and a danger to the country, Jefferson was elected to the nation's highest office in 1800 and again in 1804. Jefferson had previously served in the Continental Congress, prepared the first draft of the Declaration of Independence, and served in a variety of public capacities, including governor of Virginia, ambassador to France, secretary of state under Washington, and vice president under John Adams.

In his soft-spoken, barely audible 20-minute inaugural address, Jefferson noted that peace had prevailed during the Washington and Adams administrations, and while he couldn't guarantee that it would continue, he would seek to avoid troubles through a policy of "friendship with all nations—entangling alliances with none."[1]

Policy Decisions and Religious Practices Under Jefferson

After taking office in early 1801, and with Republican control of both the House and Senate, Jefferson set out to implement a legislative program favored by fellow Republicans. One of his first decisions was to rescind the Alien and Sedition Acts made law during the Adams administration.

Another major policy initiative of Jefferson and Secretary of Treasury Albert Gallatin (a Swiss financier who became an American citizen) was to rid the federal government of indebtedness, and to operate with a budget surplus. This led to reductions in military spending, leaving the United States at the mercy of sea powers, especially Great Britain.

Jefferson and Aaron Burr. One of the interesting stories about Burr, who was totally discredited in most of the country following his killing of Alexander Hamilton in their duel, and who was a fugitive from the law in New York and New Jersey, was that he remained in the office of vice president and continued to preside over the Senate through Jefferson's first term.

Jefferson was incensed with John Adams for what he (Jefferson) considered the last minute loading of the federal court system with Federalist justices, and he was determined to get rid of most of them. Republicans in the House of Representatives initiated impeachment proceedings against Justice Samuel Chase, who had a reputation for being strongly partisan (he actively supported Adams in the 1800 election) and was an advocate of the Alien and Sedition Acts.

As vice president, Aaron Burr presided over the Chase impeachment trial. Burr made it his "grand public finale," managing every detail. The present-day proceedings for impeachment date back to the Chase trial. When six Republicans joined with the Federalist Senators, Chase was acquitted.[2] After this trial Jefferson

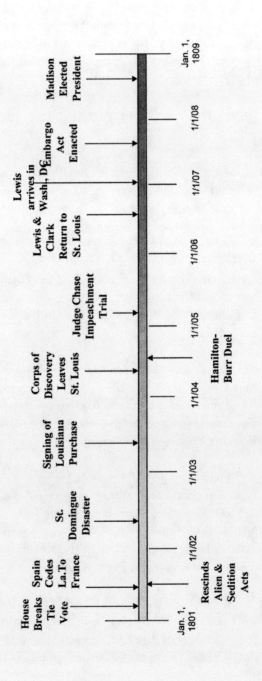

lost his enthusiasm for using the impeachment process to clear the courts of Federalist judges.

The Embargo Act of 1807 and Non-Intercourse Act of early 1809. After years of British and French interference with American shipping, Jefferson and Congress approved the Embargo Act of 1807. In effect, this act was intended to stop American shippers from either exporting or importing goods from any foreign country. The hope was that this would lead to international pressure on England and France to recognize America's free trade rights. The results were predictable—the economy of the United States, especially New England and New York, suffered tremendously.

One of Jefferson's last acts in office was to abolish the Embargo Act and replace it with the less restrictive Non-Intercourse Act, which forbade trade with *only* France and England. This act also authorized the president to end the boycotts when either country stopped violating America's neutrality rights and impressing seamen.[3] In effect, Jefferson passed a serious problem on to the Madison Administration.

Jefferson's religious practices. According to historian James Hutson, "The description of Jefferson's presidency as a rebuke to Christianity is a caricature that disregards conflicting evidence that has long been accessible." Writing to Dr. Benjamin Rush on April 21, 1803, Jefferson said, "I am a Christian in the only sense in which he (Jesus) wished any one to be."[4] In the mid 1790s, it is generally recognized that Jefferson's attitude toward Christianity changed. He became noticeably more religious, including immersing himself in biblical scholarship while he was in the White House.

Reflecting the old saying that actions speak louder than words, Jefferson "put his rejuvenated faith into practice in the most conspicuous form of public witness possible, regularly attending worship services where the delegates of the entire nation could see him—in the 'hall' of the House of Representatives…According to recollections of an early Washington insider, 'Jefferson during his whole administration, was a most regular attendant.'"[5] Worship services were nondenominational; ministers from a variety of sects preached there on Sunday mornings. "Notes taken by various congressmen about the texts preachers explicated and about the substance of their sermons make it clear that, during Jefferson's administration, the president and his fellow worshipers received a steady diet of high octane, New Testament Christianity."[6]

An interesting sidelight to worship services in the Congressional halls was that the Marine Band played. "Splendidly attired in their scarlet uniforms, the Marine musicians made a 'dazzling appearance' in the House on Sundays, as they tried to help the congregation by providing instrumental accompaniment to its psalm singing."[7] "The assistance of the Marine Band was a modest contribution to religion in the capital compared to Jefferson's decision to let executive branch buildings, the War Office and the Treasury, be used for church services."[8] The Episcopalians and Presbyterians were the most frequent users.

Hutson concluded that under Jefferson the government (or at least government buildings) became the church. This is contrary to perceptions about Jefferson's religious policies, which picture him as championing the separation of church and state.[9]

The "Wall of Separation" between church and state. In a letter to the Danbury (Connecticut) Baptists on January 1, 1802, Jefferson wrote that there "should be a wall of separation between Church and State." Two days later, Jefferson attended his first church service at the House. Hutson explained the seeming contradiction this way: "The Danbury letter and Jefferson's commencement of attendance at congressional church services fit together like hand and glove. They must be understood as being bracketed together as part of a carefully balanced strategy of words and action to convey his policy on church and state to his fellow citizens…By attending church services in Congress, Jefferson intended to send to the nation the strongest symbol possible that he was a friend of religion, hoping thereby to retain the political support of pious New England republicans who might be misled by the uncompromising sound of the 'wall of separation' metaphor in his letter to their Danbury brethren…"[10]

By way of further explanation of Jefferson's policy, Hutson said, "In his view, the government could not be a party to any attempt to impose upon the country a uniform religious exercise or observance; it could, on the other hand, support, as being in the public interest, voluntary, non-discriminatory religious activity, including church services, by putting at its disposal public property, public facilities and public personnel, including the president himself."[11]

Doing away with public financial assistance to selected churches or denominations. While he was governor of Virginia late in the Revolutionary War, Jefferson drafted a bill promoting religious liberty—the Statute for Religious Liberty—which became state law in 1786. This is one of three accomplishments etched on his grave marker (along with being the author of the Declaration of Independence and founder of the University of Virginia). The Statute for Religious Liberty would "...establish religious liberty and disestablish the Anglican Church. It would outlaw religious taxes and assessments."[12]

The Worldwide Setting for the Louisiana Purchase

In 1762, France turned New Orleans and the ill-defined Louisiana territory over to Spain as part of the Treaty of Paris ending the Seven-Years' War (known in America as the French & Indian War). The French thought of this large piece of land as a "huge white elephant."[13] The Spanish did not have a firm idea of what to do with this territory, but they realized that by controlling traffic up and down the Mississippi River, they could dominate the region, and gain leverage over the United States.

Spain closes shipping on the Mississippi River. In 1794 the Spanish announced they were closing the river and would not allow the storage and transfer of agricultural produce and goods in New Orleans. This was an obvious political ploy; Spain was not interested in seeing American expansion west where it might endanger their gold and silver mining interests in Mexico. In other words, they viewed Texas and Louisiana as a buffer zone. However, Thomas Pinckney was responsible for negotiating a treaty giving American ships the right to navigate the Mississippi for three years with the possibility of an extension. The Louisiana crisis appeared to be over.

Spain transfers ownership of Louisiana back to France. Also in 1794, Napoleon Bonaparte began developing his reputation as an artillery officer, and was soon in command of the French Army of Italy, which over the next four years, gained control of much of Europe. By the time Jefferson became president in 1801, he had reversed his favorable opinion of the French Revolution and was concerned over possible French aggression in North America.

In March 1801 reliable evidence came to Madison (Jefferson's secretary of state) that Spain planned to cede Louisiana and the Floridas back to France. In

September, Madison instructed Robert Livingston, the country's ambassador to France, to begin discussions about the seriousness of American concerns over French ownership of New Orleans. After confirming that France had in fact regained ownership of Louisiana, Jefferson wrote Livingston spelling out his views: "There is on the globe one single spot, the possessor of which is our natural and habitual enemy. It is New Orleans, through which the produce of three-eighths of our territory must pass to market, and from its fertility it will ere long yield more than half of our whole produce and contain more than half of our inhabitants. France, placing herself in that door, assumes to us the attitude of defiance."[14]

Napoleon's invasion of St. Domingue and plans for New Orleans. St. Domingue (Haiti) and the Louisiana Purchase were intimately tied. France had owned St. Domingue since 1697, "and its productivity had made it a crown jewel among France's colonial possessions...France's misadventures in St. Domingue would change American history and help to save the heart of the continent for the United States."[15]

In the years following the French Revolution, there were several slave revolts in St. Domingue, and an abortive effort by the British to take over the island (13,000 British soldiers died in the attempt). In 1801 Napoleon's brother-in-law, General Charles Leclerc, and 34,000 troops sailed to St. Domingue with the intention of going on to New Orleans after they had pacified the island. However, most of the French army were wiped out by yellow fever and fewer than 2,000 of the men were able to return to France. This misadventure was the end of French plans to occupy New Orleans. In an effort to recoup some of their losses, Napoleon and his advisors made the decision to sell Louisiana to the United States.

The Louisiana Purchase

The fact that the United States was able to purchase 875,000 square miles, then called Louisiana, doubling the size of the country, for $15 million ($17 a square mile or three cents an acre), represented the culmination of an amazing series of events. Jefferson, James Monroe, James Madison and Robert Livingston facilitated the purchase, but it would not have happened without Napoleon Bonaparte's problems, ambitions and financial needs and the Adams administration's avoidance of war with France.

During the Revolutionary War and when he was ambassador to France, Jefferson began to hear reports that the North American continent stretched 3,000 miles west to a large ocean. He and others frequently speculated about what lay beyond the Mississippi River. Jefferson was also concerned that the British, French and Spanish knew more about this vast territory than was known by the American government. He suspected that this was one reason the British held on to their forts in the Great Lakes area. The idea that these European powers might some day block American expansion to the west concerned Jefferson.

Following the war for independence, large numbers of Americans moved to the territories west of the Appalachian Mountains. "A ruling called the Northwest Ordinance of 1787 promised self-government to any new territory that had a population of at least five thousand, and full-fledged statehood would come when a population of sixty thousand was reached. With these lures, the speed of growth in the western areas was astonishing; Virginia's Kentucky County already had 140,000 residents."[16]

Livingston senses the possibility of a purchase. Robert Livingston, ambassador to France, a former governor of New York and one of the five members of the committee responsible for drafting the Declaration of Independence, had already had a distinguished career. Although his French was barely adequate, he had been in Paris long enough to sense that Napoleon Bonaparte was short on cash and that a deal for Louisiana (which he thought of as New Orleans) might be possible; he was excited by the prospect. However, Secretary of State Madison did not trust Livingston. Madison and Jefferson thought he was windy and dim-witted. Livingston was also frustrated because his letters to Madison requesting guidance on the amount he would be authorized to offer for New Orleans and Florida went unanswered.

Of Napoleon's two key advisors, Charles Maurice de Talleyrand was not in favor of disposing of Louisiana, but Francois Barbe-Marbois (treasury minister) liked the idea. Marbois had spent several years in America, spoke reasonably good English and had an American wife. He had traveled across the Atlantic with John Adams and his son, John Quincy Adams, and was friends with both. Of his two

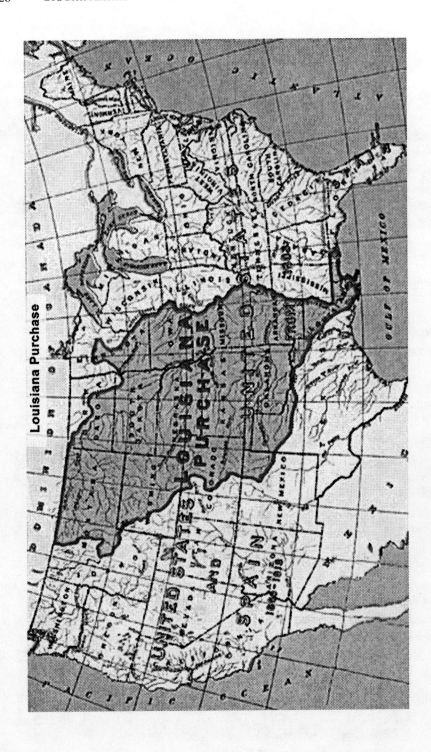

advisors, Napoleon leaned more toward Marbois' view on the advantages of selling Louisiana and the Floridas.

To make matters even more confusing, Louis Andre Pinchon, who was in charge of the French legation in Washington, was close to both Talleyrand and Napoleon. Pinchon picked up and passed on information from Madison and Jefferson, much of which was deliberate disinformation to confuse the French about America's intentions should France occupy New Orleans.

Port of New Orleans closed. For unexplained reasons, Juan Ventura Morales, the Spanish official in charge of New Orleans (the French owned the city but they had not taken possession) closed the port to American shipping in November 1802. Although the Spanish denied having ordered the closure, the port remained closed for several months. American farmers and merchants who relied on the Mississippi River were furious, and there were calls in Congress to create an army of 50,000 to take New Orleans by force. Napoleon, Talleyrand and Marbois were soon aware of the uproar, and this stimulated their desire to sell Louisiana while it still had value. In Washington, Pinchon was briefed on likely American action, and even took the unusual step of ordering Morales to open the port; Morales refused.

Monroe's role in the Louisiana Purchase. James Monroe had been ambassador to France during the Washington administration, but his pro-French comments proved embarrassing to United States' relations with England, and he was recalled. However, Monroe was trusted by Jefferson and Madison, and he was looked upon favorably by American westerners, those most impacted by decisions affecting the Mississippi River. In a letter to Livingston, Jefferson said that he was dispatching Monroe, "who will be the bearer of the instructions under which you are jointly to negotiate."[17] Although Livingston was upset, he was relieved to learn that he would not be recalled at a time when he had an opportunity to be part of what he sensed would be a historic transaction.

Napoleon's decision. On April 11, 1803, Napoleon told Marbois, "I renounce Louisiana. It is not only New Orleans that I mean to cede; it is the whole colony, reserving none of it." In discussing the selling price, Napoleon first said 100 million francs (a little less than $20 million), plus an American assumption of war claims. "Marbois told him that was more than the Americans could possibly raise, whereupon Napoleon said, 'Make it fifty million ($9.3 million) then but nothing less. I must get real money for the war with England.'" Talleyrand, hearing about the conversation later, said, "That was the fastest decline in property values in the history of the world."[18]

A few days before Monroe arrived, Talleyrand talked to Livingston about the United States purchasing all of Louisiana, not just New Orleans. The proposal had never occurred to Livingston and he had no idea how to respond. At the same time, he understood the significance of the offer.

The issues and negotiations. When Monroe arrived and Livingston told him that the French were interested in selling all of Louisiana, Monroe was puzzled; this scenario was not part of his instructions from Jefferson. The two American envoys were on their own in making a momentous decision.

Before Monroe could receive diplomatic credentials, Marbois approached Livingston with an offer to sell Louisiana for 100 million francs. Livingston said that was too much, and Marbois asked him to think it over and get back quickly with a counter offer. Livingston found Marbois' offer to be obscure because no one knew the boundaries of Louisiana, and he was unsure about whether the Floridas were included.

Although Congress had authorized only $2 million, Jefferson stuck his neck out and told Monroe (before he left for France) that he could go as high as $9 million (about 50 million francs) for New Orleans and the Floridas.

An additional factor that complicated the negotiations was that France did not have full authorization to make the sale to the United States. In acquiring the property from Spain in 1801, Napoleon had agreed that if France ever sold it, Spain would have the opportunity to repurchase Louisiana (a first right of refusal). The uncertainties created by these conditions also impacted Monroe's deliberations. "A logical price evaluation, therefore, was far from being the sole issue. The decision involved the whole philosophy of what kind of nation Americans wanted. If he made it virtually alone, Monroe had no way to know what he might be condemning his great friend in the president's house to—impeachment, perhaps? Would Jefferson want him to use the extraordinary power he had been granted for such a different purpose as doubling the size of the country?"[19] Monroe finally resolved to do what he thought was right for the United States, and not try to figure out what Jefferson would do. After he made this decision, he and Livingston were more comfortable in making a counter offer for all of Louisiana.

The deal. On April 15, 1803, the Americans offered 20 million francs plus 20 million more to relieve France of the claims for seizure of American ships, crews and cargoes, a total of 40 million francs (less than $8 million). Marbois responded that the offer was so low he would not even take it to Napoleon.

Two weeks later Marbois returned with a contract he thought that Napoleon would sign. It called for 80 million francs ($15 million, or seven times the amount Congress had authorized). Monroe and Livingston accepted this offer, and the deal was signed on May 2, 1803.

Congressional approval and the issue of its constitutionality. Monroe and Livingston sent Jefferson and Madison a detailed letter explaining the purchase. Upon receiving the letter, Jefferson was elated. When word of the purchase became public, most Americans, especially those living in the west, were ecstatic, primarily because they thought that it guaranteed access to the Mississippi River and New Orleans.

Jefferson's request of Congress to approve the treaty for the purchase of Louisiana stirred considerable debate. Of course, the westerners were firmly in favor and the middle colonies were skeptical or opposed. One point of controversy was the cost. Another issue was whether the purchase was constitutional.

The Senate ratified the treaty on October 19, 1803, and five days later the House agreed by a vote of 59-57 to meet the terms on the treaty.[20] The French transferred the territory to the United States on December 20, 1803.

The Lewis & Clark Expedition

Eighteen months prior to the purchase of Louisiana, Jefferson and his 28-year old aide, Captain Meriwether Lewis, had begun discussing an expedition to explore the west. Jefferson and Lewis were at Monticello reading a just-arrived book by Alexander Mackenzie, *Voyages from Montreal on the River St. Lawrence, Through the Continent of North America, to the Frozen and Pacific Ocean* (London, 1801). Although Mackenzie had failed to find a practical route for the fur trade, what stood out to Jefferson and Lewis was that he had made it across the continent.[21]

Jefferson and Lewis made the decision—that day—that Lewis would lead an expedition to explore the west.

There had been explorations up the Missouri River as far as present-day Mandan (near Bismarck) by white men and a few sketchy maps were available. In 1792, Captain Robert Gray, an American, had sailed into an estuary he called the Columbia River, named after his ship, and fixed its position. Other than these facts, Jefferson and Lewis knew little about what lay between Mandan and the mouth of the Columbia River. Jefferson had hoped to find an easy water passage across the country but was unaware of the Rocky Mountains and the immense barrier they represented. (Jefferson had interpreted Mackenzie's report as indicating that the mountain barrier across the continent was only 700 feet high!)

How is this for a concise mission statement? "The objective of your mission is to explore the Missouri River to the Pacific Ocean." Thomas Jefferson, July 4, 1803.[22]

Planning and preparation. As an aide to Jefferson, Lewis (who had only five years of formal schooling) received a hurried education in botany, zoology, ethnology, and astronomy. Jefferson realized he did not have the time to teach Lewis all he needed to know for the expedition and had Lewis spend the spring of 1803 in Philadelphia with several of his scientific friends who would provide him with "graduate training." In addition to medical training from Dr. Benjamin Rush, and the purchase of a supply of pills, Lewis received instruction in preserving animal and plant specimens, fossils, and how to make celestial observations by using various instruments, such as a chronometer (at $250, his most expensive purchase).

Lewis initially estimated that 10-12 men would be required for the expedition. He thought a larger number would stir up the Indians. His initial estimate of the cost ($2,500) included gifts to Indians. Being a strict constitutionalist, Jefferson puzzled over how to present the request to Congress; he finally decided to call it a scientific exploration designed to promote commerce. (Jefferson also provided Lewis with a letter guaranteeing an open-ended line of credit on the Treasury of the United States.)

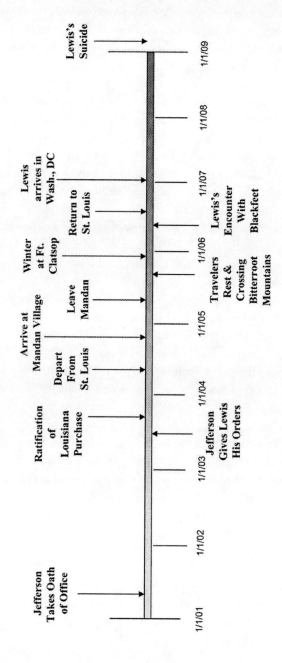

Lewis and Jefferson worked on detailed lists of equipment and supplies, and Lewis began assembling these materials in early 1803. In terms of how well Lewis anticipated the needs of the expedition, the Corps ran out of whiskey, salt, tobacco and beads. However, they had enough powder and lead to repeat the voyage. They also took along twice as much paper and ink as they used.

A few years earlier, Lewis had served in the army under William Clark, who was four years older, and they had developed a mutual liking and respect. Clark was an expert outdoorsman, skilled in surveying and a better waterman than Lewis. He also had command experience. In June 1803, Lewis and Jefferson agreed that Clark would be co-commander (something that was unheard of at the time). Lewis agreed that he would travel down the Ohio River and pick up Clark near present-day Louisville, Ky. For his part, Clark was responsible for selecting the men who would make up the Corps of Discovery. They both agreed that they wanted young, unmarried, tough frontiersmen with special skills, such as blacksmiths, carpenters, hunters and trackers, and boatmen.

Phase I—from Pittsburgh to St. Louis. Lewis had ordered a keelboat built in Pittsburgh, but when he arrived it was not ready. The keelboat, which measured 55 feet in length and eight feet in width, with a shallow draft, was completed on the last day of August, 2003. Based on a model in the visitor center on the banks of the Missouri River at Chamberlain, S.D., the keelboat was about the same size as the back of a semi-truck trailer and carried about the same cargo (12 tons).

On October 14 Lewis and his small crew met Clark at his home in Clarksville in Indiana Territory. Over the next two weeks, they began recruiting their men from hundreds of volunteers. Only two of the men who had traveled with Lewis from Pittsburgh were selected for the final expeditionary force. In late November, the expedition arrived at Wood River, upstream from St. Louis where they spent the winter. The effort required to move the keelboat against the current convinced the co-commanders that they needed more men; they added a dozen from an army post south of St. Louis.

Over the winter, they acquired two canoes, or pirogues as the captains called them, one requiring a five-man crew and the other eight men. Clark, who had experience in fighting Indians, also bought a small cannon and mounted it on a swivel on the keelboat.

The final party included 25 men plus another group of five would go as far as Mandan and then sail the keelboat back to St. Louis, carrying messages and specimens. In addition to the two captains, others making up the permanent party included Clark's slave York; George Drouillard, a skilled hunter, woodsman, trapper and scout; and Lewis's dog, Seaman.

Launching the trip. Clark and the Corps of Discovery left St. Louis on May 14, 1804. Lewis was delayed making arrangements to send an Osage chief to Washington to meet Jefferson; he joined the Corps at the village of St. Charles a week later. They added two French and Indian half-breeds, Pierre Cruzzatte and Francis Labiche, as privates and attached them to the permanent party.

The current of the Missouri River ran about five miles per hour, and faster in some places. The average daily distance the Corps made against the current was 12 miles. The amount of work to make this distance required tremendous energy; each man typically consumed 10 pounds of meat per day. Fortunately, the deer, buffalo and elk hunting was excellent for much of the trip.

By August 20, about three months after leaving St. Charles, the Corps had traveled as far as present-day Sioux City, Iowa. Sergeant Charles Floyd, who had been seriously ill, died and was buried with full military honors just south of downtown Sioux City on the east side of the river. Sergeant Floyd was the only member of the Corps of Discovery who died on the trip.

The Teton Sioux, near present-day Pierre, S.D., were known to be warlike, and they were the only tribe Jefferson had specifically warned Lewis about. Since the Tetons controlled the river, Jefferson wanted Lewis to make peace with this tribe. The Corps met its first Teton Sioux on September 23, and after several close calls—and threats by both Captains Lewis and Clark, and the Indian chiefs—the Corps was able to break away and resume its trip north.

Stephen Ambrose believed the Corps was fortunate to escape the Teton Sioux: "The captains had been exceedingly lucky. Had a firefight broken out, they and their men would almost certainly have been wiped out. They would have taken a goodly number of Sioux with them, thus making the most powerful tribe on the Missouri River the implacable enemy of the United States. It would have been years, perhaps decades, before the United States would become strong enough to

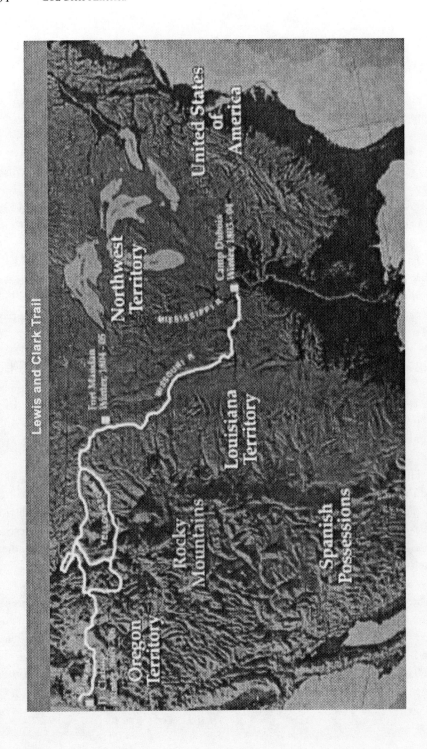

send trading parties up the river against the active opposition of the Sioux. The entire timetable of westward expansion would have been slowed."[23]

On October 8, the keelboat passed the home of 2,000 Arikara Indians. Two decades earlier, before an outbreak of smallpox, the tribe had numbered 20,000. Lewis, who went on shore to meet the chief, received a warm welcome.

First winter in Fort Mandan. On October 24, according to plan, the Corps arrived at the Mandan villages and proceeded to set up winter quarters. The Mandans, and their relatives the Hidatsa, lived in five villages of about 1,000 each. The Hidasta hunted all the way to the Rocky Mountains and were a valuable source of information on the terrain to the west.

A few days after their arrival, the captains were approached by Toussaint Charbonneau, a French Canadian who was living among the Hidasta as a trader. Charbonneau owned two squaws who had been captured by a Hidasta war party. He won the two women on a bet with their captors. Charbonneau was signed up at once and told he could pick one of his wives to accompany the Corps; he chose Sacagawea, who was 15 years old and pregnant. With the assistance of Captain Lewis, Jeane Baptiste Charbonneau was born on February 11, 1805.

Ambrose sums up the winter in Mandan this way: "Had the Mandan not been there, or had they had no corn to spare, or had they been hostile, the expedition would not have survived the winter."[24]

On April 6, several of the men and the keelboat headed back to St. Louis. They took along the lengthy notes of Lewis and Clark, 108 botanical specimens (including seeds), pressed plants, minerals, skeletons of several animals and four live magpies, a prairie dog and prairie grouse hen. Clark also included a map based on what he had observed and what had been learned from talking with the Hidasta. This shipment eventually made it to Jefferson, who proudly shared the materials with his scientific friends in Philadelphia; some of the items remain on display at Monticello.

From North Dakota to Idaho. Leaving Fort Mandan, the Corps had the two pirogues plus six small, heavily laden canoes. Other than having to make a difficult decision about which branch of the river to follow, and surviving several attacks by grizzly bears, the first part of the trip was relatively uneventful. (In the early 1800s, grizzly bears were indigenous to the plains and much feared by the Indians.)

In June, the Corps came to the Great Falls of the Missouri, a series of five falls ranging from 14 to 26 feet, and extending more than 12 miles. At this same time, Sacagawea became ill and almost died; Lewis was able to help her regain her health, an event of tremendous importance to the future of the expedition.

The portage of their canoes past the falls was started on June 22 and finished two weeks later, on July 3. Lewis was concerned; three months had elapsed since leaving Mandan, and the Corps still needed to cross the mountains and make it to the Columbia River before winter.

On July 22, Sacagawea recognized a section of river where she had lived as a young girl. She knew that what is now known as Three Forks (a few miles west of present-day Bozeman) was not far ahead. Lewis and Clark named the rivers the Gallatin, Madison and Jefferson, and proceeded up the Jefferson.

Lemhi Pass and the Shoshone Indians. The Jefferson River branched off to what was called the Beaverhead (a mountain that Sacagawea also recognized); as the river narrowed, the current became faster. The Corps, under the direction of Clark, labored up this river for two weeks, while Lewis went ahead looking for the Shoshone. He and three others hiked up what is today known as Lemhi Pass (on the border of Montana and Idaho) and crossed the Continental Divide. On August 13, Lewis saw three Indians digging roots—an old woman, a teenage girl and a child. "Through Drouillard's sign language, Lewis persuaded the woman to lead the white men to the Shoshone village," where they were met by a party of 60 warriors."[25]

The Shoshone were friendly, and Lewis was able to smoke a peace pipe with the chief, Cameahwait. Lewis noted that there were 400 horses around the village. Cameahwait said he had never crossed the mountains to the west, but there was an old man who had information on the country between the Shoshone and Nez Perce Indians, who were camped in flat country west of the Rockies. Lewis was also told that the Nez Perce had a trail through the mountains they used to travel east to hunt buffalo.

Lewis then persuaded Cameahwait and a few warriors to backtrack over Lemhi Pass to meet Clark and the main body of the Corps, and help them transport their supplies over the pass in preparation for crossing the Bitterroot Mountains. In the midst of the excitement of meeting up with Clark, "...one of the Shoshone women recognized Sacagawea...The reunited teens hugged and cried and talked, all at once, in an outburst of emotion."[26] As they began to decide how to haul all their gear west, Sacagawea began to stare at Cameahwait—he was her brother! Another celebration took place.

Traveler's Rest and over the Bitterroot Mountains. Two weeks later, on September 1, the party and their 29 newly acquired horses headed north to pick up the Nez Perce trail across the mountains. By September 9, after crossing rugged mountainous country, they arrived at the junction of a stream (Lo Lo Creek) and the Bitterroot River, eight miles south of present-day Missoula. The Shoshone guide told them that this was where they would head due west along the creek and over the Bitterroot Mountains. The Corps spent two days at this site, now called Traveler's Rest, and then began the difficult climb.

Almost two weeks later, Clark, who was out in front of the main party, broke away from the mountains into flat country where he had a friendly meeting with the first of the Nez Perce. He purchased fish and roots and sent this food back to Lewis and the rest of the Corps. It had taken 11 days for the expedition to travel the 160 miles from Traveler's Rest. This was without question the most difficult part of the trip; they had essentially no food, and the mountains represented an almost impassable barrier.

Because of the sudden change in diet and overeating, almost every member of the Corps became sick. "For almost a week, the expedition resembled a hospital ward for the critically ill more than it did a platoon of fighting men." At this point of weakness, the Nez Perce seriously considered killing the whites, and taking their weapons and supplies. However, they were talked out of it by a squaw named Watkuweis, who had been captured by the Blackfeet some years earlier, taken to Canada, and sold to a white trader. After several years, she found her way home, and told the Nez Perce that the white man had treated her better than the Indians. She said, "These are the people who helped me. Do them no harm."[27] The plot died.

Using the Indian method—placing logs over a slow burning trench fire—Clark set to work making canoes. It took four days to complete four large canoes and a small one. The Nez Perce promised to take care of the Corps' horses until they came back the following spring; Clark had the horses branded. On October 6, with both Lewis and Clark sick, they put the canoes in the water, loaded them and shoved off. This was the first time during the trip that they were going downstream, and it seemed like they were flying. Four days later they made the Snake River near present-day Lewiston, Id. By October 16, they had reached the Columbia River and a month later they were close to the Pacific Ocean on the north side of the Columbia in an area occupied by the Chinook Indians.

The Corps was rescued again, this time by the Clatsop Indians who canoed across the Columbia and sold them salmon and roots. The Corps liked the Clatsop better than the Chinooks, who constantly stole from them. "The expedition could stay on the north side, among the Chinook, or go to the south side, where the Clatsop lived and where there were more elk..."[28] But, rather than making an arbitrary decision, the captains put it to a vote (including York and Sacagawea); the south side won.

The dreary winter at Fort Clatsop. Lewis had previously been south of the Columbia and had scouted a site on a bluff, near a spring, where large trees offered shelter and fuel (near present-day Astoria, Or.). Also, the site was a few miles from the ocean where salt, a product highly valued by the Corps, could be extracted from seawater. Work on winter quarters began on December 7, and the Corps moved into Fort Clatsop by Christmas. The remainder of the winter was boring, but the Corps did not go hungry; there was plenty of elk and salmon. However, it rained all but 12 of the 106 days they spent at Fort Clatsop, and the Corps suffered from fleas (they spent hours picking them out of their clothes), colds, sniffles and rheumatism.[29] By late March, the Corps was more than ready to leave Fort Clatsop to begin its 4,000-mile trip home.

The expedition had used up 95 percent of its supplies on the trip west, and had virtually nothing to trade for food and horses on the way back to St. Louis. However, the previous fall Clark had treated an old Nez Perce Indian who had a sore knee, and he had recovered. The captains found they could pay for their keep by providing medical care, including help with red and itching eyes, which the Indians paid for with dogs (considered good eating by the Corps) and edible roots.

In early May, the Nez Perce had bad news for the Corps: the Bitterroot Mountains were still covered with snow, and no passage was possible until early June. One of the problems was the lack of grass for the horses. As they moved closer to the mountains, the Corps recovered 21 of their horses, plus saddles and ammunition. On the afternoon of June 16, after starting the day in a glade where flowers were blooming, they found themselves in winter conditions with snow eight to 10 feet deep. However, on all but one night they were able to find south-facing campsites with fresh grass. On June 30, they reached a familiar spot, Traveler's Rest, on the eastern edge of the Bitterroot Mountains.

Splitting up at Traveler's Rest. After three days at Traveler's Rest, Lewis took nine men and 17 horses and headed east through Blackfeet country, past the Great Falls with the plan to rendezvous with Clark at the confluence of the Missouri and Yellowstone Rivers near the present-day Montana and North Dakota border. Clark took the remainder of the Corps south and east to retrace the original steps of the journey; he then divided his group, with one floating down the Missouri and the other traveling east to follow the Yellowstone River to the Missouri. This was a complex plan to be carried out over a distance of 1,000 miles.

By July 13, Clark reached Three Forks and found that the canoes they had cached the previous fall were in good condition. Clark then split his group; the 11 men under Sergeant Ordway retraced their steps down the Missouri past the Great Falls to meet Lewis, while he, along with 12 members of the Corps, including York and Sacagawea, traveled east by horseback through present-day Bozeman to the Yellowstone River at present-day Livingston. However, it was not until Clark and his group reached what is now Billings, about 100 miles east of Livingston, that they found cottonwood trees suitable for making canoes to carry them to the Missouri River.

On July 15, Lewis and his group reached their cached supplies near the Great Falls. Then, Lewis and a party of three headed north through an area occupied by the Blackfeet Indians; the remainder of his group met Sergeant Ordway, who had left Clark and traveled down the Missouri River. After a run-in with several Indian boys who stole some of their horses and tried to steal their rifles (one was killed and another seriously wounded), Lewis and his small party fled south toward the Missouri River. In the meantime, the remainder of Lewis's party and Sergeant Ordway's group were waiting at the confluence of the Marias and Missouri rivers. The combined group then floated down the Missouri to meet Clark. In effect, the Corps of Discovery had split into four different groups and on August 12, rejoined at the confluence of the Yellowstone and Missouri Rivers. In itself, this was an amazing feat.

By August 17, the expedition had reached the Mandan villages, where Charbonneau, Sacagawea and Private John Colter left the Corps. Colter headed back to the mountains and became the first white man to visit what is now Yellowstone National Park. The remainder of the Corps reached St. Louis on September 23 where they received a hearty welcome from all 1,000 residents.

The tragedy of Meriwether Lewis. Lewis sent a detailed report to Jefferson, who received it with great joy. Lewis and Clark, along with a delegation of Indians, York, two sergeants and two privates, then headed east. Clark separated from Lewis to visit friends and relatives, and Lewis continued to Washington to meet with Jefferson. Lewis was the guest of honor at the White House on New Year's Day, 1807.

By today's standards, Meriwether Lewis had it made; he was a celebrity. He had a lucrative book contract for his journals and memoirs, a president who was extremely proud of him and interested in what he had learned, and a grateful country. However, Lewis had a serious mental illness (probably manic depression), which was aggravated by heavy drinking. Consequently, he did not produce a single word of the manuscript he had promised. He spent many months in deep depression that eventually ended in his suicide on the Natchez Trace in southern Tennessee three years after his return. He was 35.

Clark, on the other hand, had a long and distinguished career. He married and had 10 children, and served as Superintendent of Indian Affairs for 30 years. In addition, from 1813 to 1821, he was governor of the new Missouri Territory. Clark died at the age of 69.

Lewis & Clark Expedition—evidence of divine providence. After three years, the Corps of Discovery had been given up for lost by most Americans. Looking at this journey in its totality, and recognizing the dangers (e.g., hostile Indians, starvation, exposure to the weather, disease), it is a miracle that it was successful, with only the loss of Sergeant Floyd. Stephen Ambrose's book title, *Undaunted Courage*, is apt. There were several miracles along the way:

- Avoiding a conflict with the Teton Sioux near present-day Pierre, S.D. As Ambrose said, the entire Corps of Discovery could have easily been overpowered and killed.
- Ambrose believed that had the Mandan not been friendly and helpful, the Corps would not have survived the winter of 1804-1805.
- Having Sacagawea join the group in Mandan was a miracle. She proved to be an invaluable guide and interpreter.
- When the Corps met up with the Shoshone Indians near the border of Montana and Idaho, relationships were strengthened when the Shoshone chief met his sister, Sacagawea. Although the Shoshone were destitute, they provided food, a guide and horses for the difficult trip across the Bitterroot Mountains.
- When camped with the Nez Perce, and with nearly all of Corps sick from eating too much salmon after almost starving crossing the Bitterroot Mountains, there was a plot to kill them and take their supplies. However, an Indian woman, Watkuweis, who had been captured and spent several years in Canada with a white man, convinced the Nez Perce leaders not to harm the white men.
- Avoiding the collapse of riverbanks, falling trees and submerged logs while traveling close to the shore of the Missouri was miraculous. Lewis wrote, "we have had many hairbreadth escapes from them but Providence seems to have ordered it that we have as yet sustained no loss in consequence of them."[30]

If any one of these examples of divine favor had not occurred, the expedition could have failed. When we assign probabilities to each individual occurrence, we conclude that without these miracles, the chances of successful completion of the expedition were less than one percent.

Recap of the Jefferson Administration

Along with the Louisiana Purchase and the Lewis and Clark Expedition, Jefferson's support of freedom of religion was one of his greatest legacies as president. While president, he actively participated in worship services at the capital, thus setting an example for the rest of the country.

In terms of divine intervention, what if General Leclerc and his army had not been wiped out by yellow fever in St. Domingue, and had proceeded to New Orleans? If that had happened, it is unlikely that Louisiana would have been available, and perhaps even worse, that France would have had an even larger permanent settlement—and in a strategic location on the Mississippi River. Farmers in Ohio, Tennessee, Kentucky and what was then the western United States would have had no economical way to get their produce to market and the western expansion of the country would have been stymied. This would have undoubtedly led to armed conflict.

Is this an example of divine providence? The French would certainly not look at it that way. However, America benefited from Napoleon's missteps and the misfortune of Leclerc's army. The size of the country doubled with the stroke of a pen and a $15 million payment, and enormous new lands were opened for settlement. It is also likely that war with France was avoided.

Alexander Hamilton, no friend of Jefferson, wrote an unsigned editorial in the *New York Evening Post* published July 5, 1803, where he admitted that, "The purchase has been made during the period of Mr. Jefferson's presidency, and will, doubtless, give éclat to his administration. Every man, however, possessed of the least candour and reflection will readily acknowledge that the acquisition has been solely owing to a fortuitous concurrence of unforeseen and unexpected circumstances, and not to any wise or vigorous measure on the part of the American government."[31] Were the "fortuitous" events that made Louisiana available luck or divine providence? We believe it was the latter.

If France had occupied New Orleans and what is now the central part of the United States, it is inconceivable that peace would have prevailed in America, at least for many generations. The probability of war with France would have been at least 75 percent. In the event of war, it is far from certain that the United States would have prevailed.

In our view, God continued to pour out His blessings on the United States during the eight years of the Jefferson administration. The country avoided war with both England and France, and doubled in size. The port of New Orleans was opened for trade, and Jefferson took the initiative in exploring the west. On the negative side, the international threat posed by Napoleon reached its peak during the Madison administration.

Chapter 13

Mr. Madison's War

> *Blest with vict'ry and peace, may the Heav'n–rescued land, Praise the Pow'r that made and preserved us a nation.*
>
> —Fourth stanza, *Star Spangled Banner*

Here is the way one historian described the difficult situation facing James Madison as he took over as president: "Madison's problem was the same one every president since George Washington had faced. Britain and France were each more powerful than the United States, and each considered its war with the other more important than good relations with America. If strangling France required trampling on America's rights, Britain would trample away. If repelling Britain necessitated treating American vessels as British, France would do so. America's European troubles might not end when the European war ended, but they certainly wouldn't end before that."[1.]

The War of 1812—in New England referred to derisively as "Mr. Madison's War"—can be understood within the context of the almost continuous conflict between England and France dating back to the War of Spanish Succession and continuing through the French Revolution and the Napoleonic era. The irritations of these conflicts for the United States were not minor; in the five years preceding the outbreak of the war, France captured 558 American ships and the British captured 389.[2] Given these large numbers, and the insult to the prestige and honor of the United States, some argued that the country should have declared war on both of these European powers.

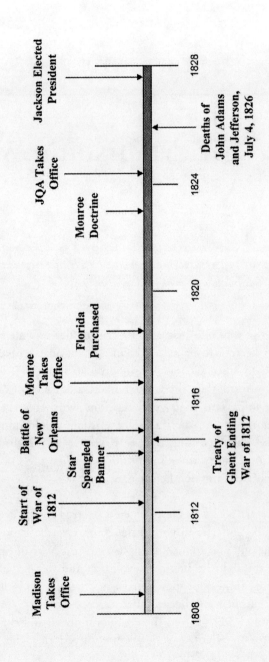

Timeline of Presidencies of Madison, Monroe and John Quincy Adams

War of 1812

Of all America's major military conflicts dating back to King Phillip's War in 1675-76 (an attack by Indians on residents of Massachusetts), the War of 1812 is perhaps the most complex in terms of understanding what precipitated the fighting, where it happened, and who won. Factors that differentiated the War of 1812 include:

- In the earlier Seven-Years' War, the French and Indians were aligned against the British and colonists; in the War of 1812, the Indians usually—but not always—fought on the side of the British.
- Leaders and residents of the western and southern states pushed the confrontation; the New England states were generally opposed to the war and provided little or no support.
- The fighting ranged on a wide front, including the Great Lakes region (e.g., what is now Detroit, Niagara Falls, Buffalo, and Toronto), Baltimore and Washington, D.C., upstate New York and western Vermont, New Orleans and on the Atlantic Ocean, often hundreds of miles at sea. It also included the Indian wars on America's western and southern frontier.
- Although some elements of American society and government wanted to use the war as an excuse to take over Canada, many of the militia refused to cross the border and fight inside Canadian provinces.

In the years following the Revolutionary War, the United States was unprepared to fight another war, a fact recognized by presidents Washington, Adams and Jefferson. In one of his first foreign policy decisions as president, Washington took the position that the United States should not become involved in European conflicts; it was a policy of neutrality, and in retrospect, a wise one. The Jay Treaty with England during Washington's tenure as president, and the treaty with France in the last days of the administration of John Adams, delayed conflicts with these two European superpowers. At the time, both of these treaties were unpopular with large segments of the population. Yet, in retrospect, they played vitally important roles in delaying what would become an almost inevitable conflict with either France or England. Many would credit these treaties to divine providence.

The western Indian wars. A series of intense conflicts with Indians were intertwined with the War of 1812. Many Americans living in the western frontier thought that the British were inciting Native Americans to attack settlers in Tennessee, Kentucky, Ohio and other border areas. There were rumors, some true, that the British were supplying weapons leading to the increasingly bloody raids on white farmers and settlers.

The Shawnee warrior Tecumseh and his brother were the main instigators of the Indian revolts that occurred prior to and during the War of 1812. Tecumseh's brother Tenskwatawa, "...the strangely charismatic figure called the Prophet," had a vision of America without white men, "...where Indians lived as they had lived since before the eldest elders could recall, at peace with nature and enjoying its bounty."[3] Tecumseh was an impressive leader. "While the Prophet spoke of a spiritual union of Indians against whites, Tecumseh traveled from village to village and nation to nation, forging a military alliance of Indians against whites."[4]

In August 1811, Tecumseh confronted William Henry Harrison, long-time Governor of Indiana Territory, and told him he would destroy village chiefs who sold their land to Americans. Harrison, in turn, warned Tecumseh about depending on the British for weapons and military support. Harrison subsequently learned that Tecumseh had approached the British in Canada about guns and supplies. He was concerned that the advantage enjoyed by the Americans—superior military technology—might be negated.

In the autumn of 1811, while Tecumseh was in the south attempting to organize resistance to the whites, Harrison launched a pre-emptive strike against the Indians at Prophetstown, a village at the mouth of the Tippecanoe and Wabash Rivers, where Tecumseh's brother had gathered a large band of warriors. In the subsequent battle, Harrison and nearly 1,300 militia lost 179 killed and wounded; the Indians lost considerably fewer. However, since the Indians abandoned the field, Harrison controlled Prophetstown, which he destroyed, and declared a victory. The Prophet escaped to Canada, but he lost his credibility with the Indians.

Harrison's victory, which was instrumental in getting him elected to the presidency ("Tippecanoe and Tyler too") was costly in that it cemented the relationship between the British and Native Americans. Furthermore, when Tecumseh returned north he led a series of devastating raids on American settlements in Indiana and Michigan.[5]

Tecumseh was also successful in encouraging aggressiveness in a group of Creek warriors, the Red Sticks, and their chief, William Weatherford. In 1813, Samuel Mims, his family and hundreds of settlers from nearby areas were huddled in Mim's Fort, a ramshackle affair north of Mobile, Ala. Mim's Fort was subsequently reinforced by a small number of troops from Louisiana. When the Red Sticks attacked the fort, "The soldiers and residents mounted what resistance they could. That attackers hesitated when five of their prophets, who had declared that the white men's bullets would split in two and pass around their bodies, fell dead from undivided rounds. But their numbers—at least a thousand—were overwhelming. The Red Sticks slaughtered every white person they could reach, and when some of the whites took refuge in the buildings of the fort, Weatherford's men set the buildings on fire and murdered them as they streamed out..."[6] There were 553 citizens and soldiers plus 453 women and children. Only 13 escaped.

As a result of the slaughter at Mim's Fort, President Madison and Tennessee Governor Blount called out the Tennessee militia under General Andrew Jackson to hunt down Chief Weatherford and his braves. Jackson ordered his 2,000 troops on a forced march to catch and punish the Red Sticks; they met at a place called Talladega. In the subsequent battle, Jackson's troops killed at least 300 Red Sticks compared with the loss of 17 of their own men.

In October 1813 Harrison and his troops finally met the British and Tecumseh, who had returned from the south, in a battle on the north bank of the Thames River near Lake Erie. The British, under General Henry Proctor, pulled back after initial fighting, but Tecumseh and his braves stood and fought. Tecumseh and 33 braves were killed. As a result of the loss of their leader, the Indians' hopes of rolling back the white Americans died. "Indian resistance would continue, but the unity he (Tecumseh) preached and imperfectly accomplished couldn't survive without its apostle and ablest practitioner. Neither whites nor Indians had ever seen his like nor (sic) would see it again."[7]

Naval battles. The United States did not have much of a navy during the War of 1812, but the few available ships played an important role. Fortunately for the country, most of the British Navy was occupied with Napoleon. Therefore, engagements between the United States and British navies tended to be small scale, and more often than not, ended in a draw.

When one travels the Great Lakes area in both Canada and the United States, it is difficult to believe that in 1812 and 1813 this was the region where most of the combat on both land and water took place. Admiral Oliver H. Perry defeated the British fleet on Lake Erie on September 10, 1813. "The *Lawrence*, his flagship, was so badly damaged that he had himself towed to the *Niagara*, from which he continued the fight until the British squadron surrendered." He then sent the famous message, "We have met the enemy and they are ours."[8]

On August 19, 1813, the 44-gun *Constitution* encountered the *HMS Guirriere*, a 36-gun frigate near the entrance to the St. Lawrence River. As the two ships maneuvered, the *Guirriere* opened fire but the cannon balls bounced harmlessly off the hull of the *Constitution*. One crew member yelled, "'Hurrah, her sides are made of iron,' or words to that effect. No matter. A legend was born, and 'Old Ironsides' she became."[9]

At 25 yards, Captain Isaac Hull ordered the gun crews of the *Constitution* to rake the *Guirriere* with a combination of cannonballs and grape. After several volleys, the rigging of the two ships became entangled, and boarding orders were trumpeted. Then the foremast of the *Guirriere* crashed on its deck and the ship lost its ability to maneuver. The captain immediately surrendered the *Guirriere*, which was so badly damaged it could not be towed to port. In transferring the crew of the *Guirriere* to the *Constitution*, it was discovered that there were 10 impressed American seaman on board—"a graphic example of one of the war's causes."[10]

The *Constitution*'s victory had important political ramifications. Congress, which had been reluctant to appropriate funds for the navy, promptly increased the navy budget from $300,000 to $2.5 million to build four 74-gun ships of the line.

Two months later, in the Atlantic Ocean 600 miles south of the Azores, the 38-gun *HMS Macedonian* encountered the 54-gun *United States* under the command of Stephen Decatur. After a brief battle, in which the *Macedonian* lost 43 killed and 71 wounded (out of a crew of 428), the British ship surrendered. The *United States,* by comparison, lost only seven killed and five wounded.

In two decades of almost incessant naval warfare, the British had lost only one naval battle, and that was a single vessel to a larger French ship. "The British were not only unaccustomed to losing, they were scarcely aware of the possibility...What in the world, wondered the British Admiralty, was going on?"[11]

Burning the White House. Despite these losses, the British had almost complete control of the waters up and down the Atlantic Coast. With Napoleon in exile in Elba and the French navy no longer a threat, the British were free to conduct a series of hit-and-run raids. They were particularly anxious to inflict damage on the southern towns since they perceived (accurately) that the South was more supportive of the war. There were virtually no precautions made for the defense of Washington, D.C. Several government leaders, including Secretary of War John Armstrong, were ambivalent on the subject. "Why should the British attack Washington?" he asked.[12]

In August 1814, a combined British force of 20 ships, 3,400 troops and 700 marines under the command of Admiral George Cockburn sailed up the Chesapeake. By August 20, the British troops were ready to march into Washington thus embarrassing the government of the United States and providing retribution for the burning of the Canadian capital of York (now Toronto) earlier in the war. After a brief fight south of the city, British troops entered Washington and burned several buildings, including the Capitol, White House, Treasury Building, State and War Department Buildings, Navy Yard and the offices of the *National Intelligencer,* an anti-British newspaper.

A sudden thunderstorm came up that afternoon. "The skies darkened almost more so than the night before, and lightning darted from black clouds to the ground." One woman stepped out of her house and confronted Admiral Cockburn with these words: "This is a special interposition of Providence to drive our enemies from our city." The British left that night.[13]

Fighting in Baltimore and the Star Spangled Banner. Baltimore, the third largest American city with a population of 45,000, was the next British target. However, Baltimore was ready; 9,000 militia had been called up. "Whereas Washington ran, Baltimore dug."[14] Fort McHenry, just outside Baltimore's inner harbor, was the key to the defense of the city.

Admiral Cockburn landed 4,000 troops 14 miles east of Baltimore with orders to advance toward the city. A few miles from Baltimore, British General Robert Ross encountered a force of 3,000 militia under the command of Brigadier General John Stricker. In the fighting, Ross was killed; it became obvious to the British that taking Baltimore by land would be costly. Admiral Cockburn decided to bombard Fort McHenry and land troops in Baltimore, thus flanking the American troops.

On September 13 Admiral Cockburn assigned five ketches with mortars capable of hurling 200-pound shells up to 4,000 yards to bombard Fort McHenry. He added the rocket vessel HMS *Erebus* to take up station three miles from the fort. Larger British ships, hampered by their deeper drafts, waited further down the river.

A huge American flag, 30 feet by 42 feet, flew above Fort McHenry. Major George Armistead, commander of the fort, had 20 cannon with a range of 2,000 yards. It was simple arithmetic and all Armistead could do was wait out the attack, which commenced during the day and continued on through the night.

An American ship, the *Minden*, under a flag of truce, was anchored among the British vessels. A Georgetown lawyer, Francis Scott Key, and a Baltimore attorney, John Skinner, were attempting a prisoner exchange, and were present during the bombardment. "The contrails of the Congreve rockets from the *Erebus* glared red across the sky. The mortars, with their fuses timed to explode above the fort and rain shrapnel and destruction upon it, appeared as giant fireworks—bombs bursting in the night sky."[15]

Dr. Beanes, a released American prisoner, asked over and over, "Can you see the flag? Is the flag still there?...Finally, as the early light of dawn tinged the eastern sky, Key was able to answer in the affirmative...Key took out an envelope and scribbled a few lines. Two days later, back in an American Baltimore, Key elaborated on his verse."[16]

The next day, September 15, the British troops east of Baltimore pulled back and boarded their ships. Within a few days, the British fleet sailed out of the Chesapeake Bay; there would be no further military campaigns in the Baltimore area.

The peace treaty with England. The English were as eager as most Americans to end the conflict; the British public was tired of the sacrifices which some referred to as "the millstone of an American war." When approached to take command of British forces, Lord Wellington, later the hero of Waterloo, read the reports on the conflict, and declined. He commented, "...that if he went to Canada, it would be only to sign a peace which might as well be signed now." [17] In other words, he saw the war as a quagmire.

At the same time the British were burning Washington, D. C. and attacking Baltimore, a five-person United States peace commission was in Ghent, Belgium, negotiating an end to the war. John Quincy Adams' close relationship with Emperor Alexander of Russia was instrumental in getting the peace process moving. Much to the delight of President Madison, Emperor Alexander encouraged both sides to begin negotiations.[18]

President Madison instructed John Quincy Adams to leave Russia to join the American peace commission as its leader. Here is how Adams summed up his feelings after signing the peace accord in December 1814: "I cannot close the record of the day without a humble offering of gratitude to God for the conclusion to which it has pleased him to bring the negotiations for peace at this place."[19]

President Madison's proclamation following the completion of the Peace Treaty of Ghent read: "A day...to be observed by the people of the United States with religious solemnity as a day of thanksgiving and of devout acknowledgment to Almighty God for His great goodness manifested in restoring to them the blessing of peace...to the same Divine Author of Every Good and Perfect Gift we are indebted for all those privileges and advantages, religious as well as civil, which are so richly enjoyed in this favored land."[20]

The Battle of New Orleans. This famous battle was fought two weeks after the signing of the peace treaty, which is not surprising given the time it took for ships to cross the Atlantic, and for word to get from the East Coast to New Orleans. In visiting the battlefield, which lies along the Mississippi River a few miles down river from New Orleans, it is difficult to understand the British strategy; they marched right into fortified American positions and as a consequence, suffered severe casualties (as many as 2,000 killed or wounded). One important side effect of the War of 1812 was the creation of a new national hero—Andrew Jackson.

Jackson had defeated Indians in several prior battles, was in command at New Orleans, and was later instrumental in bringing Florida into the country.

Benefits of the War of 1812. The war ended, for the most part, the adversarial relationship with England. In a sense, it settled several loose ends of the peace treaty that had followed the Revolutionary War, including fishing rights off Newfoundland and Labrador, and the stationing of British troops in the Great Lakes region. Under the original treaty, these troops were supposed to be withdrawn, but they were not. The War of 1812 was the last armed conflict involving Canada. This settled most remaining northern border disputes and assured that Canada would be free to continue its special relationship with both England and the United States.

What was accomplished by this war? "After the War of 1812, there was no longer any doubt that the United States of America would become a force to be reckoned with in North America and in time throughout the world. The war had forged a nation." [21] In our view, this was an extraordinary blessing.

The Barbary Pirates—A Continuing Problem

Problems with the Barbary pirates off the Mediterranean Coast of North Africa attacking American shipping went back to the post-Revolutionary War period when John Jay was secretary for foreign affairs for the Confederation Congress. As the ambassador of Tripoli justified piracy to John Adams and Thomas Jefferson, then ambassadors to England and France: "It was written in their Koran, that all nations who should not have acknowledged their authority were sinners, that it was their right and duty to make war upon them wherever they could be found, and to make slaves of all they could take as prisoners, and that every (Moslem) who should be slain in battle was sure to go to paradise."[22] "The ambassador described with some pride, how, 'each sailor (would) take a dagger in each hand and another in his mouth, and leap on board, which so terrified their enemies that very few ever stood against them.'"[23]

In 1797, during the presidency of John Adams, the American Consul to Algiers, made an unauthorized entry into a treaty with Tripoli to the effect that the United States, "is not, in any sense founded on the Christian religion (an insertion intended to clarify that the American government was not like the Mohammedan, Buddhist, or Hindu countries, where the government controls the religious life of the people)." In 1805, Congress deleted this phrase from a new treaty with Tripoli.[24] The original treaty that included the insertion is often cited by those who argue that the United States does not have a Christian heritage.

Piracy in the Mediterranean grew during the chaos of the Napoleonic Wars and the War of 1812. In fact, when the United States missed its regular annual tribute payment in 1813, the pirates attacked American shipping and took captives. However, two years following the end of the War of 1812, the United States sent a squadron under the command of naval hero Commodore Stephen Decatur, who quickly captured an Algerian flagship and another corsair, then sailed for Algiers where the Dey quickly made peace.[25]

However, Decatur's triumph was not the end of the problem. After several abortive attempts at international cooperation, in 1830 the French sent an armada and 27,000 troops to Algiers and occupied the city. The Dey capitulated and released the remaining Christian slaves, thus ending the era of the Barbary pirates.[26]

Evidence of God's Blessings During Madison's Presidency

By most accounts, Madison was not a strong president. He did not adequately prepare the country for the War of 1812, and it is a miracle that the nation survived this conflict. His selection of cabinet members was suspect, especially Secretary of the Army John Armstrong, who was caught by surprise when the British attacked Washington, D.C. Madison departed from the principles of a strong central government that he had articulated as the father of the Constitution and writer of several of *The Federalist* papers.

At the same time, he was in the difficult position throughout most of his presidency of being caught in the middle between warring France and England. As indicated earlier, neither country was much concerned about their treatment of America and its citizens who were on board ships in the Atlantic.

Madison's views on Christianity. Madison was raised in a Christian home and received his education, including his days at the College of New Jersey (Princeton), from Christian teachers, such as John Witherspoon. According to one of his biographers, "It seems clear he neither embraced fervently nor rejected utterly the

Christian base of his education. He accepted its tenets generally and formed his outlook on life within its world view."[27] It is evident that Madison was a scholar who analyzed government, and the future of the United States, from a Christian perspective.

While president, Madison continued the practice, established by Jefferson, of permitting worship services in government buildings. He was pleased with the rapid growth of Christianity, which he believed to be the result of separating churches from public financial support, and opening religion to the marketplace of ideas.

One of Madison's greatest accomplishments was *A Memorial and Remonstrance on the Religious Rights of Man*, written in 1785 in opposition to a drive to use state funds to support certain religious denominations in Virginia. "It (the paper by Madison) immediately took its place with the most important documents ever written on religious liberty." Madison defined religion as "duty owed to our creator..." and not a duty owed the government.[28] Toward the end of *A Memorial and Remonstrance*, Madison extolled Christianity "as a 'precious gift,' deplored the fate of those living, under 'the Dominion of false Religions,' and regretted that religious establishments place an 'obstacle before the victorious progress of Truth.'"[29]

Madison saw the benefits of multiple religious denominations: "If there were a majority of one sect, a bill of rights would be a poor protection for liberty. Happily for the (United States), they enjoy the utmost freedom of religion. This freedom arises from the multiplicity of sects, which pervades America, and which is the best and only security for religious liberty in any society."[30]

America's Christian heritage. The national anthem is one of the most visible examples of a contribution to the country's Christian heritage. The fourth stanza that began this chapter acknowledges that the United States is a blessed land.

President Madison "...renewed the tradition of Thanksgiving proclamations during the war of 1812. In 1814 Madison declared: 'a day of...prayer to Almighty God for the safety and welfare of these States, His blessing to their arms.'"[31] In 1815, following the peace treaty with England, Madison proclaimed another national day of prayer that included these words, "...devout acknowledgment to Almighty God for His great goodness manifested in restoring to them the blessing of peace..."[32]

Continuing religious revival. The Second Great Awakening was going strong during Madison's presidency. Madison referred, in a positive way, to the "plain, cheap meeting houses" that dominated the landscape of Virginia during the early 19th century. Many of these were built by Methodists and Baptists during one of the many rounds of revival that made up the second Awakening. Reflecting on the importance of this movement, historian James Hutson said, "During this period, revivalism, through which evangelical religion now found its expression, was 'the grand absorbing theme of American life. Few Americans could escape the evangelical orbit and fewer still wanted to."[33]

Madison was favorably impressed with the results of the revivals rolling through Virginia. "In a letter written in 1819, he seemed to relish the troubles of the Anglican—now Episcopal—church, whose places of worship, 'built under the establishment at the public expense, have in many instances gone to ruin, or are in a very dilapidated state, owing chiefly to a desertion of the flocks to other worships.'" He believed that the changes wrought by the revivals were beneficial in terms of the increase in the number of religious teachers, "the zeal which actuates them, the purity of their lives, and the attendance of people on their instructions."[34]

Divine providence. It is also interesting—some might call it divine providence—that John Quincy Adams' close relationship with Emperor Alexander of Russia contributed to the start of negotiations that ended the War of 1812. Although Emperor Alexander's initial offers were rejected by the British, these initiatives began a process that eventually led to peace.

Given the country's weak position militarily, being able to survive the War of 1812 was, in our view, evidence of divine providence.

We agree with Walter Borneman that the War of 1812 forged a nation. Many Americans believed that this was divine providence. Encouraged by both the end of the war and the Second Great Awakening, patriotism and pride in the United States were at an all-time high. The presidencies of James Monroe and John Quincy Adams, which are described in the next chapter, reinforced the belief that

America was finally able to stand on its own as an independent country capable of influencing events in the Western Hemisphere and the world.

Chapter 14

Presidencies of James Monroe and John Quincy Adams Position New Country as a World Power

America is a nation with the soul of a church.
—G. K. Chesterton in James Moore, *One Nation Under God*, xvi.

The 12 years covered by the presidencies of James Monroe and John Quincy Adams seem dull compared with those of their four predecessors. There were no major wars or involvement in European conflicts. In a sense, these years offered the United States a chance to get on its feet following the War of 1812. Monroe's tenure was referred to as the "Era of Good Feelings," but it was more than that; it was a period during which the country consolidated its gains and moved forward. And, as indicated earlier, it was a period of continuous religious revival (the Second Great Awakening).

Monroe and John Quincy Adams were not big-name Founding Fathers in the same sense as Washington, Jefferson, Franklin, Hamilton, Madison and John Adams. However, they were both part of the Revolutionary War generation;

Monroe served in the Continental Army and John Quincy Adams was with his father in Europe during the war and while the final negotiations of the peace treaty with England were proceeding.

Rather than a heavy emphasis on the major historical events that occurred during the years of the Monroe and Adams administrations, this chapter focuses on the character, major accomplishments and viewpoints of these two presidents. Their lives were intertwined in the sense that John Quincy Adams served as secretary of state under Monroe, and was the principle author of Monroe's most historic accomplishment, the Monroe Doctrine. Adams, who had tremendous respect and friendship for Monroe, gave the major address at Monroe's funeral.

James Monroe's Life and Presidency

Prior to becoming president, Monroe fought in several major battles, including Trenton, Brandywine Creek, Germantown and Monmouth, and he survived the winter at Valley Forge. Later in his life, after college and training as an attorney, Monroe was ambassador to France, returned to the United States, went back to France to play a key role in negotiating the Louisiana Purchase, was governor of Virginia, and then served as Madison's secretary of war during the latter part of the War of 1812, and as his secretary of state. He was also known for his role in the Missouri Compromise, developing new relationships with Indians, the purchase of Florida, and most importantly, the Monroe Doctrine.

As was the custom of the time, Monroe did not actively campaign for the office of president. Nevertheless, he won easily with 183 electoral votes versus 34 for Rufus King. In his first inaugural address, Monroe praised religious freedom and declared that "the favor of a gracious Providence" has guided the country. He concluded by saying that he was entering the presidency with "fervent prayers to the Almighty that He will be graciously pleased to continue to us that protection which he has already so conspicuously displayed in our favor."[1]

Monroe presided over a period of relative calm in the United States. Napoleon Bonaparte was in exile, and relations with France and England were reasonably settled. The population of the country was growing rapidly and new states and territories were being added.

Political philosophy. Although Monroe was originally opposed to ratification of the Constitution and, like Jefferson, was a staunch supporter of Republican principles, he gradually modified his thinking. For example, following his experiences during the War of 1812, he became an advocate of a standing army and strong coastal defenses. As far as Monroe was concerned, the country "should never again be exposed to such risks as a result of the traditional Republican antipathy toward military and naval expenditures."[2] This was the main thrust of his first inaugural address.

As president, Monroe saw the Republican Party as national in scope and concluded that there had to be a greater ability to compromise. "In one sense, Monroe's policies were founded upon the acceptance of compromise, or to use a more modern phrase, upon the politics of consensus."[3] This was the most important objective of his two terms. He saw himself as the head of a nation, not the head of a political party.

Acquisition of Florida. In 1817, with Andrew Jackson in command of the Army's southern forces, President Monroe ordered him to respond to Seminole Indian attacks on settlements in Georgia. Since many of the Seminoles were based in Florida, Jackson went after them. In the process he captured Pensacola, which at the time was occupied and owned by Spain. With the Seminoles subdued, Jackson set up a fort at Pensacola and returned home to Nashville to a hero's welcome.

Jackson's military efforts in Florida had international political ramifications. Secretary of State John Quincy Adams supported Jackson, as did President Monroe; most of the rest of the cabinet did not. Adams convinced the Spanish minister in Washington, Luis de Onis, that without the ability to police Florida, Spain should give up the territory. In February, 1819 Adams negotiated the Adams-Onis Treaty by which the United States purchased Florida from Spain for $5 million.[4]

Panic of 1819. This serious economic depression lasted three years. Monroe and the federal government were not of a mind to intervene, and furthermore, did not have the economic tools to do much about it. Due to its drastic curtailment of loans, the Second Bank of the United States received much of the blame for the panic, and public animosity led to the bank's eventual closure during Andrew Jackson's administration.

Poor economic conditions drove many Americans to seek land in the south and west. During this depressed period, the populations of the Mississippi and Alabama territories grew rapidly, as did those further west such as Arkansas and Missouri. Texas, which was owned by Spain until 1821 when Mexico achieved its independence, was largely uninhabited by either whites or Indians; Stephen Austin and other Americans were the first to move in.

Missouri Compromise. Midway through Monroe's first term, there was an effort to bring Missouri into the union. "The bill itself was harmless, but not the amendment of Representative James Tallmadge, Jr. of New York, who proposed to alter the Missouri bill to require the emancipation of all slaves at the age of twenty-one and to forbid the further introduction of slavery."[5] This amendment was unacceptable to the people of Missouri.

Monroe was opposed to restrictions on Missouri's admission to the United States that would violate the rights of Missouri; he noted that such conditions had not been placed on other states. The compromise of 1820 allowed Missouri into the union without restrictions, but barred slavery in areas to the north that were part of the Louisiana Purchase (e.g., Iowa, Nebraska, the Dakotas, Wyoming, Minnesota, Montana, and eastern Colorado).

Goodwill tours. Monroe continued President Washington's practice of visiting the various states. In 1817, shortly after taking the oath of office, he took a three-month tour up the East Coast through Baltimore, Philadelphia, New York and New England. He had an emotional visit to Trenton where he received a life-threatening shoulder wound. In the spring of 1819, Monroe took an extended southern and western tour visiting the Carolinas, Georgia, Tennessee, Kentucky, Indiana, what is now West Virginia, and Virginia.

Monroe often attended church in the communities he visited. "Throughout New England as well as in Pittsburgh, his visits to towns and cities included clergy in receptions and in ceremonial processions. On some Sundays Monroe went to church—usually to Episcopal services, but sometimes to those of other denominations."[6] Like his predecessors, Monroe consciously avoided favoring a particular denomination.

Election to a second term. Monroe was unopposed for re-election and other than a single electoral vote for John Quincy Adams (much to Adams' embarrassment), he was unanimously elected. Voter turnout was low. In his second inaugural address, Monroe spoke of his "firm reliance on the protection of Almighty God."[7]

Monroe Doctrine. In 1823, during Monroe's final State of the Union address, he discussed Spanish and European meddling in Central and South America. "The most important passage in John Quincy Adams' draft was the declaration that 'the American continents, by the free and independent condition which they have assumed, and maintain, are henceforth not to be considered as subject for future colonization by any European power.'"[8]

These and other paragraphs appeared in Monroe's speech and became known as the Monroe Doctrine. Many historians believe that this speech rivaled Washington's Farewell Address in terms of its long-term importance, and its underlying belief that the United States was at long last strong enough to develop and carry out its own hemispheric policies. This was James Monroe's most enduring legacy.

John Quincy Adams' Life and Presidency

John Quincy Adams had one of the longest and most impressive resumes of any of the Revolutionary War-generation presidents. When he was eight, he accompanied his mother, Abigail, to a hill where they observed the Battle of Bunker Hill. At 10, he traveled to France and the Netherlands with his father, where he became fluent in French. While in Europe, and still a teenager, he spent two years as an interpreter in Russia, Sweden, Denmark and Germany. At age 17, he took a winter trip, by himself, from St. Petersburg to Paris.

Like his father, John Quincy Adams graduated from Harvard, and then studied and briefly practiced law (which he disliked) in Massachusetts. He subsequently served as ambassador to the Netherlands and Germany, U. S. senator from Massachusetts, Harvard professor (two years), minister to Russia, leader of the commission that negotiated an end of the War of 1812, ambassador to Great Britain, and secretary of state under President Monroe.

David McCullough wrote, "John Quincy Adams, in my view, was the most superbly educated and maybe the most brilliant human being who ever occupied the executive office. He was, in my view, the greatest Secretary of State we've ever had. He wrote the Monroe Doctrine, among other things. And, he was a wonderful human being and a great writer."[9]

Adams' reading, writing and devotional habits. Adams' interest in reading and writing went back to his childhood, his years in Europe and his time at Harvard. When he was a teenager, his father urged him to read the New Testament in Greek. When he was approached to be ambassador to the Netherlands (at age 27), his primary concern was that this might cut into his reading and writing time.

In his years as a diplomat, John Quincy Adams began a lifelong habit of reading four to six chapters of the Bible every day. "It generally took him a year to finish, whereupon he would begin again. Later in life, to broaden his understanding of the text, he read the Scriptures in French and German, comparing the translations."[10] While he was American ambassador to Russia during the winter of 1811-1812, the birth of a daughter sharpened his concentration. "Previously, he had often complained of letting worldly thoughts and problems distract him from attentively reading the Bible or a sermon."[11] His goal was to be more open to divine inspiration.

Secretary of State Adams. After receiving notification that he had been selected to be President Monroe's secretary of state, he gave up chess for study of a book on biblical commentary. On his trip from London to New York in 1817, "He began discussing religion with others on board, and when a 'scoffer' became sarcastic, John promptly gave his reasons 'for the faith that is within me.'"[12]

After an exhilarating first day on the job in Washington, D.C., Adams penned these verses:

> O God, my only trust was thou
> Through all life's scenes before:
> Lo, at thy throne again I bow,
> New mercies to implore.
>
> Extend, all seeing God, thy hand,
> In mercy still decree,

And make to bless my native land
An instrument of me.[13]

Adams' major accomplishments as secretary of state during Monroe's first term included a treaty with England setting the western boundaries of the United States and Canada, and re-establishing American fishing rights off Newfoundland and Labrador. As noted earlier, he also negotiated a treaty with Spain that led to ownership of eastern Florida.

While he was secretary of state, Adams was elected president of the American Bible Society. On Sundays, he attended worship services, usually at the U. S. House of Representatives, and often listened to sermons in the morning, afternoon and evening. Adams disliked disputes among various sects and "...preferred to emphasize the sublime moral beauty of Christ's teachings, leaving issues of Protestant doctrine to faith. 'It is enough for us to know that God hath made foolish the wisdom of this world.'"[14]

By the end of his first four-year term as secretary of state, Adams finished a comprehensive report on weights and measures, including recommendations that the United States adopt the metric system. His report was considered the most scholarly study of the subject ever written; however, his recommendations attracted more interest in France and Europe than in the United States.

In Monroe's second term, clamor for independence by several of Spain's colonies in South America became a central issue. Spain was preparing to send troops to the region to quell rebellions. "Since Great Britain saw such a move as hostile to its own global interests, it proposed that the United States join it in public opposition to this enlarged Spanish intrusion in the Western Hemisphere." Adams then convinced the president and the cabinet that it would be "...wiser if the nation remained alone in warning the world that the Western Hemisphere was no longer to be intruded upon."[15] This statement led to the Monroe Doctrine described earlier.

Although Adams did not actively campaign for the presidency, the attacks by other candidates forced him to defend his record and character. As the election drew near, he knew that he would not win a majority of the electoral votes and that the outcome would be decided by the House of Representatives. His prognosis was accurate; Adams was the second president selected by the House (Jefferson was the first). Andrew Jackson had 99 Electoral College votes; Adams had 84; and Crawford 41. On the first vote of the House, Adams emerged the winner. His opponents said he gained the presidency through the "corrupt bargain," referring to the fact that Henry Clay of Kentucky threw his support behind Adams and, in the opinion of many, was rewarded with the job of secretary of state.

President Adams. Here is the last sentence of the inaugural address John Quincy Adams delivered on March 4, 1825: "...knowing that 'except the Lord keep the city the watchman waketh but in vain,' with fervent supplications for His favor, to His overruling providence I commit with humble but fearless confidence my own fate and future destinies of my country."[16]

Adams knew that the conditions surrounding his election would leave him a weak president; his predilections were correct. None of his proposals were enacted into law, and he was widely ridiculed for ideas like the establishment of a national observatory. He was an advocate for the federal government facilitating public works, such as roads and aqueducts, none of which was approved by the Congress during his tenure.

Overall, most historians describe John Quincy Adams's presidency as "lackluster." One historian said that, "His term was, if possible, even worse than his father's—a long nightmare, oppressed by a succession of alternately terrible and trivial events, which he seemed powerless to control or avoid."[17] (As noted earlier, we don't share the opinion that John Adams' presidency was a failure; the peace treaty with France avoided a war that the United States was ill-prepared to wage, and set the stage for the Louisiana Purchase.)

Loss to Andrew Jackson. According to all reports, the election of 1828 was one of the dirtiest in American history. "Adams's supporters accused Jackson and his wife, Rachel, of being adulterers and bigamists (unbeknownst to them, her divorce to a first husband had not gone through when she and Jackson married); when Mrs. Jackson died after the election, Jackson blamed the rumors for killing her."[18] Jackson won the election with 178 electoral votes to 83 for Adams. Like his father, John Quincy Adams did not attend his successor's inauguration, returning to Quincy embittered by his experience as president and his loss to Jackson, and determined not to become involved in politics. It took three years, and the pleadings of several friends, to change his mind.

Jackson took the presidential oath of office in March 1829. In his first major address to Congress late that year, in which he outlined his program for the coming years, he commended Congress "...to the guidance of Almighty God, with a full reliance on His merciful providence for the maintenance of our free institutions."[19]

Seventeen years in the House of Representatives. John Quincy Adams was the only former president elected to Congress where he served as a representative from Massachusetts from 1831 until his death in 1848. There were two issues that set him apart: establishment of the Smithsonian Institution and a dogged campaign against slavery.

Adams was one of the most cantankerous representatives who ever served in Congress. He never passed up an opportunity to fight the powers behind slavery, whether it was opposition to statehood for Texas (a slave state), gag rules preventing antislavery petitions to congress, or the *Amistad* case (slaves rebelled, killing their crew) where he defended the Africans before the Supreme Court. In short, over his last 17 years, John Quincy Adams' relentless pressure drove southern congressmen and slave owners crazy. On several occasions, southern members of Congress attempted to censure him, but he survived these votes.[20] He was a hero in the North and loathed in the South.

John Quincy Adams' Unique Historical Perspective

Adams was an outstanding orator with an unsurpassed historical perspective on the early development of the United States. For example, in an address delivered at Plymouth in 1802, Adams contrasted the motivations of the Pilgrims with the history of peoples who founded several countries: "It is your further happiness to behold, in those eminent characters (the Pilgrims), who were conspicuous in accomplishing the settlement of your country, men upon whose virtue you can dwell with honest exultation. The founders of your race are not handed down to you, like the fathers of the Roman people, as the sucklings of a wolf. You are not descended from a nauseous compound of fanaticism and sensuality, whose only argument was the sword, and whose only paradise was a brothel." To the contrary, "The great actors of the day we now solemnize were illustrious by their intrepid valor no less than by their Christian graces..." He added, "Theirs was the gentle temper of Christian kindness; the rigorous observance of reciprocal justice; the unconquerable soul of conscious integrity."[21]

Adams noted that the first European settlements on the North American continent were made "...at various times, by several nations, and under the influence of different motives. In many instances, the conviction of religious obligation formed one and a powerful inducement of the adventures; but in none, excepting the settlement at Plymouth, did they constitute the sole and exclusive actuating cause."[22]

Referring to the *Mayflower Compact*, Adams said: "One of these remarkable incidents is the execution of that instrument of government by which they formed themselves into a body politic, the day after their arrival upon the coast, and previous to their first landing. That is, perhaps, the only instance in human history of that positive, original social compact, which speculative philosophers have imagined as the only legitimate source of government. Here was a unanimous and personal assent, by all the individuals of the community, to the association by which they became a nation."[23]

In an 1821 speech commemorating the signing of the Declaration of Independence, Adams stated: "From the day of the Declaration...they (the American people) were bound by the laws of God, which they all, and by the laws of the Gospel, which they nearly all acknowledge as the rules of their conduct."[24]

In Newburyport, Mass., at a 4th of July celebration in 1837, Adams spoke of the significance of the Declaration of Independence. "Why is it that, next to the birthday of the Savior of the world, your most joyous and most venerated festival returns on this day? Is it not that, in the chain of human events, the birthday of the nation is indissolubly linked with the birthday of the Savior? That it forms a leading event in the progress of the Gospel dispensation? Is it not that the Declaration of Independence first organized the social compact on the foundation of the Redeemer's mission upon earth? That it laid the cornerstone of human government upon the first precepts of Christianity?"[25]

Speaking in New York City on the 50th anniversary of the enactment of the Constitution, Adams said: "And thus was consummated the work commenced by the Declaration of Independence—a work in which the people of the North American Union, acting under the deepest sense of responsibility to the Supreme

Ruler of the universe, had achieved the most transcendent act of power that social man in his mortal condition can perform—even that of dissolving the ties of allegiance by which he is bound to his country; of renouncing the country itself; of demolishing its government; of instituting another government; and of making for himself another country in its stead...The Revolution itself was a work of thirteen years—and had never been completed until that day (when the Constitution was ratified). The Declaration of Independence and the Constitution of the United States are parts of one consistent whole, founded upon one and the same theory of government, then new practice, though not as a theory, for it had been working itself into the mind of man for many ages, and had been especially expounded in the writings of Locke, though it had never before been adopted by a great nation in practice."[26]

In John Quincy Adams's mind, there was no question about the Christian heritage of the first immigrants to America on through those who enacted the Declaration of Independence and drafted the Constitution. Although he was a student of classical and Enlightenment philosophers, he was noticeably quiet in crediting them with the founding of America.

Evidence of God's Blessings

Given that James Monroe and John Quincy Adams served as presidents during a prolonged period of peace and prosperity, along with rapid population growth to the west, the examples of divine providence that were so obvious during the Revolutionary War and the War of 1812 were not as noteworthy. However, when we step back and look at what was taking place in America during these 12 years, several examples of providential favor stand out:

- The Monroe Doctrine—Adams' bold insight backed up by Monroe—was miraculous given that these two presidents served just a few years after the War of 1812. The country was weak, both militarily and economically, during and immediately after the war.

- The prolonged period of good economic times and major technological change (e.g., railroads, steamships, telegraph) was a sign of divine providence. Since the 1770s, there had never been a period free of major tensions or actual war, and certainly not one with as many transportation, communications and other technological improvements that blessed the lives of many Americans.

- Although we described the Second Great Awakening in a previous chapter, the spiritual events, including the establishment of benevolent societies, that took place as a part of these religious revivals peaked during the administrations of Monroe and Adams. What Tocqueville described after his 1831-32 visit reflects the combination of the Second Great Awakening and the period of economic growth and prosperity.

- A close reading of biographies of Monroe and John Quincy Adams reveals that on numerous occasions both narrowly escaped serious injuries or death. In our view, the preservation of the lives of these two Founding Fathers is evidence of divine providence.

- If we had been able to interview John Quincy Adams near the end of his life, he would have been most proud of his service in the House of Representatives, particularly his success in exposing the evils of slavery, and his successful legal defense of the survivors of the *Amistad*. Adams' Christian heritage and intensive Bible study contributed to his energetic attacks on what was often referred to as the "Slave Power." In our view, this was a prelude to the future.

The next chapter summarizes the observations of John Adams, Thomas Jefferson, Alexis de Tocqueville and others as they assessed the early development of North America and the founding of the United States. We compare the contributions of Enlightenment philosophy and Christianity to the development of America.

Chapter 15

The Role of Christianity in Founding America

America, historians remind us, was born in a seedbed of religion.
—David Brooks, *On Paradise Drive*, 117.

Not everyone agrees that religion was a key underpinning of America. Despite the evidence presented in previous chapters, many historians see religion as a minor player. As we noted earlier, a number of popular historians omit mention of the first Great Awakening and its impact on American culture and government. Other historians argue that the first Great Awakening did not happen; that this was a public relations coup on the part of revivalists.

Some argue that Enlightenment thinking, not Christianity, was the key to success in founding the United States. In an e-mail received by one of the authors, one individual put it this way: "Our nation was founded not on Christian principles but on Enlightenment ones. God only entered the picture as a very minor player, and Jesus Christ was conspicuously absent. Though for public consumption the Founding Fathers identified themselves as Christians, they were, at least by today's standards, remarkably honest about their misgivings when it came to theological doctrine, and religion in general came very low on the list of their concerns and priorities—always excepting, that is, their determination to keep the new nation free from bondage to its rule."

In his book, *Hamilton, Adams, Jefferson: The Politics of Enlightenment and the American Founding*, Darren Staloff argued that "The United States of America was forged in the crucible of the Enlightenment; no other nation bears its imprint as deeply." In describing the sources of Enlightenment thinking, he said, "Despite the absence of the word of God (or perhaps because of it), the ancients (Greeks, Romans) had produced unrivaled works of politics, ethics, philosophy, and art. Their achievements, both in culture and in virtuous civic life, demonstrated more vividly than any Rationalist geometric proof the fundamental irrelevance of religious revelation to the great issues of public life."[1]

Based on our review of the historical evidence, Staloff and others who ignore the influence of Christianity in the founding of the United States are wrong. Christian thinking and tradition were at the forefront of the early American experience. Early America developed a unique approach to religion—more tolerant of differences of opinion and in religious philosophy and practice. Moreover, the growing importance of religious freedom in America spread into other spheres, such as personal freedom, free markets, and representative democracy. In other words, religious thinking influenced (and was influenced by) numerous other aspects of young America. While conflicts between specific religious beliefs were a source of disunion in many of the European countries where most early immigrants originated, free worship and open discourse on religion were key to the unifying culture of early America.

Certainly, the Enlightenment also influenced the development of America. However, our review suggests that Enlightenment was a distant second to the growing, changing role of religion, not the other way around. Fortunately, a number of valuable resources are available to shed light on the thinking of America's Founders and those who were observing the country closely at the time. For example, the 158 letters exchanged between John Adams and Thomas Jefferson (arguably two of the most influential Founding Fathers) are instructive. Also, the classic writings of Alexis de Tocqueville, following his visit to America in 1831-1832, provide an invaluable overview of what the country was like, and how religion permeated the economy, government, institutions and personal values (e.g., character, morals, virtue).

In Their Own Words: Adams and Jefferson Look Back at the Founding

John Adams and Thomas Jefferson had been friends when they collaborated on the Declaration of Independence, and again when they served as ambassadors to England and France, respectively, in the years following the Revolutionary War. However, the two Founders had a falling out during the second Washington administration and relationships deteriorated even further during the campaign and election of 1800, in which Jefferson defeated Adams. In fact, Adams was so piqued that he left town before Jefferson's inauguration.

Encouraged by Dr. Benjamin Rush, a mutual friend of both men, Adams broke the ice by writing Jefferson on New Year's Day, 1812. The resumption of their friendship led to 158 letters (109 from Adams and 49 from Jefferson) over the next 14 years. Adams wrote to Jefferson, "You and I ought not to die before we have explained ourselves to each other."[2] And that is what they proceeded to do, often with a touch of humor and humility, much to the benefit of all who are interested in the two Founders' perceptions of America's early development.

Adams to Jefferson on the central role of the principles of Christianity. Writing about the Declaration of Independence, Adams stated clearly that he believed principles of Christianity had a key role in America's founding: "The *general principles*, on which the Fathers achieved independence, were the only Principles on which that beautiful Assembly of young Gentlemen could Unite...And what were these *general principles*?...I answer, the general Principles of Christianity, in which all these Sects were United; And the *general Principles* of English and American Liberty, in which all those young Men United, and which had United all Parties in America in Majorities sufficient to assert and maintain her Independence. Now I will avow, that I then believed, and now believe, that those general Principles of Christianity are as eternal and immutable as the Existence and Attributes of God; and that those Principles of Liberty are as unalterable as human Nature and our terrestrial, mundane (solar) System."[3]

Views about sectarianism. Both Adams and Jefferson disliked the dogmatism of most religious sects. In reflecting upon the writings and teachings of several denominational leaders, Adams wrote to Jefferson, "This would be the best of all Worlds if there was no Religion in it." However, Adams followed with this statement: "Without Religion this World would be Something not fit to be mentioned in polite Company, I mean Hell."[4]

Jefferson responded: "If, by *religion*, we are to understand *Sectarian dogmas*, in which no two of them agree, then your exclamation on that hypothesis is just, 'that this would be the best of all possible worlds, if there were no religion in it.' But, if the moral precepts innate in man and made a part of his physical constitution, as necessary for a social being, if the sublime doctrines of philanthropism, and deism taught us by Jesus of Nazareth in which all agree, constitute true religion, then, without it, this would be, as you again say, 'something not fit to be named, indeed a Hell.'"[5]

Personal religious comments. Upon hearing of the death of Abigail Adams, Jefferson wrote, "…it is of some comfort to us both that the term is not very distant at which we are to deposit, in the same cerement (shroud), our sorrows and suffering bodies, and to ascend in essence to an ecstatic meeting with the friends we have loved and lost and whom we shall still love and never lose again. God bless you and support you under your heavy affliction."[6] In his later years, Jefferson concluded nearly all of his letters to Adams with sentences that included, "May God bless you." Adams responded, "I believe in God and in his Wisdom and Benevolence: and I cannot conceive that such a Being could make such a Species as the human merely to live and die on this Earth. If I did not believe a future State I should believe in no God."[7]

Reflections on the death of Adams and Jefferson by their contemporaries. Speaking at Feneuil Hall in Boston in 1826, shortly after the deaths of Adams and Jefferson, Daniel Webster declared: "It cannot be denied, but by those who would dispute against the sun, that with America, and in America, a new era commences in human affairs. This era is distinguished by Free Representative Governments, by entire religious liberty, by improved systems of national intercourse, by a newly awakened, and unconquerable spirit of free inquiry, and by a diffusion of knowledge through the community, such as has been before altogether unknown and unheard of. America, America, our country, fellow-citizens, our own dear and native land, is inseparably connected, fast bound up, in fortune and by fate, with these great interests. If they fall, we fall with them; if they stand, it will be because we have upholden them."[8]

Webster included religious liberty as one of the nation's "great interests." Based on their letters, both Adams and Jefferson viewed Godly and enlightened people as essential ingredients of peace, strong government, and an innovative, productive and prosperous country.

When President John Quincy Adams learned that his father and Thomas Jefferson had died on the same day—July 4, 1826, the fiftieth anniversary of American independence—he saw "visible and palpable marks of Divine favor," a feeling widely shared throughout the nation.[9]

The Acute Observations of a Visitor: Alexis de Tocqueville

During his 1831-1832 visit to the United States, Alexis de Tocqueville was both surprised and favorably impressed by the influence of religion and attributed much of the success of the new country to the large number of Americans who were professing Christians.

Christianity, patriotism and education. Everywhere Tocqueville traveled in the United States, he "...encountered the conviction, fostered by the evangelical juggernaut, that for the United States to prosper there must be an 'association between religion and patriotism.'"[10] Tocqueville concluded: "I do not know whether all the Americans have a sincere faith in their religion, for who can search the human heart? but I am certain they hold it to be indispensable to the maintenance of republican institutions. This opinion is not peculiar to a class of citizens or to a party, but it belongs to the whole nation, and to every rank of society."[11]

Tocqueville said that America was settled primarily by Protestants and that the contract between religion and politics remained in place: "The greatest part of British America was peopled by men who, after having shaken off the authority of the Pope, acknowledged no other religious supremacy; they brought with them into the New World a form of Christianity which I cannot better describe than by styling it a democratic and republican religion. This sect contributed powerfully to the establishment of a democracy and republic, and from the earliest settlement of the emigrants politics and religion contracted an alliance which has never been dissolved."[12]

On his visit to New England, Tocqueville noted: "...every citizen receives the elementary notions of human knowledge; he is moreover taught the doctrines and the evidences of his religion, the history of his country, and the leading features of its Constitution."[13] He also noted that, "In the Eastern States the instruction and practical education of the people have been most perfected, and religion has been most thoroughly amalgamated with liberty."[14]

Factors assuring success in America. Tocqueville argued that there are three characteristics of a country and its people that lead to success—(1) physical attributes, such as location, climate and natural resources, (2) constitution (type of government, which is where the Enlightenment philosophers had their greatest impact), and (3) manners (what might also be called virtue, character or values, and where religion may have had its greatest impact).

Tocqueville pointed out that many countries in Europe and South America were well endowed with natural resources and with reasonable forms of government, but they were not able to preserve democracy. For citizens of the United States, he believed it was the manners of the people that made the difference. He said that manners are the same as "mores," including the moral and intellectual condition of a people.[15]

Related to the three factors, Tocqueville said, "I am convinced that the most advantageous situation and the best possible laws cannot maintain a constitution in spite of the manners of a country; whilst the latter may turn the most unfavorable positions (location and resources) and the worst laws to some advantage."[16] He said that this was the most important finding from his research: "The importance of manners is a common truth to which study and experience incessantly direct our attention. It may be regarded as a central point in the range of human observation, and the common termination of all inquiry. So seriously do I insist upon this head, that if I have hitherto failed in making the reader feel the important influence which I attribute to the practical experience, the habits, the opinions, in short, to the manners of the Americans, upon the maintenance of their institutions, I have failed in the principal object of my work."[17]

Tocqueville's emphasis on manners is contrary to Jared Diamond's finding in *Guns, Germs & Steel* that over the past 13,000 years, location was the main factor determining the future of civilizations. Diamond's compelling arguments about the importance of domesticating plants and animals and developing a food supply are difficult to refute over the longer sweep of world history. However, it appears that Tocqueville's perspective is shorter term, looking at the previous two or three centuries. In this light, we accept Tocqueville's thesis on the primacy of manners as valid. Even more important to our analysis of the impacts of Christianity on the development of the United States, we find that the evidence is indisputable that almost all Americans viewed the situation the same way that Tocqueville did. The early Christian heritage of the first immigrants, and the impacts of the two Awakenings on religious beliefs and actions, plus freedom of religion (doing away with state-supported churches) and an emphasis on education represented the major elements of the "manners" observed by Tocqueville.

Relative to the connection between religion and a virtuous people, Tocqueville said: "Despotism may govern without faith, but liberty cannot." In other words, religion is much more important in democracies or republics, and it is essential in making them work. He concluded that when the centralized control of government eases off, the moral tie (religion) must increase proportionately if a society is to escape destruction.[18] This is consistent with the beliefs of *all* of the Founding Fathers.

Tocqueville, like others cited in earlier chapters, believed that Christianity and liberty (our second criterion for evaluating God's blessings) leaned on each other. Later in his life, he wrote this unequivocal statement: "I have never been more convinced than I am today that only liberty…and religion, through a combined effort, are capable of raising men out of the mire in which democratic equality naturally plunges them as soon as one of these two supports is lacking."[19]

The Supporting Role of the Enlightenment

Taken in the context of what we have learned about early America, the notion that the Enlightenment was the dominant force in the founding of America is an unwarranted revision of history. It seems clear that early American leaders were influenced by Enlightenment thinking, but that they viewed it in the context of their purpose, their environment and their religious beliefs. As far as we can tell, the notion that the Enlightenment was a dominant factor and that Christianity was less important would have seemed quite strange to the Founders.

The Enlightenment was a supplement to early American thinking. There is no doubt that many of the Founders—John Adams, Thomas Jefferson, Alexander

Hamilton, and John Jay among them—benefited from their studies of the Greek and Roman classics and from the writings of John Locke, David Hume, Adam Smith and other Enlightenment philosophers. However, they appeared to have chosen carefully which elements to adopt and integrate into their thinking and which to reject. By and large, they rejected the atheist aspects of the Enlightenment movement as it evolved in France.

Also, the vast majority of Americans had not read—and were not interested in reading—the works of Enlightenment philosophers. The more common bond across America was the King James Bible. One historian put it this way: "The rise of evangelical Christianity in the early republic is, in some measure, a story of the success of common people in shaping the culture after their own priorities rather than the priorities outlined by gentlemen such as the framers of the Constitution."[20]

Scientific enlightenment was seen as an outgrowth of Christianity. As noted earlier in this book, scientific advances were seen as the outgrowth of leading Christian thought, not as a competitor. Rodney Stark, author of *The Victory of Reason,* argued "The rise of science and technology was not an extension of classical learning. It was the natural outgrowth of Christian doctrine: nature exists because it was created by God. In order to love and honor God, it is necessary to fully appreciate the wonders of his handiwork. Because God is perfect, his handiwork functions in accord with *immutable principles.* By the full use of our God-given powers of reason and observation, it ought to be possible to discover these principles…These were the crucial ideas that explain why science arose in Christian Europe and nowhere else."[21]

Stark also noted that the first two universities appeared in Paris and Bologna in the middle of the 12th century. Oxford and Cambridge were established about 1200 AD. More than 20 additional European universities were established in the 13th century. These were the universities where science was born. "Keep in mind that these were deeply Christian institutions: all the faculty were in holy orders and, consequently, so too were most of the famous early scientists."[22]

Enlightenment thinking on the value of the individual was integrated with religious concepts. Clearly, the Founders were influenced by seventeenth century Enlightenment philosophers, such as John Locke. However, these concepts were integrated with their religious convictions. When some later historians argued that secular philosophers were the thought leaders who figured most prominently in establishing the United States, Stark countered: "Many (secular political theorists) also express admiration for John Locke's seventeenth-century works as a major source for modern democratic theory, seemingly without the slightest awareness that Locke explicitly based his entire thesis on Christian doctrines concerning moral equality. Most textbook accounts of the birth of our nation now carefully ignore the religious aspects, as if a bunch of skeptics had written these famous lines from the Declaration of Independence. 'We hold these truths to be self-evident, that all men are created equal, that they are endowed by their Creator with certain unalienable Rights, that among these are Life, Liberty, and the Pursuit of Happiness.'"[23]

Many American Founders rejected the atheistic elements of the Enlightenment in France. Adams and Jefferson are often referred to as followers of the Enlightenment as well as being political philosophers in their own right. Here is what Adams said about the French Enlightenment philosophers: "They seemed to believe that whole Nations and Continents had been changed in the Principles, Opinions, Habits and Feelings by the Sovereign Grace of their Almighty Philosophy, almost as suddenly as Catholics and Calvinists believe in instantaneous Conversion…And what was their Philosophy? Atheism, pure unadulterated Atheism…The Universe was Matter only and eternal; Spirit was a Word Without meaning; Liberty was a Word Without a Meaning…This was their Creed and this was to perfect human Nature and convert the Earth into a Paradise of Pleasure." Adams concluded: "We all curse Robespierre and Bonaparte, but were they not both such restless, vain extravagant Animals as Diderot and Voltaire?" Referring to Voltaire and Bonaparte, Adams wrote that they were, "Both equally heroes and equally Cowards."[24]

In another letter, Adams continued to raise doubts about the wisdom of several French Enlightenment philosophers and leaders: "Who shall take the side of God and Nature? Brachmans? Mandarins? Druids? Or, Tecumseh and his Brother the Prophet? Or shall We become Disciples of the Philosophers? And who are the Philosophers? Frederick? Voltaire? Rousseau? Buffon (he claimed that American people and animals were inferior to those in Europe)? Diderot? Condercet? These Philosophers have shown them selves as incapable of governing mankind as the Bourbons or the Geulphs."[25]

Tocqueville and others saw the distinction between the French and American movements. As a Frenchman and Roman Catholic who grew up during the Napoleonic period, and a scholar familiar with Enlightenment philosophy, Tocqueville was interested in the question of why the United States avoided the decline of Christian influence typical of European nations and other countries. He found that the conventional wisdom articulated by many Enlightenment philosophers to be in error: "The philosophers of the eighteenth century explained the gradual decay of religious faith in a very simple manner. Religious zeal, said they, must necessarily fail, the more generally liberty is established and knowledge diffused. Unfortunately, facts are by no means in accordance with their theory. There are certain populations in Europe whose unbelief is only equaled by their ignorance and their debasement, whilst in America one of the freest and enlightened nations in the world fulfills all the outward duties of religious fervor."[26]

Reflecting the historic ground broken by Christianity in the United States following the first Great Awakening, British historian Paul Johnson observed, "Thus for the first time since the Dark Ages, a society came into existence in which institutional Christianity was associated with progress and freedom, rather than against them."[27] In response to those who credit the founding of America to Enlightenment thinking, he observed: "The essential difference between the American Revolution and the French Revolution is that the American Revolution in its origins, was a religious event, whereas the French Revolution (influenced by the French Enlightenment philosophers) was an anti-religious event."[28]

In his essay, *The Baffling Americans*, Italian writer Luigi Barzini also concluded that it was Christianity, not Enlightenment philosophy, that led to America's success: "What few imitators have understood is that the secret of the United States' tremendous success was in reality not merely technology, know-how, the work ethic, the urge to succeed or plain greed. It was a spiritual wind that drove the Americans irresistibly ahead from the beginning. What was behind their compulsion to improve man's lot was an all-pervading sense of duty, the submission to a God-given imperative, to a God-given code of personal behavior, the willing acceptance of all the necessary sacrifices, including death in battle."[29]

The Connection between Christianity and Liberty

As Jonathan Edwards, the great Puritan theologian, understood the situation in the early 1700s, well before the Declaration of Independence, God is intimately involved in governing the universe, and as such He is interested in the maximum autonomy for human beings, who are His creation.[30] God wants people to be free—or autonomous—so they have alternatives, or choices, for their lives; for those who choose to voluntarily follow Christ, God is pleased. God can't be pleased when people have little or no individual freedom, and therefore have no opportunity to make free choices of who they will follow and how they will invest their lives.

The spread of Christianity in America, especially the initial Puritan settlements in New England and the first Great Awakening, influenced early Americans' desire for liberty, and helped set the stage for the Declaration of Independence and the Revolutionary War. In further support of this conclusion, these words are carved on one wall of the Jefferson Memorial in Washington, D.C.: "God who gave us life gave us liberty. Can the liberties of a nation be secure when we have removed a conviction that these liberties are the gift of God?"

Almost all of the Founding Fathers agreed with John Witherspoon, president of the College of New Jersey (Princeton) and a signer of the Declaration of Independence, that "civil and religious liberty leaned on each other."[31] Writing two years before the Declaration of Independence, Alexander Hamilton said, "Remember civil and religious liberty always go together, if the foundation of one is sapped, the other will fall..."[32] In a paper published in 1776, John Jay connected freedom and God. "If then, God hath given us freedom, are we responsible to Him for that, as well as other talents? If it be our birthright, let us not sell it for a mess of pottage, nor suffer it to be torn from us by the hand of violence. If the means of defense are in our power and we do not make use of them, what excuse shall we make to our children and our Creator?"[33]

Historian Mark Noll noted that by the time of the French & Indian War, most evangelical Christians in America were "...far more willing to embrace a republican picture of the political world than most evangelicals in Britain." He went on: "In the mid-eighteenth century, republicanism meant a distrust of centralized political power, a commitment to checks and balances in government, a fear of political enslavement and belief in an interlocking relationship among liberty, law and natural rights. Republican theory also drew a close connection between the morals of a people and the safety of its government—virtue in the public made it more likely that government would flourish, vice more likely that it would become tyrannical."[34] He observed that the implications of these differences in religious views and the role of government between the colonies and England were large, and explain why a substantial proportion of Christians in America, especially those touched by the first Great Awakening, willingly supported the war for independence.[35]

More than half a century after the Declaration of Independence, Tocqueville observed: "The Americans combine the notions of Christianity and of liberty so intimately in their minds, that it is impossible to make them conceive the one without the other…" He went on, "Thus religious zeal is perpetually stimulated in the United States by the duties of patriotism."[36] In other words, Tocqueville viewed Christianity, liberty and patriotism as intertwined. This was one of the main themes of the Second Great Awakening.

In summarizing the connection between religion and freedom, Jon Meacham wrote, "Looking back at the Founding is neither an exercise in nostalgia nor an attempt to deify the dead, but a bracing lesson in how to make a diverse nation survive and thrive by cherishing freedom and protecting faith. And faith and freedom are inextricably linked…"[37] Meacham went on, "The story of how the Founders believed in faith and freedom, and grappled with faith and freedom, has particular resonance in our era."[38]

The American Difference

America took its own unique path. Americans rejected perpetuation of the sectarian religious strife they had experienced in Europe, and they rejected the movement towards atheism that many Enlightenment thinkers in Europe later embraced. Instead, they developed a culture in which religious freedom was a core concept.

The step from religious freedom to other individual freedoms was a short one. This was consistent with early Enlightenment thinking and with religious freedom. Americans embraced science and the scientific method and found them too to be consistent with religious and personal freedom. Open discourse, freedom of expression, scientific debate, religious debate—these were all seen as of the same cloth, all part of the fabric of this new culture. All were to a degree woven from the diversity in Americans' religious beliefs.

Instead of letting sectarian religious differences cause division, early Americans chose to have religion in general, and the values or mores it imbeds, serve as the unifying basis for their society. Religious values, broadly defined, became the key underpinning of democratic society.

Americans were aware that they were inventing a new form of society. However, they did not see this as solely the act of man. Most Founders saw themselves as being led by and carrying out the will of God. And in carrying out God's will, they frequently invoked, and saw themselves receiving, the blessings of divine providence. How God watched over and blessed America is the subject of the next and final chapter of this book.

Chapter 16

God Has Blessed America

In the designs of Providence, there are no mere coincidences.
—Pope John Paul II, 1982.

Historian and speaker Stephen Mansfield observed, "One of the signs of a great society is the diligence with which it passes culture from one generation to the next. This culture is the embodiment of everything the people of that society hold dear: its religious faith, its heroes, and its traditions, arts and ceremonies. When one generation no longer esteems its own heritage and fails to pass the torch to its children, it is saying in essence that the foundational principles and experiences that make the society what it is are no longer valid."[1]

One of the reasons we prepared this book is our belief that many Americans, including those who often write about the founding of the United States, appear to be ignoring a key element of the country's heritage. As discussed in the previous chapter, some historians argue that America's heritage is based on the thinking and writing of Enlightenment philosophers. While that may be part of it, we believe that objective research shows there is much, much more to the story. Our experience in performing the research for this book is consistent with that of the historian who wrote: "History is vividly clear about the importance of God in the founding of our nation…Indeed, to study American history is to encounter God again and again."[2]

Ignoring or downplaying America's religious underpinnings means failing to learn from history. America is unique in that it was deliberately founded as an alternative to sectarian religious strife. Also, the religious mores that were common to the major sects in early America were seen as the key link in establishing a common culture and a participative democracy. If the Founders had catered to sectarian differences, or failed to build on the religious mores that were common at the time, American and world history would have been radically altered.

Did God have a hand in this? As best we can tell, He had a big hand in it. This final chapter explores the evidence that God did indeed bless America, and it offers our hopes for how we interpret and use these blessings.

The Evolution of a Christian Heritage

The evidence presented in previous chapters shows that America's heritage has been shaped by Christian men and women, their prayers, and their sacrifices. Even though the Jamestown Settlement was primarily a commercial venture, the initial settlers, who were part of the Church of England, celebrated communion the day they arrived and built a chapel soon thereafter. The second group of immigrants, the Pilgrims who landed at Plymouth, bound themselves together with the *Mayflower Compact*, the first written covenant relationship between a North American people and God. The Puritans, who began arriving in the Boston area a decade later, were intent upon establishing a distinctive Christian community and were seriously committed to living and working in ways they believed would please God.

In our view, the unique Christian heritage of early America developed in three waves:

1. The first wave, which lasted a little more than 100 years, featured the immigration of tens of thousands of Christians, mostly Protestants, who arrived from England and other northern European countries, and who were members of many different sects. Although freedom from state-sponsored churches was not universal until 1833, New York, Pennsylvania, New Jersey, Maryland, and Rhode Island avoided this restriction from the outset.

2. By 1730, Puritanism in New England was running out of steam, and religious fervor in the Middle Colonies and the South had leveled off. This set the stage for the second wave: the Great Awakening led by George Whitefield, Jonathan Edwards, the Tennets and others. Two decades later, this series of religious revivals left the colonies with 1,500 churches and several new Christian colleges (e.g., Princeton, Brown and Dartmouth). During the years of the Great Awakening, church attendance soared, with more than half of all Americans regularly attending churches of their choice in the years immediately preceding the Revolutionary War.

3. The third wave, which began shortly after the signing of the peace treaty with England ending the Revolutionary War, included a series of revivals led by Methodists, especially Francis Asbury and his band of itinerant preachers, and by Baptists and Presbyterians. The Second Great Awakening, plus rapid population growth west of the Appalachian Mountains, fueled an explosion in the number of churches, a dramatic increase in church attendance and the establishment of many non-denominational benevolent organizations (e.g., missionary societies, Bible societies, Sunday school unions, abolitionist movements). The United States that Alexis de Tocqueville observed during his 1831-1832 visit reflected the results of all three waves, especially the third.

Speaking at Plymouth at a commemoration of the landing of the Pilgrims, John Quincy Adams uttered these prophetic words linking the Christian heritage of the country to its future: "Two centuries have not yet elapsed since the first European foot touched the soil, which now constitutes the American Union. Two centuries more and our numbers must exceed those of Europe itself...so let us never forget that the glory and greatness of all our descendants is in our hands. Preserve in all their purity, refine, if possible, from all their alloy, those virtues, which we this day commemorate as the ornament of our forefathers."[3]

In terms of what the Pilgrims wrought, Adams said, "The revolutions of time furnish no previous example of a nation shooting up to maturity and expanding into greatness with the rapidity which has characterized the growth of the American people." He went on, "Let us unite in ardent supplication to the Founder of nations and the Builder of Worlds, that what then was prophecy may continue unfolding into history—that the dearest hopes of the human race may not be extinguished in disappointment, and that the last (the United States) may prove the noblest empire of time."[4]

The first presidential inauguration in New York City provided additional evidence of the Christian heritage of the newly organized United States. In the days preceding the inauguration, many Americans attended church services and prayed for the country. Washington took the oath of office with his hand on a Bible, and immediately following his inaugural address, the entire leadership of the country walked to St. Paul's Chapel for a worship service.

Harvard historian Samuel Huntington summed the Christian heritage of the United States this way: "America was founded in large part for religious reasons and religious movements have shaped its evolution for almost four centuries. By every indicator, Americans are far more religious than the people of other industrialized countries. Overwhelming majorities of white Americans, of black Americans, and of Hispanic Americans are Christians. In a world in which culture and particularly religion shape the allegiances, the alliances and the antagonisms of people on every continent, Americans could again find their national identity and their national purpose in their culture and religion."[5]

Divine Providence Preceded by Prayer

While many historians speak of "miracles" in describing unusual occurrences, especially during the Revolutionary War, they usually do not take the next step and attribute these miracles to God or divine providence. What would constitute evidence of providence? Let us suggest that if (a) the people of God pray for divine intervention, (b) miracles happen, (c) these miracles further events that might be interpreted to be in God's will, and (d) the faith of those doing the interpreting is consistent with the concept of divine providence, it is reasonable to suggest that providence may very well have been at work.

The role of prayer in early America has been documented by many. James Moore spent eight years and considered 30,000 sources in his history of prayer in America. He concluded, "Take away the very real, palpable presence of prayer throughout the American experience, and we would be nothing more than a shadow of ourselves today." Moore went on, "To dismiss prayer in the life of America is to embark on a fool's errand. Prayer has been and always will be an integral part of the national character."[6]

Moore went on: "If American history can be likened to a great musical composition, prayer must be seen as an integral and powerful theme throughout the piece. At times it is softer; louder at others. It has its own rhythm, its own pulse. It is always there, fundamentally contributing to whatever melody may be playing. Most important, it is an integral component to the arrangement. To remove it is to take away the depth, the breadth, and the richness of what gives the work, at least in part, its special character."[7]

What is the evidence supporting Moore's assertion on the importance of prayer in the founding of America? He cited several examples, including these:

- More than half of all ministers stepped forward and offered their services to the Revolutionary War effort. "From pulpit to battlefield, ministers across the colonies called on their congregations to pray continuously for the Revolutionary cause."[8]
- While attending an all-night prayer vigil on New Year's Eve in Philadelphia, and after receiving an urgent request for funds from General Washington, Robert Morris realized what he needed to do. "Walking out of the church in the middle of the night, he went from door to door, rousing wealthy friends and acquaintances from their sleep and asking for their help."[9] By the end of the day, he had secured the $50,000 Washington needed.
- In speaking to the Constitutional Convention in 1787, Benjamin Franklin reflected back to the time of the Revolutionary War. In addressing George Washington, the presiding officer, Franklin said, "Our prayers, Sir, were heard, and they were graciously answered. All of us who were engaged in the struggle must have observed frequent instances of a superintending Providence in our favor."[10]

Moore concluded: "American prayer and the spirituality that it evokes are part of America's history. Without prayer the political, cultural, religious, social, and even military annals of our nation would have been radically different from what they are today...even global history would have taken a far different path in the absence of American prayer."[11] Our findings are consistent with those of Moore.

When he was leaving Boston for Philadelphia to attend the first Continental Congress, John Adams wrote: "A most kindly and affectionate meeting we had, and about four in the afternoon we took our leave of them, amidst the kind wishes and fervent prayers of every man in the company for our health and success. The scene was truly affecting, beyond all description affecting..."[12] Tocqueville attended a meeting where a Catholic priest offered a long prayer that included these words: "Lord, turn not Thou Thy face from us, and grant that we may always be the most religious and the freest people of the earth."[13] Based on Moore's research and our own studies, these types of prayers were common in early America, and they appear to have been answered.

Reverend Charles Coffin is as obscure as Tocqueville is famous; however, he was quite prominent in his time. Coffin believed that the survival of the American republic was dependent on religious revival and prayer. In an 1833 letter, Coffin explained why the United States had been so hospitable to evangelicalism in general and revivalism in particular: "Never was there any other country settled, since Canaan itself, so much for the sacred purposes of religion, as our own. Never did any other ancestry, since the days of inspiration, send up so many prayers and lay such ample foundations for the religious prosperity of their descendants, as did our godly forefathers. It is a fact, therefore, in perfect analogy with the course of Providence, that there never has been any other country so distinguished for religious revivals as our own."[14]

James Moore, Alexis de Tocqueville and Charles Coffin come to a conclusion ignored by most historians—the power of the prayers of early Americans. Based on our research, it seems certain that Americans like the Catholic priest Tocqueville observed prayed fervently and often for the future of their country. An emphasis on prayer is consistent with the evangelical Christianity that blossomed during the two Great Awakenings. The many congressional days of prayer and fasting, which were taken seriously by the people of the country, are additional evidence of the importance of prayer to the founding generations.

Miraculous Events

Extraordinary or miraculous events were plentiful in the founding of America. Numerous examples have been cited earlier in this book. Consider, for example, the following.

What if early Americans had not been prepared for self-government? There were at least six factors underlying the American experience that pushed the colonies toward freedom and a new kind of governance. It is difficult to believe these were accidental.

1. The bulk of early colonists came from the British Isles or northern Europe, where local autonomy was strongest.
2. These early immigrants were weary of constant imperial wars and sought greater freedom from government restriction. They welcomed the Protestant Reformation in Europe and in Britain, largely apart from the state church.
3. They sought new economic opportunity, including the availability of land, and were willing to work hard and risk their lives to achieve it.
4. They were disgusted with corrupt political/governance systems and being manipulated by the few.
5. The lack of well established social restrictions (e.g., by class or wealth) created opportunity for upward mobility.
6. In America, they had enjoyed 150 years of only marginal interference from the home government in London and experienced considerable self-government in local, colonial affairs. They became accustomed to autonomy and increasingly viewed it as a birthright.

The mentality and experience of the colonists was well summed in 1775 by Edmund Burke in a three-hour speech to the English Parliament: "These colonists were Englishmen born with a free spirit, what is more, Englishmen in whom religion 'is in no way worn out or impaired; and their mode of professing it is also one main cause of this free spirit. The people are Protestants; and of that kind, which is most adverse to all implicit submission of mind and opinion...'"[15]

What if there had been no first Great Awakening? The Great Awakening was a pivotal event in America's history. There is compelling evidence that the religious revivals of the mid 18th century broke down class barriers and helped unify a diverse and heterogeneous group of people scattered over 1,500 miles of difficult terrain, thus imbuing them with a strong desire to unite and govern their own affairs. John Adams and others agreed that without revival and the support of many ministers, the Declaration of Independence and Revolutionary War would not have been possible. The country would have lacked the unity and resolve to proceed with the drive for independence, and the perseverance to succeed in the face of the greatest military power in the world.

What if George Washington had been disabled or killed? Washington was truly the indispensable man of the American Revolution and the founding of the country. Looking back, Washington had at least eight narrow escapes during the Revolutionary War and another in the French & Indian War. In this first conflict, Washington was the only British officer not killed or wounded in Braddock's Massacre; he escaped with four bullet holes in his coat and had two horses shot out from under him. Washington wrote later, "...the miraculous care of Providence...protected me beyond all human expectation."[16]

Assuming there was a 50 percent chance of sustaining either a serious wound or being killed in any of the eight close combat situations Washington faced during the Revolutionary War, and the same chance of surviving Braddock's Massacre, the probabilities of his surviving unscathed to the end of the war would have been less than two tenths of one percent. Was this luck or divine providence? Washington thought it was providence.

What if unusual weather had not aided the Continental Army? In previous chapters, we have described several incidents involving unusual weather conditions that helped—or saved—the Continental Army.

- *Rainstorm at Dorchester Heights.* Once the British discovered cannon on Dorchester Heights, a strong force boarded boats and crossed to the base of the hills in preparation for a direct assault. However, a storm—some said one of the strongest they had ever seen—came up suddenly forcing the British to withdraw to Boston.

- *Fortuitous fog.* Nearly all historians agree that had Washington not evacuated his army from Brooklyn Heights, he would have been killed or hung as a traitor. The Revolutionary War would have been over. Was the rain, wind and fog an accident, or was it God's protection for Washington and the army? David McCullough and other historians refer to it as miraculous. The atmospheric conditions that prevailed those fateful August days were extremely rare for New York. There was perhaps one chance in a thousand of the rain, winds and fog coming together as they did.

- *Frozen road to Princeton.* In early January 1777, Washington and his army were trapped in Trenton and facing General Cornwallis and 7,000 elite British troops. It had rained and the roads were knee deep in mud. However, during the night a cold snap froze the ground allowing Washington and his army to march to Princeton where they surprised and defeated 700 British troops.

- *Storm delayed the British fleet.* While General Cornwallis was trapped at Yorktown, a heavy wind damaged the British fleet in New York harbor as it was preparing to transport 6,000 troops to relieve Cornwallis.

- *Cornwallis foiled by heavy winds and rains.* A few days later, as the combined American and French armies began to inch forward, Cornwallis attempted to evacuate his army across the York River to the Gloucester Peninsula. From there, he hoped to fight his way north to New York to join General Clinton. However, with less than one-third of his troops across the river, a violent storm damaged many of his boats and prevented additional troops from leaving Yorktown.

Historians generally agree that unusual weather patterns favored the Continental Army. Was this an accident of nature or divine providence? Most of the political and military leaders of the United States at that time credited providence.

What if General Howe had joined General Burgoyne at Albany? Was the American victory at Saratoga an example of God's blessings? The troops thought so. Oliver Boardman, a soldier, wrote home: "'the Hand of Providence work'd wonderfully in Favour of America,' and he hoped that every heart would be affected by 'the wonderful goodness of God in delivering So many of our cruel unnatural Enemies into our hands, & with so little loss on our Side...'"[17]

A historian said, "Many if not most of the American soldiers had an abiding faith in the Almighty and His influence on the affairs of men, and Boardman's thoughts were echoed in letters throughout the army by soldiers who considered the victory as something of a miracle, wrought by the Lord."[18] In our view, and in the writings of several historians, this viewpoint was typical of American soldiers.

What if Cornwallis and his army had escaped Yorktown? Historian Richard Ketchum described the situation facing Washington during the summer of 1781: "As he had demonstrated on so many occasions during this long war, George Washington was a gambler—he had to be, given the paucity of his resources and the odds against him. Now, with recruiting almost at a dead end and his army dwindling day by day, he had no choice but to head for Virginia, hoping against hope that de Grasse's fleet would materialize on schedule."[19]

What if the French naval squadron had not shown up? It had happened before. Another possibility was that the British navy might have driven off Admiral de Grasse, and Washington's army would have been stranded between New York and Virginia, open to attack by both General Clinton's forces and Cornwallis' army. "And—the all important fact—these disparate allied forces had to come together at precisely the same moment. All things considered, it appeared that only a miracle could make it happen."[20] As we calculated earlier, the probability of all these actions taking place at precisely the right time was less than one percent.

What if there had been no Second Great Awakening? In addition to the growth in churches and church membership, the best way to grasp the importance of the Second Great Awakening is to read Alexis de Tocqueville. He found that the United States was a religious country and that Christianity influenced people to become more educated, more industrious and more virtuous. He concluded that the manners (character) of the people were more important in the success of the United States than its constitution and republican form of government, or its vast natural resources.

It is difficult to contemplate what might have happened in America without the positive effects of the second wave of revivals. The struggles to function as a single country rather than as a loose network of states and territories would have been overwhelming. Maintaining order on the frontier would have been a huge challenge. The Second Great Awakening stimulated institutions of higher learning, abolition of slavery, greater roles for women, patriotism, and under-girded a struggling central government.

What other unusual events benefited the United States? In addition to the examples of divine providence just cited, there were several other unusual events that contributed to America's success during its founding period:

- *Ratification of the Jay Treaty.* The treaty was unpopular, especially with the Republicans who viewed it as a sellout to the British. History has shown that John Jay negotiated a very good treaty that avoided war with England at a time when the United States was totally unprepared for such a conflict.

- *John Adams and the peace treaty with France.* This treaty prevented a declared war with France. If the Adams administration, with the strong support of Congress and the people of the United States, had declared war on France, there would have been no opportunity to purchase Louisiana.
- *Napoleon's failed efforts in St. Domingue (Haiti) opened way for the Louisiana Purchase.* The French army was decimated by yellow fever and could not continue on to New Orleans. Napoleon subsequently decided to sell Louisiana.
- *Negotiating a favorable peace treaty to end the War of 1812.* The Treaty of Ghent established the United States' boundaries in Maine and in the western part of the continent (Michigan, Wisconsin, Minnesota and west to Montana), and set the stage for long-term peaceful relations with England and Canada.

All of these events had momentous consequences for the United States, and all depended on the right breaks. Was this divine providence? Almost every American thought so.

How was early America able to develop outstanding leadership? Most students of history marvel at the quality of leadership that emerged in the British North American colonies, especially during the 1770s and continuing through the next half-century. There were Washington, John Adams, Franklin, Hamilton, Jefferson, and Madison, all of whom played multiple roles. Even those readers who do not believe in divine providence would agree that early America was blessed with exceptional leadership.

Then there was the second tier of leaders, all outstanding men in their own right. These included John Quincy Adams, Samuel Adams, Nathaniel Greene, Andrew Jackson, John Jay, Henry Knox, John Marshall, James Monroe, and John Witherspoon. Where there were other leadership needs, important contributors came from Europe, such as Marquis de Lafayette, Baron von Steuben, and Thomas Paine. Since he played a key role in preparing the country for independence, George Whitefield also falls into this category. Francis Asbury, an Englishman, led the Methodists to tremendous growth in the years following the war. There were others.

These men were far from perfect, and they often had conflicting views. It would be no exaggeration to say that some of the country's Founding Fathers strongly disliked, and, in some cases, hated each other. Yet these men worked toward a common purpose benefiting from their individual strengths, thus accomplishing the improbable.

It was not just the Founding Fathers. Cokie Roberts and Carol Berkin have written about the role of women in the founding period of the country. Most notable among them were Martha Washington, who joined her husband in winter quarters and nursed him to health in Morristown in 1777; Abigail Adams, who influenced and encouraged both John Adams and her son, John Quincy Adams; Kitty Greene, wife of General Nathaniel Greene; and Eliza Hamilton, wife of Alexander Hamilton. Obviously there were many more women who played important supporting roles, including keeping homes, farms and businesses functioning, and raising families.

As Harvard historian Bernard Bailyn pointed out, British North America was parochial; compared with England and other parts of Europe, it was the backwaters. It was not a place where one would expect to find outstanding leaders. That makes the leadership that emerged in the years leading up to the drive for independence that persevered during the war, and continued through the first 40 years of the new republic, even more amazing. America was truly blessed.

The Presence of Providence and Obligations of the Blessed

We began this book by posing the question whether a phrase frequently used by political leaders or sung at baseball games during the seventh-inning stretch—*God Bless America*—represents patriotic fervor or historic reality. Our conclusion is that both are real. Americans fervently want to be blessed and prosper, and we truly have been blessed.

Author David Brooks noted that new Americans, especially the Puritans, saw God's hand at work. "They interpreted their abundance as part of a Divine Plan, as the latest and last in a series of God's dispensations. This meant that Americans had a specific destiny, a specific role to play in the history and culmination of the universe."[21] If one believes in the possibility of providence, then he/she would almost certainly see evidence of providence in the founding of America.

Those who have been blessed have an obligation. David McCullough summed it up this way: "The laws we live by, the freedoms we enjoy, the institutions that we take for granted—as we should *never* take for granted—are all the work of other people who went before us. And to be indifferent to that isn't just to be ignorant; it is to be rude."[22]

We do not want to be ungrateful or rude; this is our main reason for writing this book. We believe it is a responsibility—and privilege—to honor God and those who went before us in founding the United States of America.

Even as we are thankful for America's past, we pray that the concepts, which began as unique to America, will survive and thrive for many generations to come.

Chapter Endnotes

The system of referencing used in this book links chapter endnotes to the bibliography. The brief endnotes are intended to be a guide to the appropriate bibliographical citation. This method is intended to eliminate duplication.

Where the author cited has more than one book listed in the bibliography, the specific book is identified in the endnote. For example, James Hutson, the first reference listed in Chapter 1, has two books in the bibliography, as does Paul Johnson, endnote 13 below.

Chapter 1. In Pursuit of Freedom—The Seeds That Influenced the Founding of America

1. Hutson, *The Founders on Religion*, 179.
2. Marty, 42.
3. Weir, 347.
4. Shelley, p. 270.
5. Bobrick, 24-75, 135.
6. Bobrick, 216-217.
7. Bobrick, 262.
8. Noll, *America's God*, 371.
9. Shelley, 261.
10. Shelley, 261.
11. Shelley, 261.
12. Marty, 41.
13. Johnson, *A History of the American People*, 6-7.
14. Taylor, 61.

15. Taylor, 61-63.
16. Stark, 169.
17. Trevelyan, 134.
18. Marty, 49.
19. Roberts, J. M., 250.
20. Marty, 20.
21. Stark, 185.
22. McDougall, 32.
23. Roberts. J. M., 251.
24. Swisher, 29.
25. Carden, 198.
26. Swisher, 39.
27. Swisher, 10-13.
28. Taylor, 292.
29. Roberts, J. M., 261.
30. Taylor, 293.
31. McDougall, 169.
32. McDougall, 170-171.
33. McDougall, 172-175.
34. Roberts, J. M., 294.
35. Stark, 12.
36. Kramnick, xi.
37. Himmelfarb, 19.
38. Swisher, 89.
39. Taylor, 302.
40. Taylor, 314.
41. Taylor, 318.
42. McDougall, 156.
43. Taylor, 324.
44. Marty, 20.
45. Noll, *America's God*, 372.
46. Stiles, 118-119.
47. Stiles, 117.

Chapter 2. Settlement Patterns in Early America—A Diversity of Motivations

1. Tocqueville, 31.
2. Harrell, 3.

3. Taylor, 33.
4. McDougall, 29.
5. Moore, 13.
6. Kurlansky, 51.
7. Coffin, 38.
8. Coffin, 38.
9. Harrell, 16.
10. Harrell, 18.
11. Taylor, 92.
12. Taylor, 78-79.
13. Simmons, 7 and 17.
14. Ross and Deveau, 16.
15. Ross and Deveau, 14-21.
16. Ross and Deveau, 10-12
17. Simmons, 18.
18. Taylor, 118.
19. Marty, 54-55.
20. Marty, 57.
21. McDougall, 45.
22. Taylor, 130.
23. Coffin, 45.
24. Coffin, 45-46.
25. Marshall and Manuel, 120.
26. Marty, 60.
27. Schweikart and Allen, 28.
28. Clark, 17.
29. Taylor, 165-166.
30. McDougall, 49.
31. McDougall, 51.
32. Shorto, 308.
33. McDougall, 69.
34. Bremer, 179.
35. Taylor, 159.
36. Shelley, 345.
37. Moore, 34.
38. Taylor, 136.
39. McDougall, 48.
40. McDougall, 64.

41. Schweikart and Allen, 34.
42. McDougall, 51.
43. Shorto, 277-278.
44. Shorto, 278.
45. Taylor, 263.
46. Taylor, 223.
47. Taylor, 225-226
48. Taylor, 226
49. Taylor, 237.
50. McDougall, 85.
51. *Fundamental Constitution of Pennsylvania*, 1682.
52. McDougall, 86.
53. Taylor, 241.
54. Taylor, 243.
55. Johnson, *A History of the American People*, 89.
56. Taylor, 384.
57. Taylor, 384.
58. Taylor, 385.
59. Ross and Deveau, 64-65
60. Schweikart and Allen, 53.
61. Simmons, 40.
62. Noll, *The Old Religion in a New World*, 47.
63. Hutson, *Religion and the Founding of the American Republic*, 18.
64. Latourette, 954.
65. Taylor, 339.
66. Bailyn, *The Ideological Origins of the American Revolution*, 32-33.

Chapter 3. The Impact of the Great Awakening: The Emergence of Discontent

1. Bailyn, *The Ideological Origins of the American Revolution*, 160.
2. Fischer, *Liberty and Freedom*, 196.
3. Butler, 179.
4. Clark, 272
5. Johnson, *A History of the American People*, 110.
6. Johnson, *A History of the American People*, 110.
7. Johnson, *A History of the American People*, 116.
8. Schweikart and Allen, 44.
9. Latourette, 958.

10. Lambert, *Inventing the "Great Awakening,"* 56.
11. Lambert, *Inventing the "Great Awakening,"* 56.
12. Noll, *The Rise of Evangelicalism*, 72.
13. Latourette, 958-959.
14. Latourette, 959.
15. Noll, *The Rise of Evangelicalism*, 77-78.
16. Noll, *The Rise of Evangelicalism*, 92.
17. Noll, *The Rise of Evangelicalism*, 83.
18. Noll, *The Rise of Evangelicalism*, 86.
19. Mansfield, *Forgotten Founding Father*, 47.
20. *George Whitefield's Journals*, 45.
21. *George Whitefield's Journals*, 47.
22. Noll, *The Rise of Evangelicalism*, 87.
23. Noll, *The Rise of Evangelicalism*, 99.
24. Lambert, 90.
25. Noll, *The Rise of Evangelicalism*, 104.
26. Noll, *The Rise of Evangelicalism*, 109.
27. Marsden, *Jonathan Edwards*, 206.
28. Taylor, 347.
29. Hutson, *Religion and the Founding of the American Republic*, 29.
30. Marsden, *Jonathan Edwards*, 209.
31. Marsden, *Jonathan Edwards*, 209.
32. Isaacson, 110.
33. Isaacson, 111.
34. Holifield, 1.
35. Mansfield, *Forgotten Founding Father*,108.
36. Mansfield, *Forgotten Founding Father*,103.
37. McDougall, 133.
38. Hutson, *Religion and the Founding of the American Republic*, 35.
39. Johnson, *A History of the American People*, 116.
40. Nash, 8-9.
41. Noll, *America's God*, 76.
42. Bailyn, *The Ideological Origins of the American Revolution*, 303.
43. Nash, 11.
44. Taylor, 342.
45. Taylor, 342.
46. Noll, *A History of Christianity in the U. S. and Canada*, 163.
47. Hutson, *Religion and the Founding of the American Republic*, 24.

48. Latourette, 960.
49. Taylor, 349.
50. Noll, *The Rise of Evangelicalism*, 181.
51. Noll, *The Rise of Evangelicalism*, 183.
52. Noll, *The Rise of Evangelicalism*, 185.
53. Newman, 670.
54. Newman, 673.
55. Noll, *America's God*, 32, 33 and 162.
56. Boorstin, *The Americans: The Colonial Experience*, 179.
57. Boorstin, *The Americans: The Colonial Experience*, 179-180.
58. Hutson, *Religion and the Founding of the American Republic*, 25.
59. Taylor, 339.
60. McDougall, 133.
61. Johnson, *A History of the American People*, 115.
62. Bushman, xi.
63. Moore, 50-51.
64. Harrell, 119.
65. Middlekauff, 338.
66. Mansfield, *Forgotten Founding Father*, 112.
67. McDougall, 134.
68. Schweikart and Allen, 97.
69. Middlekauff, 49 and 51.
70. Bushman, xiv.

Chapter 4. Prelude to the Declaration of Independence

1. McDougall, 209.
2. Stiles, xxii.
3. Cunningham, *In Pursuit of Reason*, 24.
4. Cunningham, *In Pursuit of Reason*, 25.
5. Cunningham, *In Pursuit of Reason*, 26.
6. Stahr, 37.
7. Fleming, *Liberty! The American Revolution*, 96.
8. Moore, 57.
9. Stahr, 43.
10. Founding Fathers Quotes, Web site, 4.
11. Hutson, *Religion and the Founding of the American Republic*, 54.
12. McCullough, *John Adams*, 91.
13. Wallbuilders Web site, *America Seeks God in a Time of War*, 2.

14. Stiles, 112.
15. Ferling, *A Leap in the Dark*, 159.
16. McCullough, *John Adams*, 98.
17. Middlekauff, 3.
18. McDougall, 236.
19. McDougall, 237.
20. McCullough, *John Adams*, 102.
21. McCullough, *John Adams*, 118.
22. McCullough, *John Adams*, 118-119.
23. Cunningham, *In Pursuit of Reason*, 47.
24. Fleming, *Liberty! The American Revolution*, 176.
25. Ferling, *A Leap in the Dark*, 169.
26. Johnson, *A History of the American People*, 208.
27. Roberts, Cokie, 75-76.
28. Congressional Record—Senate, 11514.
29. McCullough, *John Adams*, 65.
30. McDougall, 227.
31. McDougall, 227-228.
32. Fleming, *Liberty! The American Revolution*, 98.
33. Fleming, *Liberty! The American Revolution*, 105.
34. Middlekauff, 278.
35. McDougall, 232.
36. McDougall, 233.
37. Fleming, *Liberty! The American Revolution*, 142.
38. Novak and Novak, 65.
39. McCullough, *1776*, 60.
40. McCullough, *1776*, 83-85.
41. Flexner, 74-75.
42. McDougall, 252.
43. Roberts, Cokie, *Founding Mothers*, 71-72.
44. Wood, 140.
45. Brands, *The First American*, 453.
46. Brands, *The First American*, 3.
47. Brands, *The First American*, 471.
48. Brands, *The First American*, 470.
49. Wood, 11.
50. Fleming, *Liberty! The American Revolution*, 157.
51. Chadwick, *The First American Army*, 100.

52. Chadwick, *The First American Army*, 120.
53. Chadwick, *The First American Army*, 128-129.
54. Nelson, 311.
55. Fleming, *Liberty! The American Revolution*, 166.
56. Chadwick, *The First American Army*, 132.
57. Noll, *America's God*, 78.
58. Noll, *America's God*, 73.
59. Noll, *America's God*, 64.
60. Noll, *America's God*, 65.
61. Noll, *America's God*, 77.
62. Schweikart and Allen, 71.
63. Chadwick, *The First American Army*, 111.
64. Hutson, *Religion and the Founding of the American Republic*, 38.
65. McDougall, 237.

Chapter 5. The Revolutionary War—The First Months

1. Schiff, 63.
2. Cowley, 49.
3. Cowley, 52-53.
4. Cowley, 53.
5. Spivey, 148.
6. Flexner, 84.
7. Flexner, 90.
8. Novak and Novak, 80.
9. Fischer, *Washington's Crossing*, 209, 214-215.
10. Chadwick, *George Washington's War*, 20.
11. Fischer, *Washington's Crossing*, 259.
12. Fleming, 229.
13. Chadwick, *The First American Army*, 154.
14. Chadwick, *George Washington's War*, 73.
15. Chadwick, *George Washington's War*, 99.
16. Chadwick, *George Washington's War*, 112.
17. Flexner, 102.
18. McDougall, 256.
19. Chernow, 98.
20. Ketchum, Richard, *Saratoga*, 436.
21. Chadwick, *The First American Army*, 206.
22. Middlekauff, 504.

23. Stahr, 82.

Chapter 6. The Revolutionary War—Years of Survival

1. Chadwick, *George Washington's War*, 213.
2. Fleming, *Liberty! The American Revolution*, 280.
3. Stahr, 88.
4. Chadwick, *George Washington's War*, 294-295.
5. Chadwick, *George Washington's War*, 233.
6. Chadwick, *George Washington's War*, 234.
7. Chadwick, *George Washington's War*, 235.
8. Chadwick, *George Washington's War*, 239.
9. Chadwick, *George Washington's War*, 243.
10. Wood, 190.
11. Fleming, *Liberty! The American Revolution*, 282.
12. Chadwick, *George Washington's War*, 297.
13. LaHaye, 111.
14. Hutson, *Religion and the Founding of the American Republic*, 52.
15. Chadwick, *George Washington's War*, 298.
16. Flexner, 123.
17. Chadwick, *George Washington's War*, 304.
18. Flexner, 125.
19. Fleming, *Liberty! The American Revolution*, 284.
20. Chadwick, *George Washington's War*, 306.
21. Fleming, *Liberty! The American Revolution*, 291-292.
22. Chadwick, *George Washington's War*, 312 and 318.
23. Chadwick, *George Washington's War*, 333-334.
24. Chadwick, *George Washington's War*, 387.
25. Chadwick, *George Washington's War*, 374-376.
26. Chadwick, *George Washington's War*, 395-396.
27. Chadwick, *George Washington's War*, 398.
28. Thomas, 133.
29. Thomas, 157.
30. Thomas, 191-192.
31. Thomas, 194-197.
32. Thomas, 199.
33. Hutson, *Religion and the Founding of the American Republic*, 54.
34. Hutson, *Religion and the Founding of the American Republic*, 56-57.
35. Raphael, 96.

36. Chadwick, *George Washington's War*, 397.
37. Novak and Novak, 31.
38. Wood, 192.
39. Wood, 194.
40. Wood, 196-198.

Chapter 7. The Southern Campaigns: Defeat, Then Victory at Yorktown

1. Middlekauff, 443.
2. Chadwick, *George Washington's War*, 354.
3. Middlekauff, 440.
4. Fleming, *Liberty! The American Revolution*, 300.
5. Fleming, *Liberty! The American Revolution*, 307.
6. Middlekauff, 463.
7. Fleming, *Liberty! The American Revolution*, 313.
8. Ketchum, Richard, *Victory at Yorktown*, 111.
9. Fleming, *Liberty! The American Revolution*, 314.
10. Ketchum, Richard, *Victory at Yorktown*, 117.
11. Fleming, *Liberty! The American Revolution*, 316.
12. Ketchum, Richard, *Victory at Yorktown*, 136.
13. Ketchum, Richard, *Victory at Yorktown*, 34.
14. Ketchum, Richard, *Victory at Yorktown*, 137.
15. Ketchum, Richard, *Victory at Yorktown*, 138.
16. Fleming, *Liberty! The American Revolution*, 323.
17. Fleming, *Liberty! The American Revolution*, 322-323.
18. Ketchum, Richard, *Victory at Yorktown*, 139.
19. Ketchum, Richard, *Victory at Yorktown*, 142.
20. Ketchum, Richard, *Victory at Yorktown*, 142-143.
21. Fleming, *Liberty! The American Revolution*, 324.
22. Ketchum, Richard, *Victory at Yorktown*, 152.
23. Ketchum, Richard, *Victory at Yorktown*, 153.
24. Ketchum, Richard, *Victory at Yorktown*, 6.
25. Ellis, *His Excellency George Washington*, 134.
26. Schweikart and Allen, 86.
27. Ketchum, Richard, *Victory at Yorktown*, 191-192.
28. Fleming, *Liberty! The American Revolution*, 330.
29. Fleming, *Liberty! The American Revolution*, 329.
30. Ellis, *Founding Brothers*, 130.

31. Fleming, *Liberty! The American Revolution*, 330.
32. Fleming, *Liberty! The American Revolution*, 331.
33. Ketchum, Richard, *Victory at Yorktown*, 266.
34. Hutson, *The Founders on Religion*, 181-182.
35. Ketchum, Richard, *Victory at Yorktown*, 266-267.
36. Ketchum, Richard, *Victory at Yorktown*, 267.
37. Hutson, *The Founders on Religion*, 177.
38. Hutson, *The Founders on Religion*, 177.
39. Fleming, *Liberty! The American Revolution*, 336-337.
40. Isaacson, 402.
41. Isaacson, 407.
42. Isaacson, 408.
43. Isaacson, 409.
44. Stahr, 193.
45. Stahr, 195.
46. Fleming, *Liberty! The American Revolution*, 339.
47. Fleming, *Liberty! The American Revolution*, 340.
48. Stiles, 356.
49. Fleming, *Liberty! The American Revolution*, 340 and 343.
50. Hutson, *The Founders on Religion*, 179.
51. Hutson, *The Founders on Religion*, 19.

Chapter 8. The Chaos of the Articles of Confederation and the Need for Change

1. Middlekauff, 623.
2. Berkin, *A Brilliant Solution*, 5.
3. Van Doren, 6-7.
4. Ketcham, Ralph, *James Madison*, 185.
5. Van Doren, 6-7.
6. Ferling, *A Leap in the Dark*, 280.
7. Eidsmoe, 43.
8. Brookhiser, *Gentleman Revolutionary*, 31.
9. Bowen, 97.
10. Bowen, 98.
11. Ketcham, Ralph, *James Madison*, 193.
12. Ketcham, Ralph, *James Madison*, 191-192.
13. Lambert, *The Founding Fathers and the Place of Religion in America*, 4.
14. Van Doren, 91-92.

15. Van Doren, 93.
16. Van Doren, 93.
17. Van Doren, 94.
18. Ketcham, Ralph, *James Madison*, 219.
19. Ketcham, Ralph, *James Madison*, 226.
20. Berkin, *A Brilliant Solution*, 108.
21. Wills, *Negro President*, 2.
22. Wills, *Negro President*, 6.
23. Brookhiser, *Gentleman Revolutionary*, 85.
24. Middlekauff, 666.
25. Bowen, 189.
26. Bowen, 217.
27. Hutson, *Religion and the Founding of the American Republic*, 77.
28. Brookhiser, *Gentleman Revolutionary*, 87.
29. Brookhiser, *Gentleman Revolutionary*, 88.
30. Brookhiser, *Gentleman Revolutionary*, 91.
31. Brookhiser, *Gentleman Revolutionary*, 91-92.
32. Bowen, 229.
33. Hutson, *Religion and the Founding of the American Republic*, 62.
34. Hutson, *Religion and the Founding of the American Republic*, 64.
35. Hutson, *Religion and the Founding of the American Republic*, 64.
36. Bailyn, *The Ideological Origins of the American Revolution*, 184.
37. Bowen, 135.
38. Bowen, 135.
39. Bowen, 140.
40. Van Doren, 15.
41. McDougall, 312.
42. McDougall, 312.
43. Huntington, *The Wall Street Journal*, June 18, 2004.
44. Bowen, 125.
45. Bowen, 126.
46. Bowen, 127.
47. Meacham, 87-88.

Chapter 9. Managing Change—The Ratification of the New Constitution

1. Bailyn, *The Ideological Origins of the American Revolution*, 334.
2. Middlekauff, 679.

3. Bailyn, *To Begin the World Anew*, 107-108.
4. Bailyn, *To Begin the World Anew*, 112-113.
5. Stahr, xiii.
6. Scigliano, 8.
7. Scigliano, 8-9.
8. Stiles, 118.
9. Scigliano, 9.
10. Scigliano, 9.
11. Scigliano, 16.
12. Scigliano, 22.
13. Bailyn, *To Begin the World Anew*, 117.
14. Scigliano, 61.
15. Bailyn, *To Begin the World Anew*, 120-121.
16. Bailyn, *To Begin the World Anew*, 123.
17. Bailyn, *To Begin the World Anew*, 124.
18. Scigliano, 143.
19. Scigliano, 155.
20. Scigliano, 549.
21. Berkin, *A Brilliant Solution*, 163.
22. Bailyn, *To Begin the World Anew*, 104.
23. Ketcham, Ralph, *James Madison*, 251.
24. Ketcham, Ralph, *James Madison*, 251.
25. Berkin, *A Brilliant Solution*, 190.
26. Simon, 25.
27. Berkin, *A Brilliant Solution*, 190.
28. Hutson, *Religion and the Founding of the American Republic*, 78.
29. Hutson, *Religion and the Founding of the American Republic*, 78.
30. *Journal of the First Session of the Senate of the United States of America*, 104.
31. Noll, *One Nation Under God?* 65.
32. Noll, *One Nation Under God?* 65.
33. Gingrich, 50-51.
34. Johnson, *A History of the American People*, 209.
35. Tolson, 45.
36. Marsden, *Jonathan Edwards*, 123-124.
37. Noll, *A History of Christianity in the United States and Canada*, 144.
38. Noll, *The Rise of Evangelicalism*, 214.
39. Ferling, *A Leap in the Dark*, 160.
40. Bailyn, *To Begin the World Anew*, 136.

41. Bailyn, *To Begin the World Anew*, 136 and 140.
42. Bailyn, *To Begin the World Anew*, 141.
43. Bailyn, *To Begin the World Anew*, 144-145.
44. Noll, *One Nation Under God?* 70.

Chapter 10. The Second Great Awakening—Lasting Influences

1. Askew and Pierard, 77.
2. Marty, 175.
3. Hatch, 3.
4. Tocqueville, 356.
5. Hutson, *Religion and the Founding of the American Republic*, 108.
6. Hutson, *Religion and the Founding of the American Republic*, 103.
7. Noll, *A History of Christianity in the United States and Canada*, 171-173.
8. Hatch, 3.
9. Noll, *A History of Christianity in the United States and Canada*, 171-172.
10. Marty, 170.
11. Hempton, 205.
12. Marty, 171.
13. Noll, *A History of Christianity in the United States and Canada*, 173.
14. Hempton, 68.
15. Hempton, 121-123.
16. Hempton, 137-138.
17. Hempton, 139.
18. Marty, 170.
19. Noll, *A History of Christianity in the United States and Canada*, 174.
20. Askew and Pierard, 78.
21. Askew and Pierard, 78.
22. Noll, *A History of Christianity in the United States and Canada*, 168.
23. Hardman, 125.
24. Hatch, 17.
25. Hardman, 126.
26. Hutson, *Religion and the Founding of the American Republic*, 101.
27. Hutson, *Religion and the Founding of the American Republic*, 102.
28. Shelley, 386-387.
29. Noll, *A History of Christianity in the U. S. and Canada*, 167.
30. Moore, 86.
31. Hutson, *Religion and the Founding of the American Republic*, 103.
32. Noll, *A History of Christianity in the U. S. and Canada*, 167.

33. Hatch, 3.
34. Noll, *A History of Christianity in the U. S. and Canada*, 178.
35. Noll, *A History of Christianity in the U. S. and Canada*, 179.
36. Noll, *A History of Christianity in the U. S. and Canada*, 180.
37. Noll, *A History of Christianity in the U. S. and Canada*, 175.
38. Noll, *A History of Christianity in the U. S. and Canada*, 176.
39. Noll, *A History of Christianity in the U. S. and Canada*, 187.
40. Noll, *A History of Christianity in the U. S. and Canada*, 185.
41. Hutson, *Religion and the Founding of the American Republic*, 111.
42. Hutson, *Religion and the Founding of the American Republic*, 106.
43. Noll, *A History of Christianity in the U. S. and Canada*, 180-181.
44. Noll, *The History of Christianity in the U. S. and Canada*, 200.
45. Harrell, 202.
46. Marty, 239-240.
47. Noll, *The History of Christianity in the U. S. and Canada*, 204.
48. Harrell, 203.
49. Noll, *The History of Christianity in the U. S. and Canada*, 205.
50. Johnson, *A History of the American People*, 307.
51. Levy, 144.
52. Levy, 183.
53. Marsden, *The Soul of the American University*, 70-71; 276.
54. Marsden, *The Soul of the American University*, 134, 150, and 209.
55. Wilentz, 266-267.
56. Noll, *America's God*, 167.
57. Noll, *America's God*, 163.
58. Hutson, *Religion and the Founding of the American Republic*, 35.
59. Noll, *A History of Christianity in the United States and Canada*, 153.
60. Hatch, 6.
61. Hardman, 169.
62. Hutson, *Religion and the Founding of the American Republic*, 113.
63. Hardman, 243.
64. McDougall, 511.
65. Noll, *The Rise of Evangelicalism*, 243.
66. McDougall, 508.
67. Hutson, *Religion and the Founding of the American Republic*, 100.

Chapter 11. Nation Building—Challenges and Triumphs of the First 12 Years

1. Ferling, *A Leap in the Dark*, 487.
2. McDougall, 321.
3. Morrison, 317.
4. Gingrich, 49.
5. Gingrich, 49.
6. *Journal of the First Session of the Senate of the United States of America*, 26.
7. Gingrich, 49.
8. Flexner, 220.
9. Flexner, 220-221.
10. Cunliffe, 76-77.
11. Cunliffe, 77.
12. Flexner, 258.
13. Flexner, 236.
14. Morrison, 327.
15. Morrison, 326.
16. Flexner, 279-280.
17. Flexner, 279-280.
18. Stahr, 314-315.
19. Stahr, 327.
20. Stahr, 338.
21. Ellis, *Founding Brothers*, 136.
22. Morrison, 344.
23. Ellis, *Founding Brothers*, 121-122.
24. Freeman, 862-863.
25. Wallbuilders Web site, "George Washington's Farewell Address," 10-11.
26. McDougall, 362.
27. Taranto, 23.
28. McCullough, *John Adams*, 495.
29. McCullough, *John Adams*, 495.
30. McCullough, *John Adams*, 501,
31. *The Phenix/Windham Herald*, April 12, 1798, Wallbuilders Web site, 2.
32. Hutson, *Religion and the Founding of the American Republic*, 82.
33. McCullough, *John Adams*, 511.
34. McCullough, *John Adams*, 534.
35. McCullough, *John Adams*, 552.

36. Ferling, *A Leap in the Dark*, 487.
37. Ferling, *A Leap in the Dark*, 466.
38. Marty, 158.
39. Johnson, *A History of Christianity*, 427.
40. McCullough, *John Adams*, 551.

Chapter 12. Thomas Jefferson—A Change in Direction?

1. Ferling, *A Leap in the Dark*, 486.
2. Simon, 208-217.
3. Borneman, 40.
4. Hutson, *Religion and the Founding of the American Republic*, 83.
5. Hutson, *Religion and the Founding of the American Republic*, 84.
6. Hutson, *Religion and the Founding of the American Republic*, 86.
7. Hutson, *Religion and the Founding of the American Republic*, 89.
8. Hutson, *Religion and the Founding of the American Republic*, 89.
9. Hutson, *Religion and the Founding of the American Republic*, 91.
10. Hutson, *Religion and the Founding of the American Republic*, 92-93.
11. Hutson, *Religion and the Founding of the American Republic*, 93.
12. Amos and Gardiner, 158.
13. Cerami, 11.
14. Cerami, 58.
15. Cerami, 45.
16. Cerami, 10.
17. Cerami, 146.
18. Cerami, 164-165.
19. Cerami, 193.
20. Kukla, 306-307.
21. Ambrose, *Lewis & Clark, Voyage of Discovery*, 26.
22. Ambrose, *Lewis & Clark, Voyage of Discovery*, unnumbered page.
23. Ambrose, *Lewis & Clark, Voyage of Discovery*, 68.
24. Ambrose, *Lewis & Clark, Voyage of Discovery*, 79.
25. Ambrose, *Lewis & Clark, Voyage of Discovery*, 134.
26. Ambrose, *Lewis & Clark Voyage of Discovery*, 139.
27. Ambrose, *Lewis & Clark, Voyage of Discovery*, 176-177.
28. Ambrose, *Lewis & Clark, Voyage of Discovery*, 176.
29. Patton, 144.
30. Phillips, 109.
31. Kukla, 290.

Chapter 13. Mr. Madison's War

1. Brands, *Andrew Jackson*, 157.
2. Miller and Molesky, 110.
3. Brands, *Andrew Jackson*, 165.
4. Brands, *Andrew Jackson*, 166.
5. Harrell, 263.
6. Brands, *Andrew Jackson*, 194-195.
7. Brands, *Andrew Jackson*, 205.
8. Johnson, *A History of the American People*, 262.
9. Borneman, 84.
10. Borneman, 87.
11. Borneman, 91-92.
12. Borneman, 222.
13. Borneman, 232.
14. Borneman, 238.
15. Borneman, 245.
16. Borneman, 246.
17. Wills, *Henry Adams and the Making of America*, 369.
18. Nagel, 210-211.
19. Borneman, 270.
20. Gingrich, 52.
21. Borneman, 304.
22. Stahr, 218.
23. Stahr, 218.
24. Federer, 166.
25. Earle, 251.
26. Earle, 252.
27. Ketcham, Ralph, 47.
28. Amos and Gardiner, 166.
29. Hutson, *Religion and the Founding of the American Republic*, 73.
30. Ketcham, Ralph, 166.
31. Gingrich, 52.
32. Gingrich, 52.
33. Hutson, *Religion and the Founding of the American Republic*, 99.
34. Hutson, *Religion and the Founding of the American Republic*, 96-97.

Chapter 14. Presidencies of James Monroe and John Quincy Adams Position New Country in the World

1. Holmes, 119-120.
2. Ammon, 345.
3. Ammon, 366-367, 380.
4. Remini, 80-92.
5. Ammon, 449.
6. Holmes, 122-123.
7. Holmes, 120.
8. Ammon, 481-482.
9. McCullough, *Imprimis, April 2005*, 6.
10. Brookhiser, *America's First Dynasty*, 66.
11. Nagel, 202.
12. Nagel, 235.
13. Nagel, 242-243.
14. Nagel, 260-262.
15. Nagel, 270.
16. Barleby.com Web site.
17. Brookhiser, *America's First Dynasty*, 93.
18. Brookhiser, *America's First Dynasty*, 95.
19. Brands, *Andrew Jackson*, 437.
20. Brookhiser, *America's First Dynasty*, 108.
21. John Quincy Adams, Oration at Plymouth, Dec. 22, 1802, The Free Lib. Web site, 8.
22. John Quincy Adams, Oration at Plymouth, Dec. 22, 1802, The Free Lib. Web site, 9.
23. John Quincy Adams, Oration at Plymouth, Dec. 22, 1802, The Free Lib. Web site, 11.
24. John Quincy Adams, an address in Washington, D.C., July 4, 1821.
25. John Quincy Adams, July 4, 1837 speech, Newburyport, Massachusetts, Web site, 2.
26. John Quincy Adams, New York Historical Society, April 30, 1839, Web site, 8.

Chapter 15. The Role of Christianity in Founding America

1. Staloff, 3 and 9.
2. McCullough, *John Adams*, 607.

3. Cappon, 339-340.
4. Cappon, 509.
5. Cappon, 512.
6. Cappon, 529.
7. Cappon, 530.
8. Cappon, xlix.
9. Nagel, 312.
10. Hutson, *Religion and the Founding of the American Republic*, 114.
11. Tocqueville, 353.
12. Tocqueville, 346.
13. Tocqueville, 364.
14. Tocqueville, 372.
15. Tocqueville, 345-346.
16. Tocqueville, 373.
17. Tocqueville, 373.
18. Tocqueville, 355.
19. Tocqueville, xxxix.
20. Hatch, 9.
21. Stark, 22-23.
22. Stark, 53.
23. Stark, 76.
24. Cappon, 464-466.
25. Cappon, 445.
26. Tocqueville, 355-356.
27. Johnson, *A History of Christianity*, 428.
28. Johnson, *A History of the American People*, 117.
29. Brooks, 115-116.
30. Marsden, *Jonathan Edwards*, 504.
31. McDougall, 312.
32. Freeman, 33.
33. Stahr, 73.
34. Noll, *The Rise of Evangelicalism*, 185.
35. Noll, *The Rise of Evangelicalism*, 186.
36. Tocqueville, 353-354.
37. Meacham, 5.
38. Meacham, 6.

Chapter 16. God Has Blessed America

1. Mansfield, *The Character and Greatness of Winston Churchill,* 199.
2. Gingrich, 45.
3. John Quincy Adams, Dec. 22, 1802, The Free Lib. Web site, 15-16.
4. John Quincy Adams, Dec. 22, 1802, The Free Lib. Web site, 7 and 16.
5. Huntington, *The American Enterprise,* 20.
6. Moore, xiii and xxiii.
7. Moore, xxiii.
8. Moore, 60.
9. Moore, 63.
10. Moore, 69.
11. Moore Web site, November 21, 2005.
12. Stiles, 40.
13. Tocqueville, 349.
14. Crawford, 249.
15. McDougall, 230.
16. Flexner, 26.
17. Ketchum, Richard, *Saratoga,* 436
18. Ketchum, Richard, *Saratoga,* 437.
19. Ketchum, Richard, *Victory at Yorktown,* 152.
20. Ketchum, Richard, *Victory at Yorktown,* 153.
21. Brooks, 255-256.
22. McCullough, *Imprimis,* April 2005, 2.

Selected Bibliography

Biographies and American History

Alexander, J. K. *Samuel Adams: America's Revolutionary Politician*, Rowman & Littlefield Publishers, Inc., 2002.

Ambrose, Stephen. *Undaunted Courage*, Simon & Schuster, 1996.

Ambrose, Stephen. *Lewis & Clark, Voyage of Discovery*, National Geographic Society, 1998.

Ammon, H. *James Monroe: A Quest for National Identity*, University Press of Virginia, 1990.

Amos, Gary and Richard Gardiner. *Never Before In History*, Foundation for Thought and Ethics, 2004.

Asch, Ronald G. *The Thirty Years War: The Holy Roman Empire and Europe, 1618-1848*, St. Martin's Press, 1987.

Askew, Thomas A. and Richard V. Pierard. *The American Church Experience: A Concise History*, Baker Academic, 2004.

Bailyn, Bernard. *To Begin the World Anew*, Alfred A. Knopf, 2003.

Bailyn, Bernard. *The Ideological Origins of the American Revolution*, The Belknap Press of Harvard University Press, 1992.

Berkin, Carol. *A Brilliant Solution: Inventing The American Constitution*, Harcourt, Inc., 2002.

Berkin, Carol. *Revolutionary Mothers: Women in the Struggle for America's Independence*, Alfred A. Knopf, 2005.

Black, Jeremy. *Eighteenth Century Europe*, 1700-1789, Macmillan Press, 1990.

Bobrick, Benson. *Wide as the Waters: The Story of the English Bible and the Revolution It Inspired*, Penguin Books, 2002.

Bonney, Richard. *The Thirty Years War: 1618-1648*, Osprey Publishing, 2002.

Boorstin, Daniel J. *The Americans: The Colonial Experience*, Random House, 1958.

Boorstin, Daniel J. *The Americans: The National Experience*, History Book Club, New York, 1965.

Borneman, Walter R. *1812: The War That Forged A Nation*, HarperCollins Publishers, 2004.

Bowen, Catherine D. *Miracle at Philadelphia: The Story of the Constitutional Convention, May to September 1787*, Little, Brown & Company, 1966.

Bradford, William. *The History of Plymouth Colony*, Walter Black, 1948.

Brands, H. W. *The First American: The Life and Times of Benjamin Franklin*, Anchor Books, 2000.

Brands, H. W. *Andrew Jackson: His Life and Times*, Doubleday, 2005.

Bremer, Francis J. *John Winthrop, America's Forgotten Founding Father*, Oxford University Press, 2003.

Brodie, F. M. *Thomas Jefferson, An Intimate History*, W. W. Norton & Company, 1974.

Brookhiser, Richard. *America's First Dynasty: The Adamses, 1735-1918*, Free Press, 2002.

Brookhiser, Richard. *Gentleman Revolutionary: Gouverneur Morris—The Rake Who Wrote the Constitution*, Free Press, 2003.

Brookhiser, Richard. *Alexander Hamilton, American*, Simon & Shuster, 2000.

Brookhiser, Richard. *What Would the Founders Do?* Basic Books, 2006.

Brooks, David. *On Paradise Drive*, Simon & Schuster, 2004.

Bushman, Richard. *The Great Awakening: Documents on the Revival of Religion*, Atheneum, 1970.

Butler, Jon. *Awash in a Sea of Faith: Christianizing the American People*, Harvard University Press, 1990.

Cairns, Trevor. *The Old Regime and the Revolution*, Lerner Publications, 1980.

Cameron, Richard. M. *Methodism and Society in Historical Perspective*, Abingdon Press, 1961.

Cappon, Lester J. *The Adams-Jefferson Letters: The Complete Correspondence Between Thomas Jefferson and Abigail and John Adams*, A Clarion Book, Published by Simon and Schuster. 1959.

Carden, Allen. *Puritan Christianity in America, Religion and Life in Seventeenth-Century Massachusetts*, Baker Book House Company, 1990.

Cerami, Charles A. *Jefferson's Great Gamble*, Sourcebooks, Inc., 2003.

Chadwick, B. *George Washington's War*, Sourcebooks, Inc., 2004.

Chadwick. B. *The First American Army*, Sourcebooks, Inc., 2005.

Chalfant, J. W. *America: A Call to Greatness*, published by the author, 2003.

Chernow, R. *Alexander Hamilton*, The Penguin Press, 2004.

Clark, Charles. E. *The Eastern Frontier: The Settlement of Northern New England, 1610-1763*, University Press of New England, 1983.

Coffin, Robert P. T. *Kennebec: Cradle of Americans*, Down East Books, 1937.

Coral Ridge Ministries. Speeches of the Reclaiming America For Christ Conference 2000, *Tipping the Scales: Restoring righteousness to a nation in the balance*, 2000.

Cowley, Robert. *What Ifs? of American History*, G. P. Putnam's Sons, 2003.

Crawford, Michael J. *Seasons of Grace*, Oxford University Press, 1991.

Cunliffe, Marcus. *The American Heritage History of the Presidency*, Simon and Schuster, 1968.

Cunningham, Noble E., Jr. *In Pursuit of Reason: The Life of Thomas Jefferson*, Ballantine Books, 1987.

Cunningham, Noble E., Jr. *The Presidency of James Monroe*, University of Kansas Press, 1996.

Diamond, Jared. *Guns, Germs, and Steel: The Fates of Human Societies*, W. W. Norton & Company, 1999.

Earle, Peter. *The Pirate Wars*, St. Martin's Press Inc., 2005.

Eidsmoe, John. *Christianity and the Constitution*, Baker Book House Company, 1987.

Ellis, Joseph J. *Founding Brothers: The Revolutionary Generation*, Vintage Books, A division of Random House, 2000.

Ellis, Joseph J. *American Sphinx: The Character of Thomas Jefferson*, Vintage Books, A division of Random House, 1998.

Ellis, Joseph J. *After the Revolution: Profiles of Early American Culture*, W. W. Norton & Company, 1979.

Ellis, Joseph J. *His Excellency George Washington*, Vintage Books, 2004.

Federer, W. J. *America's God and Country: Encyclopedia of Quotations*, Amerisearch Inc., 2000.

Ferling, John. *Adams vs. Jefferson: The Tumultuous Election of 1800*, Oxford University Press, 2004.

Ferling, John. *A Leap in the Dark: The Struggle to Create the American Republic*, Oxford University Press, 2003.

Fischer, D. H. *Washington's Crossing*, Oxford University Press, 2004.

Fischer, D. H. *Liberty and Freedom: A Visual History of America's Founding Ideas*, Oxford University Press, 2005.

Fleming, Thomas. *Duel: Alexander Hamilton, Aaron Burr and the Future of America*, Basic Books, 1999.

Fleming, Thomas. *Liberty! The American Revolution*, Viking, 1997.

Flexner, James Thomas. *Washington: The Indispensable Man*, Little, Brown and Company, 1969.

Freeman, Joanne B. *Alexander Hamilton Writings*, The Library of America, 1961.

Fritz, Charles. *An Artist with the Corps of Discover*, Farcountry Press, 2004.

George Whitefield's Journals, The Banner of Truth Trust, 1960.

Gingrich, Newt. *Winning the Future*, Regnery Publishing, Inc., 2005.

Gura, Philip F. *Jonathan Edwards: America's Evangelical*, Hill and Wang, 2005.

Hardman, Keith J. *The Spiritual Awakeners*, Moody Press, 1983.

Harrell, David E., Jr., et. al. *Unto a Good Land: A History of the American People, Volume 1* (to 1900), Wm B. Eerdmans Publishing Company, 2005.

Harris, Sam. *The End of Faith: Religion, Terror and the Future of Reason*, W. W. Norton & Company, 2005.

Hart, Gary. *God and Caesar in America: an Essay on Religion and Politics*, Fulcrum Publishing, 2005.

Hatch, Nathan O. *The Democratization of American Christianity*, Yale University Press, 1989.

Hempton, David. *Methodism: Empire of the Spirit*, Yale University Press, 2005.

Herman, A. *How the Scots Invented the Modern World*, Three Rivers Press, 2001.

Himmelfarb, Gertrude. *The Roads to Modernity: The British, French, and American Enlightenments*, Alfred A. Knopf, 2004.

Holifield, E. B. *Theology in America: Christian Thought from the Age of the Puritans to the Civil War*, Yale University Press, 2003.

Holmes, David. L. *The Religion of the Founding Fathers*, Ash Lawn-Highland and The Clements Library, 2003.

Hutson, James H. *Religion and the Founding of the American Republic*, Library of Congress, 1999.

Hutson, James. H. *The Founders on Religion: A Book of Quotations*, Princeton University Press, 2005.

Isaacson, Walter. *Benjamin Franklin: An American Life*, Simon & Shuster, 2003.

Johnson, Paul. *A History of the American People*, HarperPerennial, 1996.

Johnson, Paul. *A History of Christianity*, A Touchstone Book, Published by Simon & Schuster, 1976.

Johnson, Paul. *George Washington: The Founding Father*, Eminent Lives Collection, HarperCollins, 2005.

Jones, Landon Y. *The Essential Lewis and Clark*, HarperCollins Publishers, 2000.

Journal of the First Session of the Senate of the United States of America, City of New York, March 4, 1789.

Keegan, John. *The Napoleonic Wars*, Gunther E. Rothenberg, 2001.

Kennedy, D. J., with Newcombe, J. *What If America Were A Christian Nation Again?*, Thomas Nelson Publishers, 2003.

Ketcham, Ralph. *James Madison*, The University Press of Virginia, 1990.

Ketchum, Richard M. *Victory at Yorktown: The Campaign That Won The Revolution*, Henry Holt and Company, 2004.

Ketchum, Richard. M. *Saratoga: Turning Point of America's Revolutionary War*, Henry Holt and Company, 1997.

Ketchum, Richard M. *The American Heritage Book of the Revolution*, American Heritage Publishing Co., 1950.

Ketchum, Richard. M. *The Winter Soldiers: The Battles for Trenton and Princeton*, Henry Holt and Company, 1973.

Ketchum, Richard M. *The American Heritage Book of the Revolution*, Simon and Schuster, 1958.

Kramnick, Isaac. *The Portable Enlightenment Reader*, Penguin Books, 1995.

Kukla, Jon. *A Wilderness So Immense, The Louisiana Purchase and the Destiny of America*, Alfred A. Knopf, 2003.

Kurlansky, Mark. *Cod: A Biography of the Fish That Changed the World*, Penguin Books, 1997.

LaHaye, Tim. *Faith of Our Founding Fathers*, Wolgemuth & Hyatt, 1987.

Lambert, Frank. *Inventing the "Great Awakening,"* Princeton University Press, 1999.

Lambert, Frank. *The Founding Fathers and the Place of Religion in America*, Princeton University Press, 2003.

Land, Richard. *Imagine! A God-Blessed America*, Broadman & Holman Publishers, 2005.

Lane, Jason. *General and Madame de LaFayette: Partners in Liberty's Cause in the American and French Revolutions*, Taylor Trade Publishing, 2003.

Latourette, K. S. *A History of Christianity*, Harper & Brothers, 1953.

Levy, Andrew. *The First Emancipator: The Forgotten Story of Robert Carter, the Founding Father Who Freed His Slaves*, Random House, 2005.

Mansfield, Stephen. *Forgotten Founding Father: The Heroic Legacy of George Whitefield*, Highlands Books, 2001.

Mansfield, Stephen. *The Character and Greatness of Winston Churchill*, Cumberland House, 1995.

Markham, J. David. *Napoleon's Road to Glory*, Brassey's, 2003.

Marsden, George M. *Jonathan Edwards, A Life*, Yale University Press, 2003.

Marsden, George M. *The Soul of the American University*, Oxford University Press, 1994.

Marshall, P., and Manuel, D. *The Light and the Glory*, Fleming R. Revell, 1977.

Marty, M. E. *Pilgrims in Their Own Land: 500 Years of Religion in America*, Penguin Books, 1984.

McCullough, David. *John Adams*, Simon & Shuster, 2001.

McCullough, David. *1776*, Simon & Shuster, 2005.

McDougall, W. A. *Freedom Just Around the Corner, A New American History, 1585-1828*, HarperCollins Publisher, 2004.

Meacham, Jon. *American Gospel: God, the Founding Fathers, and the Making of a Nation*, Random House, 2006.

Middlekauff, Robert. *The Glorious Cause: The American Revolution, 1763-1789*, Oxford University Press, 2005.

Miller, John J. and Mark Molesky. *Our Oldest Enemy: A History of America's Disastrous Relationship with France*, Broadway Books, 2004.

Miller, Lee. *Roanoke: Solving the Mystery of the Lost Colony*, Penguin Books, 2000.

Moore, James P. Jr. *One Nation Under God: The History of Prayer in America*, Doubleday, 2005

Morrissey, Brendon. *Yorktown 1781: The world turned upside down*, Osprey Publishing, 1997.

Morrison, Samuel Eliot. *The Oxford History of the American People*, Oxford University Press, 1965.

Nagel, Paul C. *John Quincy Adams: A Public Life, A Private Life*, First Harvard University Press Paperback Edition, 1999.

Nash, Gary B. *The Unknown American Revolution: The Unholy Birth of Democracy and the Struggle to Create America*, Viking, 2005.

Nelson, James. L. *Benedict Arnold's Navy*, McGraw Hill, 2006.

Newman, A. H. *A Manual of Church History, Vol. II,* The American Baptist Publication Society, 1931.

Noll, Mark A. *The Rise of Evangelicalism: The Age of Edwards, Whitefield and the Wesleys,* InterVarsity Press, 2003.

Noll, Mark A. *America's God,* Oxford University Press, 2002.

Noll, Mark A. *A History of Christianity in the United States and Canada,* William B. Eerdmans Publishing Company, 1992.

Noll, Mark A. *One Nation Under God? Christian Faith & Political Action in America,* Harper & Row, Publishers, 1988.

Noll, Mark A. *The Old Religion in a New World,* Wm. B. Eerdmans, 2002.

Novak, Michael and Jana. *Washington's God,* Basic Books, 2006.

Paine, Thomas. *Common Sense and Other Writings,* Barnes & Noble Classics, 2005.

Paton, Bruce C. *Lewis & Clark: Doctors in the Wilderness,* Fulcrum Publishing, 2001.

Philbrick, Nathaniel, *Mayflower,* Viking, 2006.

Phillips, Brad. *Lewis & Clark, Part 1, From Jefferson's Parlor to the Great Plains,* Apricot Press, 2003.

Pole, J. R. *The Federalist,* Hackett Publish Co., 2005.

Raphael, Ray. *Founding Myths: Stories that Hide our Patriotic Past,* The New Press, 2004.

Remini, Robert V. *Andrew Jackson,* Twayne Publishers, 1966.

Remini, Robert V. *John Quincy Adams,* Henry Holt & Co., 2002.

Roberts, Cokie. *Founding Mothers: The Women Who Raised Our Nation,* William Morrow, 2004.

Roberts, J. M. *A History of Europe,* The Penguin Press, 1997.

Ross, Sally and Deveau, Alphonse. *The Acadians of Nova Scotia, Past and Present*, Nimbus Publishing Limited, 1992.

Roll, Eric. *A History of Economic Thought*, Prentice-Hall, Inc., 1964.

Schiff, Stacy. *A Great Improvisation: Franklin, France, and the Birth of America*, Henry Holt & Company, 2005.

Schweikart, Larry and Allen, Michael. *A Patriot's History of the United States*, Sentinel, 2004.

Scigliano, R. *The Federalist: A Commentary on the Constitution of the United States*, The Modern Library, 2000.

Shelley, Bruce L. *Church History in Plain Language*, Thomas Nelson Publishers, 1995.

Shorto, Russell. *The Island at the Center of the World*, Vintage Books, a Division of Random House, 2005.

Simmons, R. C. *The American Colonies: From Settlement to Independence*, David McKay Company, Inc. 1976.

Simon, James F. *What Kind of Nation? Thomas Jefferson, John Marshall and the Epic Struggle to Create a United States*, Simon & Shuster, 2002.

Spivey, Larkin. *Miracles of the American Revolution: Divine Intervention and the Birth of the Republic*, Allegiance Press, 2004.

Stahr, Walter. *John Jay*, Hambledon and London, 2005.

Staloff, Darren. *Hamilton, Adams, Jefferson: The Politics of Enlightenment and the American Founding*, Hill & Wang, 2005.

Stark, Rodney. *The Victory of Reason: How Christianity led to Freedom, Capitalism, and Western Success*, Random House, 2005.

Stiles, T. J. *The American Revolution: First-Person Accounts by the Men Who Shaped Our Nation*, A Perigee Book, 1999.

Stryker, William S. *The Battles of Trenton and Princeton*, Old Barracks Association, 2001.

Swisher, Clarice. *The Glorious Revolution*, Lucent Books, 1993.

Taranto, James, and Leo, Leonard. *Presidential Leadership: Rating the Best and the Worst in the White House*, Wall Street Journal Books published by Free Press, 2004

Taylor, Alan. *American Colonies*, Viking, 2001.

Thomas, Evan. *John Paul Jones: Sailor, Hero, Father of the American Navy*, Simon & Shuster, 2003.

Thomson, Ralph E. and Matthew. *David Thomson, 1592-1628, First Yankee: The Story of New Hampshire's First Settler*, Piscataqua Pioneers, 1997.

Thomson, Jr., Meldrim. *One Hundred Famous Founders*, Mt. Cube Farm, 1994.

Tocqueville, Alexis de. *Democracy in America*, A Bantam Classic, 2000.

Trevelyan, Raleigh. *Sir Walter Raleigh*, Henry Holt and Company, 2002.

Van Doren, Carl. *The Great Rehearsal: The Story of the Making and Ratifying of the Constitution of the United States,* The Viking Press, 1948.

Van Ens, Jack R. *How Jefferson Made the Best of Bad Messes*, Majesty, Inc., 2000.

Weir, Alison. *Henry VIII: The King and His Court*, Ballantine Books, 2001.

Wetzel, Charles. *James Monroe*, Chelsea House, 1989.

Wilentz, Sean. *The Rise of American Democracy*, W. W. Norton & Company, 2005.

Wills, Garry. *Henry Adams and the Making of America*, Houghton Mifflin Company, 2005.

Wills, Garry. *Negro President: Jefferson and the Slave Power*, Houghton Mifflin Company, 2003.

Wood, Gordon S. *The Americanization of Benjamin Franklin*, The Penguin Press, 2004.

Articles and Other Documents

Abbott, Greg, "Thou Shalt Not Mess With Texas," *The Wall Street Journal*, March 2, 2005, A16.

Andrews, John. "Scoffers of all faiths: Go ahead and hoot." *The Denver Post*, March 20, 2005, 5E.

Congressional Record—Senate, "The Signers of the Declaration of Independence," July 2, 1976, S 11513 and S 11514.

Huntington, S. P. "Under God," *The Wall Street Journal*, June 16, 2004.

Huntington, S. P. "Are We a Nation 'Under God'?" *The American Enterprise*, July/August 2004.

McCullough, David. "Knowing History and Knowing Who We Are," *Imprimis*, April 2005.

McGurn, W. "Review/Books—Who Are We?" *The Wall Street Journal*, May 21, 2004.

Rosenbaum, D. E. "In Times of Trouble, the Founding Fathers Sell Well," *The New York Times*, July 4, 2004.

Spencer, Jim. "A survivor's simple plea: respect," *The Denver Post*, January 28, 2005, 1D.

Tolson, Jay. "Divided, We Stand," *U. S. News & World Report*, August 8, 2005, 42-48.

Trachtenberg, J. A. "Behind America's Infatuation With the Founding Fathers," *The Wall Street Journal*, April 12, 2004, B1 and B3.

About the Authors

DEAN C. CODDINGTON

Coddington is a senior consultant with McManis Consulting, based in the Denver area. In 1970, he co-founded BBC Research & Consulting, an economic research firm, and served as a managing director of that firm until mid 1997. He has been with McManis since that time. From 1959 to 1970, Coddington worked as a research economist with the University of Denver's Research Institute; his areas of expertise included local and regional economic development, federal research and development policy, and socioeconomic impact assessment.

Coddington received his BS degree (1954) in civil engineering from South Dakota State University, and his MBA degree (1959) from the Harvard Business School. He served as an Air Force installation engineering officer in England after his graduation from South Dakota State University.

In health care, Coddington has supervised marketing research and strategic planning assignments for hospitals, medical groups, health plans and industry associations in all parts of the United States. With Keith Moore, he has co-authored nine health care books, and has written more than 100 articles (including four in the *Harvard Business Review*) on subjects ranging from factors driving health care costs to strategies for survival in the hospital industry. He has given speeches or led seminars before dozens of health care organizations.

He is past chairman of the board of trustees of 328-bed Swedish Medical Center in the Denver area, and also served on the board of directors of the Colorado Neurological Institute. He is past president of the Colorado Harvard Business School Club. Coddington presently serves on the boards of three Denver area not-for-profit organizations: Doctors Care (medical services for uninsured children); Town Hall Arts Center (a Littleton professional theater group); and Southwest Counseling Associates (20 Christian therapists).

Coddington is a member of Mission Hills Church, and has served as moderator, Sunday school teacher, and strategic planning facilitator for both the church and for Denver Seminary. Since 1977, he has been the leader of a men's prayer time that meets Saturday mornings, and is also a part of a community men's Bible study. He and his wife Judy have four children and seven grandchildren.

RICHARD L. CHAPMAN

Chapman has a BS in history and political science and a minor in economics from South Dakota State University (1954); an MPA in public administration from Syracuse University (1958); and a PhD in political science, also from Syracuse (1967). He also has one year of graduate studies, as a Rotary Fellow, at Cambridge University in England.

In 1986, Chapman helped organize the Milliken Chapman Research Group, and in 1988, was the principal of Chapman Research Group; both organizations were located in Littleton, Colo. Chapman Research specialized in policy management and technology applications research.

For four years in the early 1980s, Chapman directed the Management and Application of Science and Technology program at the University of Denver's Research Institute. In the 13 years prior to this, he managed a wide variety of research programs for the National Academy of Public Administration in Washington, D.C., where he was director of research and vice president.

Earlier in his career, he served in various government posts, including staff director and legislative consultant for a South Dakota congressman. He also served as a professional staff member and chief advisor to the Research and Technical Programs Subcommittee of the Committee on Government Operations, U. S. House of Representatives, and he was deputy director of research for the South Dakota Legislative Research Council.

His experience in executive agencies of the federal government includes positions in the Office of Secretary of Defense, the Bureau of the Budget in the Executive Office of the President, and the National Institutes of Health. From 1955 to 1957, he served as an officer in the U. S. Army, including a tour of duty in Korea.

In his professional career, Chapman has published one book and more than 75 research reports, articles and other documents.

Chapman is active in professional, civic, community, and church organizations. He was a member of the Technology Transfer Society, where he served on the national board for eight years, and as a member of the American Association for the Advancement of Science.

He is on the board of directors, and past chairman, of the South Dakota State University Foundation. He is a member of Our Father Lutheran Church in Centennial where he teaches early church history. He and his wife Marilyn have five children and 13 grandchildren.

Index

Most sub-categories in this index are arranged chronologically rather than alphabetically.

Abolitionists (abolition of slavery) 197, 284, 291
Acadia (Acadians; Cajuns) 10, 12, 28
Adams, Abigail 72-73, 79, 272, 293
Adams, John 21, 44, 85, 87, 292
    Boston Massacre 74
    Continental Congress 68, 70-72
    Peace Commission 144-145
    President 213-217
    Avoiding war with France 204, 213-217, 245, 264, 292
Adams/Jefferson letters 270-273
Adams, John Quincy 257-258, 273, 292
    Youth 225, 261
    Harvard 261-262
    Ambassador to Russia 251, 261
    Religion & Bible study 262-263, 268
    Treaty of Ghent 251
    Secretary of State 259, 262-263
    President 264
    Orations 265-267, 284-285
    U. S. House of Rep.. 265
    Opposition to slavery 265, 268

Adams, Samuel 67, 70, 74, 76, 292
Alexander, Emperor (Russia) 251, 255
Alien and Sedition Acts 213, 219
Allen, Ethan 78, 83
Allen, Richard 196
Amistad case 265, 268
Andre, Maj. John 121
Annapolis 124, 147, 150-152, 156
Appalachian Mountains 187, 191, 225, 284
Arnold, Benedict 43
    Ticonderoga 78
    Canadian invasion 82
    Arnold's Navy 83, 86
    Saratoga 103
    Traitor 120-121, 125
    British officer 134
Articles of Confederation 142, 150-152, 161, 174, 181
Asbury, Francis 59, 187-189, 193, 284, 292

Baltimore 35, 189, 196, 245, 249-240, 251, 260

Baptists 57-58, 99, 150, 175-176, 180, 193, 199, 284
Barbados (Goose Creek Men) 18, 36, 38, 42
Barbary Pirates 252-253
Beecher, Lyman 184, 191, 193, 195
Bennington, Battle of 103
Bible 2, 5-6, 20, 124, 201, 204, 216, 276
Bill of Rights 150, 168, 174-176, 178-179, 182
Black churches 197
Boudinot, Elias 142-143
Bound Brook, NJ 118-119
Boston Massacre 74
Boston Tea Party 67, 74-75, 80
Bradford, William 31
Brandywine Creek, Battle of 100, 112, 125, 258
Brooklyn Heights 86, 90, 106, 289
Bunker Hill (Breed's Hill), Battle of 43, 65, 76-77, 78, 86, 90, 103
Burgoyne, General Johnny 76, 100-105, 107-108
Burke, Edmund 75, 288
Burr, Aaron 219-221

Cabots, John and Sebastian 25
Calvin, John (Calvinism) 6-7, 19, 40, 186
Camden, Battle of 132-133
Carolinas 22, 36, 40, 128, 133, 136, 260
Cartier, Jacques 23, 25, 26
Casualties
   Rev. War 83, 92, 93-95, 97, 100, 108, 113, 128, 130, 133, 141-142
   War of 1812 246-247, 251
Catholics (Roman Catholics) 7, 11, 15, 34, 35, 38, 39, 57, 75, 84, 200
Champlain, Samuel de 26, 28
Charlestown (Charles Town) 36, 118, 130-131, 135
Chauncy, Rev. Charles 61
Christian heritage of America xi, 11, 30, 40-41, 61, 124, 198, 200-201, 254, 267, 282, 283-284, 285
Church growth
   Following Great Awakening 56-59, 284
   Second Great Awakening 198-200
Church of England (Anglican) 2, 4-7, 11-12, 30-31, 36, 49, 51, 59, 132, 179-180, 185, 187, 200-201, 255, 283
Coverdale, Miles 5
Clinton, Gen. Henry 76, 118, 122, 128, 130-131, 134-135, 136, 142
Cod fishing 25, 145
Coffin, Rev. Charles 31, 287
Colleges/universities
   Harvard 42, 60, 198, 261-262
   Yale 42, 48, 60, 142, 184, 190-191, 195
   William & Mary 42, 60
   Princeton (College of NJ) 60, 148, 165, 198, 253, 279, 284
   Columbia (Kings College) 60
   Dartmouth 60, 284
   Brown 60, 284
   Hampden-Sydney 190, 198
   Virginia 223
   Oberlin 194
   Others 60, 194, 198

Confederation Congress 142, 147, 153, 155, 161-162, 64, 169, 252
Congregationalists (see also Puritans) 6, 42, 56-57, 58, 60, 67, 85, 150, 153, 180, 185, 193, 198-199, 201
Constitution (U. S.)
  Annapolis Convention 150-152
  Sacrifices 153-154
  Madison's role 154-156
  Virginia plan 155, 157-158
  Confidentiality 157
  Committees 158
  Compromises 153, 158-160
  Three-Fifths Rule (federal ratio) 159-160
  Ratification 168-170, 175-177, 182
  International impacts 163, 180-182
Continental Congress
  1774 67-68
  1775 68-69
  1776 68-73
  During Rev. War 111-112, 114-115, 118, 124, 128, 132
Cornwallis, Gen. Charles 95-97, 107, 127, 132-142, 148, 289-291
Cortes, Hernando 8
Cowpens, Battle of 133-134
Cromwell, Oliver 11

Danbury Baptists 179, 222
D'Estaing, Admiral 117-118, 130
Decatur, Admiral Stephen 248, 253
Debt (indebtedness) 14, 20, 73, 146, 151, 219

Declaration of Independence 72-73, 86, 88, 144, 148, 149-150, 180, 212, 218, 223, 266-267, 277-278,
de Grasse, Admiral 127, 136-140, 147-148, 291
de Soto, Hernando 25
Deism (deists) 86, 272
Disease 26, 32, 39, 82, 84, 98-99, 113, 224, 235, 240, 242, 292
Dorchester Heights 76, 79, 86, 289
Duche, Rev. Jacob 68
Dutch Reformed Church 6, 46-47, 56
Dwight, Timothy 190-191, 195

Economic conditions; inflation 30, 71, 106, 109, 259-260, 268
Edwards, Jonathan 44, 48-49, 53, 59, 61, 180, 186, 190, 194, 278, 284
Embargo Act 221
Emigration to America 28-41
English Civil War 11-12
Enlightenment xi, 15-16, 37-38, 70-71, 172, 191, 221, 267-268, 269-270, 274, 275-278, 280, 282
Enthusiasm; emotionalism (religious) 46, 59-61, 109, 191
Era of Good Feelings 257
Establishment Clause (First Amendment) 178-179

Federalist, The 150, 156, 162, 168-175, 177, 181-182, 253
Federalists (political party) 209, 211, 214
First Amendment 178-180, 180, 182
Fort Stanwix, Battle of 103
Franklin, Benjamin
  Years in England 79-81

Continental Congress 69, 84, 87
  Years in France 105, 114, 125-126, 135-136
  Peace Treaty 144-145, 147
  Constitutional Convention 165-166, 175
Freedom (liberty) and Christianity xii, 44, 56, 62-63, 71, 84-86, 165, 184, 185, 189, 201-202, 270-271, 273, 275, 278-280, 288
Frelinghuysen, Rev. Theodore 46-48
French & Indian War (Seven-Years' War) 14, 19-20, 39, 62, 73, 78, 81, 223, 239, 279, 289
French Revolution 16, 19, 39, 163, 209, 214, 224, 243, 278

Gage, Gen. Thomas 75-76, 85
Gallatin, Albert 219
Gates, Gen. Horatio 103, 113, 132
Germaine, Lord 128
Germantown, Battle of 100-101, 106, 112, 258
Gerry, Eldridge 215
Glorious Revolution (England) 12, 16
Great Awakening, First 43-63, 182, 279
  Breakout of revival in America 46-49
  Whitefield's second trip to colonies 53-54
  Size of crowds 53-54
  Negative reactions 45, 61
  Impact of Great Awakening 44, 45, 56-58, 84, 186-187, 269, 284, 288
Great Awakening, Second 182, 184-202, 241, 255, 257, 268, 284

Comparisons with First Awakening 186-187
  Timothy Dwight/Yale 190-191
  Camp meetings 191-192
  Charles Finney 193-194
  Benevolent societies 194-195
  Role of women 190, 195-196
  Impact on culture 195
  Impact on Blacks 195-197
  Educational institutions 198
  Denominational shifts 198-200
  Lifestyle, morality; virtue 201, 280
Greene, Gen. Nathaniel 77, 92, 99, 112, 118, 133-134, 292
Guilford Court House, Battle of 133-134

Hakluyt, Richard 10
Half-Way Covenant (see also Puritans) 42, 59
Hamilton, Alexander 203, 211, 279, 293
  Revolutionary War 141
  Constitutional Convention 150, 152
  The Federalist papers 168, 175-177
  Secretary of Treasury 206, 208-209
  Leader of Federalist Party 209
  Duel with Aaron Burr 219
Hancock, John 68
Harrison, William Henry 246-247
Henry, Patrick 65, 177
Hessians 70, 86, 88, 90, 93-95, 103-105, 121-122, 130
Howe, Gen. William 76, 85, 88, 90, 100-101, 106-108, 114, 128, 290
Hudson, Henry 23, 26, 100

Hudson River 10, 25, 26, 33, 40, 78, 86, 92, 100-101, 118
Huguenots 4, 6, 26, 34
Hutchinson, Anne 35
Hutchinson, Thomas 80

Impressment 210
Intolerable Acts 75

Jackson, Andrew 194, 247, 251-252, 259, 264-265, 292
Jamestown Settlement 30-31, 283
Jay, John 2, 20, 67, 108, 112, 144-146, 153, 162, 169, 182, 252, 276, 279, 291-292
Jay Treaty 145, 204, 207, 210-212, 245, 291
Jefferson, Thomas 85, 88
   Role in Continental Congress 69, 72, 218
   Governor of Virginia 134-135
   Ambassador to France 218
   Secretary of State 218
   President 218-230, 241-242
   Worship in federal buildings 221-222, 241
Jenkins' Ear, War of 13-14
Jews (Jewish people) 9, 18, 34, 38, 57
Jones, John Paul 122-123
Judson, Adoniram 194-195

Kennebec River 22, 31, 43, 82
Key, Francis Scott 250
King Charles I 11-12
King George III 67, 70, 128, 143
King Henry VIII 5, 19
King James I 6
King Louis XVI 210

King Phillip's War 245
King, Rufus 159
Kings Mountain, Battle of 133
Knox, Henry 78, 86, 95, 98, 206, 292
Kosciuszko, Col. Thadeus 101

Lafayette, Marquis 100, 114, 116, 117-118, 134-138, 148, 292
Lake Champlain 78, 82-83, 86, 101
Laurens, Henry 111
Laurens, John 144-145
Lee, Arthur 105, 125
Lee, Gen. Charles 116
Lee, Richard Henry 65, 71
Lexington and Concord 75-76
Lewis & Clark Expedition 239
   Getting started 230-233
   Teton Sioux 233-235, 241
   Mandan 235, 241
   Charbonneau and Sacagawea 235, 241
   Heading west 236-239
   Nez Perce 237-238, 239, 241
   Fort Clatsop 239
   Return trip 239-240
   Tragedy of Meriwether Lewis 240
Livingston, Robert 72, 224-228
Locke, John 16, 267, 276-277
Log College 48
Long Island, Battle of 88-91, 106
Louisbourg (Nova Scotia) 14
Louisiana Purchase 223-229, 242
   St. Domingue disaster 224, 292
   Closing New Orleans 227
   Napoleon's renunciation 227-228
   Monroe and Livingston 234, 227-229
   Setting the price 227-229

Ratification 229
Loyalists 82, 118, 128, 132, 142
Luther, Martin 2-4, 7, 19
Lutheran Church 57

Madison, James
    Father of Constitution 150, 152
    The Federalist papers 168
    Bill of Rights 175, 178
    Secretary of State 225
    President 253
    War of 1812 (see separate section)
    Religious views 253-254
Marbois, Francois Barbe-225-229
Marshall, John 177, 214-215, 218, 292
Massasoit, Chief 32
Mayflower 21, 31-32
Mayflower Compact 32, 266, 283
McGready, James 191-192, 201
McHale, Allen 147-148
Mercer, Gen. Hugh 97
Methodists 49, 51, 59-60, 153, 185-190, 192-193, 195-196, 198-199, 201, 284
Minuit, Peter 33
Minutemen 76
Missouri Compromise 260
Monmouth Court House, Battle of 109, 114-117, 124-125
Monroe, James xiii, 292
    Revolutionary War 95, 258
    Governor of Virginia 258
    Louisiana Purchase 224, 227-229, 258
    Sec. of State and Army 258
    President 258-261

Monroe Doctrine 258, 261-262, 263, 267
Montgomery, Gen. Richard 81-82
Moravians 49-51, 112-113
Morgan, Daniel 82, 103, 133-134
Morris, Gouverneur 112, 158-159, 161-162, 164, 175, 204
Morris, Robert 154, 286
Morristown 96-99, 109, 112, 113, 119-120, 121-122, 124-125,
Mutinies (Continental Army) 120, 122

Napoleon Bonaparte 19, 214, 216, 223-229, 242, 247, 249, 258, 292
New Orleans 38-39, 209, 223-225, 227-229, 242, 245, 292
New Orleans, Battle of 251-252
Newburyport, Mass. 43-44, 55, 266
Newport, RI 57, 117-118, 130, 134-138, 141, 148
North, Lord 69, 74, 80, 133, 143
Northwest Ordinance 151, 210, 225
Nova Scotia (see Acadia)

Oglethorpe, James 13, 37
Oneida Evangelical Association 193
Oxford University 50, 276

Paine, Thomas 20, 71, 180, 292
Peace Commission (Rev. War) 144-145
Penn, William 37
Perry, Admiral Oliver 248
Pinchon, Louis Andre 227
Pinckney, Charles C. 213
Pietists 49

Pilgrims 5, 21-22, 31-34, 38, 40, 265, 283-284
Piracy 8, 252-253
Popham, George 22
Prayer (days of fasting & prayer) 67, 68, 69-70, 115, 179, 251, 254-255, 285-287
Presbyterians 6, 57-58, 60, 67, 85, 99, 112, 132, 150, 153, 190-193, 198-199, 201, 222, 284
Press (British and American) 97, 128
Princeton, Battle of 96-97, 107, 289-290
Printed material (religious) 34-35, 54, 124, 199
Propaganda (disinformation) 106, 113-114
Protestant Reformation (see Reformation)
Providential (divine providence) xii, 21, 23, 33-34, 42, 68, 72, 84, 86, 90, 95, 105, 108, 117, 125-126, 140, 142-143, 148, 147-147, 150, 163, 166-167, 170, 179, 183, 202, 216-217, 241, 242, 249, 255, 267, 273, 281, 282, 290
Puritans 4, 6-8, 10-12, 19, 22, 33-36, 38, 42, 45, 56, 59, 278, 283, 293

Quakers 22, 36-37, 40-41, 56-57, 60, 67, 112-113, 198-199
Quebec City 12, 25, 28, 43, 81-82
Queen Elizabeth I 5, 10

Raleigh, Sir Walter 21
Rall, Col. Johann 93-95, 107
Randolph, Edmund 155, 177
Reformation 2-4, 7, 20

Roanoke Colony 21-22
Robbins, Chaplain Ammi 83
Rochambeau, Count de 135-138, 148
Rush, Dr. Benjamin 71, 85, 221, 230, 271

San Agustin (Florida) 12, 26
Santa Fe, NM 38-39
Saratoga, Battle of 84, 101-105, 127, 290
Savannah 26, 37, 50-51, 130, 135, 138
Schuyler, Gen. Phillip 81, 101, 107
Science & technology 14-15, 20, 276
Shays' Rebellion 152-153, 171-172
Seven-Years' War (see French & Indian War)
Slavery 17-19, 30, 42, 159, 166, 187, 194, 196-197, 201, 260, 265, 268, 291
Sons of Liberty 74
Spanish Armada 8-9, 21-22
Spanish Empire xii, 7-10, 18-19
Springfield, Battles of 109, 121-122, 124, 130
Squanto 22, 32
Stark, Gen. John 103
St. Clair, Gen. Arthur 101
Stamp Act 74
Star Spangled Banner 243, 249-250,
Statute for Religious Liberty 223
Steuben, Baron von 114-115, 116, 125, 292
Stiles, Ezra 142
Stone, Barton 192, 201
Stuyvesant, Peter 33
Sunday School unions 194, 284

Talleyrand, Charles Maurice de 214, 225, 227-228, 228
Tarleton, Col. Banastre 133
Tecumseh 246-247
Tennets, William and Gilbert 46-48, 186, 191, 284
Thirty-Years' War 10-11, 17, 35
Thirty-Nine Articles (Queen Elizabeth) 5, 31
Thomas, Gen. John 82
Three-Fifths Rule (federal ratio) 159-160, 216
Ticonderoga, Fort 78-79, 82-83, 86, 101-102, 105, 107
Tilgham, Tench 142
Tocqueville, Alexis de xiii, 23, 185, 270, 273-275, 278, 284, 287, 291
Townshend Acts 74
Trenton, Battle of 93-96, 106
Tyndale, William 5

Valcour Island, Battle of 83
Valley Forge 101, 106-115, 116-119, 124-125, 158, 160, 164, 258
Verazzano, da Giovanni 25
Vergennes, Comte de 126, 135-136
Vikings 23
Virginia Plan (see Constitution)
Virtue; virtuous people 7, 60, 162-163, 201, 213, 216, 274-278, 279-280, 291

War of Jenkins' Ear (War of Austrian Succession) 13-14
War of 1812 245-252
    Causes 218, 243, 245, 248
    Western Indian wars 246-247
    Naval battles 247-249
    Burning of Capital 249, 253
    Baltimore 249-250
    Treaty of Ghent 145, 251
    Battle of New Orleans 251-252
    Benefits 252, 255
Washington, George
    French & Indian War 289
    Continental Congress 68-69
    Commander-in-Chief 69, 78-79, 88-101, 106-107, 109-122, 124-126, 135-147
    Constitutional Convention 150, 156-157, 164
    Inauguration 204-206
    President 206-210, 212
    Setting precedents 204-209, 216-217
    Farewell Address 212-213, 216
Washington, Martha 99, 207, 293
Wayne, Gen. Anthony 119
Wesley, Charles 46, 49-51, 189
Wesley, John 49-51, 189
Weymouth, George 22-23
Whitefield, George 43-46, 50-55, 58, 62, 85, 186, 193, 196, 201, 284, 292
William of Orange 12
Williams, Roger 35
Williamsburg 65, 67, 140
Winthrop, John 32, 34, 41, 58, 182
Witherspoon, John 148, 279, 292
Wycliffe, John 8

XYZ Affair 214

Yorktown, Battle of 127, 135-143, 147-148, 290-291

978-0-595-85644-2
0-595-85644-6

Printed in the United States
64763LVS00008B/25